Spanish

vocabulary handbook

Mike Zollo

Berlitz Publishing
New York   Munich   Singapore

Spanish Vocabulary Handbook

CONTACTING THE EDITORS
Every effort has been made to provide accurate information in this publication, but changes are inevitable. The publisher cannot be responsible for any resulting loss, inconvenience, or injury. We would appreciate it if readers would call our attention to any errors or outdated information by contacting Berlitz Publishing, 95 Progress Street, Union, NJ 07083, USA. Fax: 1-908-206-1103. email: comments@berlitzbooks.com

Cover photo © PunchStock/Medioimages

Printed in Singapore by Insight Print Services (Pte) Ltd., August 2006.

The Author:
Written by **Mike Zollo**, an experienced teacher, author and chief examiner. He is the chairman of the Association for Language Learning Spanish and Portuguese Committee.

The Series Editor:

Christopher Wightwick is a former UK representative on the Council of Europe Modern Languages Project and principal inspector of Modern Languages for England.

CONTENTS

How to Use This Handbook   *vii*

A   **Introduction**

The Vocabulary of the Spanish Language   *2*
Conventions Used in This Handbook   *10*

B   **Vocabulary Topics**

1   *Functional Words*   *12*

2   *Where? — Position & Movement*   *14*

2a	Position	14
2b	Directions & Location	16
2c	Movement	18

3   *When? — Expressions of Time*   *20*

3a	Past, Present & Future	20
3b	The Time, Days & Dates	24

4   *How Much? — Expressions of Quantity*   *26*

4a	Length & Shape	26
4b	Measuring	28
4c	Numbers	30
4d	Calculations	32

5   *What Sort Of? — Descriptions & Judgments*   *34*

5a	Describing People	34
5b	The Senses	36
5c	Describing Things	38
5d	Evaluating Things	40
5e	Comparisons	42
5f	Materials	43

6   *The Human Mind & Character*   *44*

6a	Human Character	44
6b	Feelings & Emotions	46
6c	Thought Processes	48
6d	Expressing Views	50

7   *Human Life & Relationships*   *54*

7a	Family & Friends	54
7b	Love & Children	56
7c	Life & Death	58

8 *Daily Life* 60

8a	The House	60
8b	The Household	62
8c	Furnishings	64
8d	Daily Routine	66

9 *Shopping* 68

9a	General Terms	68
9b	Household Goods & Toiletries	70
9c	Clothing	72

10 *Food & Drink* 74

10a	Drinks & Meals	74
10b	Fish & Meat	76
10c	Vegetables, Fruit & Dessert	78
10d	Cooking & Eating	80

11 *Health & Illness* 82

11a	Accidents & Emergencies	82
11b	Illness & Disability	84
11c	Medical Treatment	86
11d	Health & Hygiene	88

12 *Social Issues* 90

12a	Society	90
12b	Poverty & Social Services	92
12c	Housing & Homelessness	94
12d	Addiction & Violence	96
12e	Prejudice	98

13 *Religion* 100

| 13a | Ideas & Doctrines | 100 |
| 13b | Faith & Practice | 102 |

14 *Business & Economics* 104

14a	The Economics of Business	104
14b	At Work	106
14c	Pay & Conditions	108
14d	Finance & Industry	110
14e	Banking & the Economy	112

15 *Communicating with Others* 114

15a	Social Discourse	114
15b	Comments & Interjections	116
15c	Mail / Post & Telephone	118
15d	Computers	120

16 Leisure & Sport   122

   16a   Leisure   122
   16b   Sporting Activity   124
   16c   Sports & Equipment   126

17 The Arts   128

   17a   Appreciation & Criticism   128
   17b   Art & Architecture   130
   17c   Literature   132
   17d   Music & Dance   134
   17e   Theater & the Movies / Theatre & Cinema   136

18 Media   138

   18a   General Terms   138
   18b   The Press   140
   18c   Television & Radio   142
   18d   Advertising   144

19 Travel   146

   19a   General Terms   146
   19b   Going Abroad & Travel by Boat   148
   19c   Travel by Road   150
   19d   Travel by Air   154
   19e   Travel by Rail   156

20 Vacation / Holidays   158

   20a   General Terms   158
   20b   Accommodations & Hotel   160
   20c   Camping & Self-Service / -Catering   162

21 Language   164

   21a   General Terms   164
   21b   Using Language   166

22 Education   168

   22a   General Terms   168
   22b   School   170
   22c   School Subjects & Examinations   172
   22d   Further & Higher Education   174

23 Science: The Changing World   176

   23a   Scientific Study & Life Sciences   176
   23b   Physical Sciences   178
   23c   The Earth & Space   180

24 The Environment: The Natural World — 182

24a	Geography	182
24b	The Animal World	184
24c	Farming & Gardening	186
24d	Weather	188
24e	Pollution	190

25 Government & Politics — 192

25a	Political Life	192
25b	Elections & Ideology	194

26 Crime & Justice — 196

26a	Crime	196
26b	Trial	198
26c	Punishment	200

27 War & Peace — 202

27a	War	202
27b	Military Personnel & Weaponry	204
27c	Peace & International Relations	206

C Appendices

3b	Clocks & Watches
4d	Mathematical & Geometrical Terms
5b	Parts of the Body
6a	Human Characteristics
8b	Tools
9a	Shops, Stores & Services
9a	Currencies
9c	Jewelry / Jewellry
9c	Precious Stones & Metals
10c	Herbs & Spices
10d	Cooking Utensils
10d	Smoking
11b	Illness & Disability
11c	Hospital Departments
13b	Holidays & Religious Festivals
14b	Professions & Jobs
14b	Places of Work
14b	Company Personnel & Structure
15c	Letter-Writing Formulae
15d	Computer Hardware
15d	Computer Software
15d	Computer Printing
16a	Hobbies
17b	Architectural Terms
17c	Publishing
17d	Musicians & Instruments
17d	Musical Forms
17d	Musical Terms
17e	Movie / Film Genres
19a	Means of Transportation
19b	Ships & Boats
19c	Parts of the Car
19c	Road Signs
20a	Tourist Sights
20a	On the Beach
20a	Continents & Regions
20a	Countries
20a	Oceans & Seas
21a	Main Language Families
21a	Languages & Nationalities
21b	Grammar
21b	Punctuation
22b	Stationery
23a	Scientific Disciplines
23b	Chemical Elements
23b	Compounds & Alloys
23c	The Zodiac
23c	Planets & Stars
24b	Wild Animals
24b	Birds
24b	Parts of the Animal Body
24c	Trees
24c	Flowers & Weeds
25b	Political Institutions
27b	Military Ranks
27c	International Organizations

D Subject Index

How to Use This Handbook

This Handbook is a carefully ordered work of reference covering all areas of Spanish vocabulary and phrasing. It is based on the thesaurus structure of the Council of Europe's Threshold Level, expanded to include other major topics, especially in the fields of business, information technology, and education. Unlike a dictionary, it brings together words and phrases in related groups. It also illustrates their usage with contextualized sample sentences, often in dialogue form. This enables learners and users of the language to:

- refresh and expand their general knowledge of vocabulary;
- review systematically, using the word groups to test their knowledge from Spanish to English and vice versa;
- extend their knowledge of authentically Spanish ways of saying things by studying the sample sentences;
- support their speaking and writing on a given topic, when the logical arrangement of the sections will often prompt new ideas as well as supply the means of expressing them.

THE STRUCTURE OF THE HANDBOOK

The Handbook is divided into four parts:

A   Introduction: The Vocabulary of the Spanish Language

A concise account of the ways in which Spanish creates compound words and phrases in order to express more complex ideas. (For a more extensive treatment of this topic, see the Berlitz *Spanish Grammar Handbook*.)

B   Vocabulary Topics

Ninety-six Vocabularies, grouped under twenty-seven major areas of experience. Most Vocabulary Topics are divided into a number of sections, so that words and phrases are gathered together into closely related groups. Almost all sections contain sample sentences showing the vocabulary in use. Wherever it makes sense to do so, these sentences are linked together to form short narratives or dialogues that help to fix them in memory. In some Vocabularies the lists of words and phrases are both extensive and more independent of context, so that the role of the sample sentences is reduced.

C   Appendices

Lists of specific terms such as the names of countries or musical instruments. These are linked to the Vocabularies by clear cross-references.

D   Subject Index

An alphabetical index of topics and themes, enabling you to locate quickly the area you are interested in.

LOCATING THE RIGHT SECTION

The Handbook can be approached in two ways.

• If you are not sure which topic will be best suited to your needs, start with the Contents on page iii. This will give you a general picture of the areas covered. You can then browse through the sections until you find the one you want.

• Alternatively, if you have a specific topic in mind, look it up in the Subject Index at the end of the book. This will take you directly to the relevant Vocabulary Topic or Appendix. To help you find what you are looking for, topics are often listed more than once, under different headings. Within most sections there are cross-references to other, related areas.

A

INTRODUCTION

The Vocabulary of the Spanish Language

Conventions Used in This Handbook

The Vocabulary of the Spanish Language

1   The Origins of Spanish

Modern Castilian Spanish (**castellano**) is derived from Vulgar Latin, the Latin spoken by ordinary Romans, which also gave rise to other Romance languages, including other languages and dialects of the Iberian Peninsula. The Castilians won political and military dominance over much of Spain, so it was their dialect that eventually became the national language of Spain. Thus, Spanish comes from the same source as, for example, Italian, French, and Portuguese, and almost all other Iberian Peninsular languages, such as **catalán, valenciano,** and **gallego.**

Much vocabulary in English also comes from Latin, either via Norman French or other Romance languages; and in more recent times (largely in the fields of science or culture), directly from Latin. Hence, Spanish and English have a lot of vocabulary in common, and many words new to you in Spanish will be recognizable from English or any other Romance language you may know.

Spanish has also imported words from many other languages over the centuries, among them Arabic (e.g., **algodón** 'cotton'), French (e.g., **boutique**), English (e.g., **márketing**) and Latin American Indian languages (e.g., **tomate** 'tomato'). Many of the more recent importations are from English, mostly in the fields of sports, pop music, business, science, and computing. It is worth noting that verbs based on imported words are almost always in the **-ar** verb family, e.g., **dopar, esnifar, xerocopiar.**

Some imported words more or less keep their original spelling, but with pronunciation adapted to Spanish: this is usually the case with words adopted in written form (e.g., 'iceberg'). Words imported through spoken language on the other hand tend to do the opposite, and have spelling adapted to keep the pronunciation similar, such as is the case with **fútbol**. It is interesting to compare two words with similar meanings — **jersey** and **suéter:** the former was probably adopted from written English and is now usually pronounced in Spanish as something like 'hersei'; the latter was obviously adopted in spoken form, and a form of spelling was evolved to produce the right sound when said aloud.

2 *Important Grammatical Features*

Awareness of these will help you to categorize words and get to their base form. (For full treatment of Spanish structures, consult the Berlitz *Spanish Grammar Handbook*.)

2a *The Noun Phrase*

(i) *Gender*

All Spanish nouns are either **masculine** or **feminine** in gender. As a general rule:

• most words for female people or animals are in the **feminine** group, and most male people or animals are in the **masculine** group.

• most masculine words end in **-o,** and most words ending in **-o** are masculine

• most feminine words end in **-a,** and most words ending in **-a** are feminine

BUT there are exceptions:

el taxist*a, el* map*a, la* radi*o, la* fot*o*

(ii) *Number*

All nouns and adjectives ending in a vowel add **s** to form their plural, those ending in a consonant add **-es.**

el niño → los niños   la carta → las cartas
el papel → los papeles   la mujer → las mujeres

There are a few exceptions. For these, consult the Berlitz *Spanish Grammar Handbook*.

(iii) *Articles*

There are four words for 'the' in Spanish:

el = masculine singular   **el chico, el perro, el papel**
la = feminine singular   **la chica, la vaca, la verdad**
los = masculine plural   **los chicos, los gatos, los taxis**
las = feminine plural   **las chicas, las ratas, las fotos**

Nouns listed in this Handbook are accompanied by **el / la, los / las,** to show you which gender they belong to.

There are four words for 'a / some' in Spanish:

un = masculine singular	**un chico, un perro, un papel**
una = feminine singular	**una chica, una vaca, una verdad**
unos = masculine plural	**unos chicos, unos gatos, unos taxis**
unas = feminine plural	**unas chicas, unas ratas, unas fotos**

(iv)   Agreement of adjectives

Adjectives have to match the noun they describe in **gender** and **number.** Therefore, they can have four forms: masculine singular and plural, feminine singular and plural. Those ending in **-e,** however, have the same form for masculine and feminine. This often gives rise to apparently rhyming phrases — learn the following as useful examples to remind you:

el niñ*o* mal*o*	**un*os* tor*os* brav*os***
un*a* palom*a* blanc*a*	**l*as* isl*as* bonit*as***

BUT

un hombre inteligent*e*	**unas casas grand*es***

Note that the masculine singular form is usually listed in this Handbook.

2b   Verb Forms

Different verb forms exist for each person referred to and for each tense, and the verb ending is crucially important. On the whole, Spanish does not use subject pronouns — words such as **yo** 'I,' **él** 'he,' **nosotros** 'we,' and so on — because the actual verb form reveals who is doing the action as well as what is being done and when. Since Spanish pronunciation is very faithful to its spelling and vice versa, Spanish has never really developed the need to use subject pronouns all the time, and it reserves them for emphasis or to avoid ambiguity.

• Here are the six forms of a typical regular verb of the **-ar** verb family in the present tense, with the subject pronouns given in brackets. You will see that the verb forms are all clearly different and that most end in a vowel, an **n,** or an **s.**

hablar	to speak
(yo) habl*o*	I speak
(tú) habl*as*	you speak (familiar singular)
(él / ella / usted) habl*a*	he / she / speaks, you speak (formal singular)

(nosotros/as) habl*amos*	we speak
(vosotros/as) habl*áis*	you speak (familar plural)
(ellos/ellas/ustedes) habl*an*	they speak, you speak (formal plural)

• Some verbs are affected by the spelling change described as vowel stretching (see Section 4). Here is an example — note that not all forms are affected.

pensar	to think
(yo) p*i***enso**	I think
(tú) p*i***ensas**	you think (familiar singular)
(él/ella/usted) p*i***ensa**	he/she/thinks, you think (formal singular)
(nosotros/as) pensamos	we think
(vosotros/as) pensáis	you think (familar plural)
(ellos/ellas/ustedes) p*i***ensan**	they think, you think (formal plural)

Apart from the **-ar** verb family, other regular verbs belong to the **-er** and **-ir** verb groups. For other forms and for more information, consult the Berlitz *Spanish Verb Handbook*.

• In this Handbook, verbs are usually given in the 'I' form of the present tense (e.g., '*I* speak' **hablo**). If you come across a particular verb form, you need to work back to this form to find it in this Handbook, or to the infinitive part of the verb to find it in a dictionary.

3 *Guessing Unknown Words*

For various reasons, several letters or combinations of letters changed in written form in the transition from Latin to modern Castilian Spanish. If you are aware of these, you can quite easily work out the meanings of many words that are similar in English but not otherwise easily recognizable. Often the changed Castilian form and a form closer to Latin exist side by side, though sometimes with slightly different meanings.

(i) *'vowel stretching' of **e**, **o**, and **u***

e → **ie**, and **o** → **ue**; and in addition, sometimes **e** → **i**, **o** → **u** and, **u** → **ue**.

e → **ie**: b**i**en	= well; cf. Latin/Italian 'b**e**ne,' English 'b**e**neficial'
o → **ue**: b**ue**no	= good; cf. French 'b**o**n,' English 'b**o**unty'
e → **i**: p**i**do	= I ask for, from **pedir**; cf. 'p**e**tition'

INTRODUCTION

o → u: d*u*rmió   = he slept, from **dormir;** cf.
'd*o*rmitory'

u → ue: ag*üe*ro   = aug*ur*

(ii)   *sc, sp, st*

You may notice that some native speakers of Spanish speaking English tend to put an 'e-' at the beginning of words starting with 'sc-,' 'sp-,' 'st-.' This is because many such words in English, French, and so on, tend to begin in Spanish with **esc-, esp-, est-;**

e + sc: *esc*uela   = *sc*hool
e + sp: *esp*añol   = *Sp*anish
e + st: *est*udiante   = *st*udent

(iii)   **ll**

Castilian Spanish often uses **ll** instead of 'cl,' 'fl,' and 'pl' at the beginning of words.

cl → ll: *ll*amar   = to call; cf. *cl*aim (call)
fl → ll: *ll*ama   = *fl*ame (also the South American animal)
pl → ll: *ll*ano   = *fl*at, *pl*ain

(iv)   *f / h*

Castilian Spanish often uses **h** instead of 'f,' and two words with similar meanings but different spellings often coexist.

h ↔ f: *h*ogar   = hearth +
       *f*uego   = fire; cf. '*fo*cus'
       *h*ijo   = son; cf. '*fi*lial' and French '*fi*ls'

(v)   *w / g*

Especially at the beginning of words, Spanish tends to use **g** or **gu** instead of 'w.'

w ↔ g: (el País de) *G*ales   = *W*ales; cf. **Galicia**
       *gu*erra   = *w*ar; cf. **guerrilla / gu**errillero

Note: **w**hisky is often pronounced or written **gu**isky.

(vi)   *x / j*

Spanish usually uses **j** where English uses '**x**.'

x → j: Mé*j*ico   = Mexico   fi**j**o   = fi*x*ed

(vii)   *g / h*

Spanish sometimes begins words with **h** instead of 'g.'

g → h: *h*ermano   = brother; cf. '*g*ermane'

Note: G with **e** and **i** sounds like h.

(viii)   *ph / f*

Spanish does not allow 'ph' spellings, and uses **f** instead.

pro*f*eta	= pro*ph*et
geogra*f*ía	= geogra*ph*y
*f*armacia	= *ph*armacy

(ix)   *Double consonants*

Spanish has fewer double consonants than English. However, **cc, ll, rr** are all very common and; **nn** occurs in a few words, usually ones beginning with the prefix **in-**.

*in*necesario   = unnecessary (**in-** negating/opposite)

*in*novar   = to innovate (**in-** meaning into)

4   *Cognates and Derivatives*

Many Spanish words can be identified in a straightforward way, either because of their similarity to known words in other languages (*cognates*), or by being derived from known words in Spanish itself with bits added at the beginning or end of the word (*derivatives*). In the case of the latter, you can often derive a word by knowing how similar words are built from a base word, and you can work out the meaning of a word by 'undressing' it to get back to the base word at its core. Beware though of **amigos falsos** — words that look the same but have different meanings.

4a   *Cognates*

(i)   English words absorbed into Spanish without change of meaning.

álbum, récord, líder, fútbol, mánager

Note: Many have spellings adapted into Spanish as we have seen before.

(ii)   Spanish words with common equivalents in English or ones that English has borrowed from Spanish.

paella, matador, fiesta, aficionado

(iii)   Words identical in form to their English equivalent.

casual, panorama

(iv)   Words similar in form to their English equivalent.

documento, militar, sistema, clima, movimiento, millón

(v)   Verbs whose stem is identical or similar in form to the English equivalent.

admirar, contener, consistir, aplaudir

(vi)   Words with frequently occurring suffixes with English equivalents.

libertad, posibilidad, indicación, potencia

Note the equivalent English and Spanish suffixes:

-dad	= '-ty,' e.g., **ciudad** 'city'; **capacidad** 'capacity'
-ción	= '-tion,' e.g., **acción** 'action'; **elección** 'election'
-ía, -ia	= '-y,' e.g., **energía** 'energy'; **farmacia** 'pharmacy'

4b   *Derivatives: Word Building and Undressing*

(i)   Words whose meaning is determined by common prefixes or suffixes, but whose base element is already known or easily identifiable.

con-: contener   **des-: deshacer, desnudo**
dis-: disuadir   **in-/im-: incorrecto, imposible**
re-: revolver   **sub-: submarino, subcontinente**
-able: salud > saludable   **-ería: zapatero > zapatería**
-miento: pensar > pensamiento   **-oso: arena > arenoso**

(ii)   Nouns denoting people and other concepts, with endings such as -ero/a, -or/a, -ista.

-ero/-era: zapatero, niñera
-ista: pianista, taxista
-or/-ora: pintor, pescador

These are mostly based on another noun or a verb.

(iii)   Adverbs formed by adding the ending -**mente** to adjectives.

totalmente, activamente

> *Note:* In Spanish most adverbs end in -**mente,** just as in English most end in '-ly.' This ending is usually added to the feminine form of the adjective.

(iv)   Adjectives with ending -**able,** equivalent to English '-able' or '-ible.'

imaginable, admirable

(v)   Adjectives with ending -**oso / -osa,** equivalent to English '-ous.'

religioso, furioso, vigoroso, vicioso

(vi)   Adjectives with ending -**és / esa, -(i)ense, -eno / a, -eño / a,** equivalent to English '-ese' or '-(i)an,' usually indicating place of origin.

inglés, japonesa, canadiense, chileno, brasileña

(vii)   Diminutives ending in -**ito, -illo, -ico**

señorito, panecillo, casita, perico

(viii)   Augmentative and pejorative suffixes such as -**ón / ona, -azo, -ucho.**

hombrón, mujerona, manotazo, casucha

(ix)   Compound nouns, consisting of combinations of known words.

abrelatas, sacacorchos, cortacésped

(x)   Words derived from adjectives.

tranquilizar, ensuciar, limpieza

(xi)   Words mainly derived from verbs, with endings -**ante** or -**ente, -iente.**

cantante, oyente, comiente

(xii)   Common acronyms and initials, often in a different order.

UNO   **ONU - Organización de las Naciones Unidas**
NATO   **OTAN - Organización del Tratado del Atlántico del Norte**
Note:
USA   **EEUU - los Estados Unidos** (Plural words have doubled-up letters when given as acronyms.)

Conventions Used in This Handbook

a) Nouns
Nouns are given in the singular form preceded by the definite article.

el (pl. **los**) indicates masculine gender
la (pl. **las**) indicates feminine gender
Feminine words beginning with stressed **a-** or **ha-** are usually used with **el.**

Nouns referring to professions are generally given in the masculine form only, except for the list of professions in App. 14b, where the feminine is included.

b) Verbs
Verbs are in the first person, except when inappropriate. In the sample sentences both familiar and polite forms of 'you' are used as appropriate in that particular context. Sometimes both are given.

c) Adjectives
Adjectives are in the masculine singular form.

Abbreviations

adj	adjective	m	masculine
adv	adverb	pl	plural
f	feminine		

Symbols

( )   a part of a translation that is optional: **el juzgado (de lo) penal**
/   alternative word(s): **la historia / el cuento de terror** = **la historia de terror** or **el cuento de terror**
,   an alternative translation: 'I resign' **dimito, renuncio**
[ ]   an alternative used in Latin American Spanish: 'computer' **el ordenador, [la computadora]**
➤   a cross-reference to a vocabulary or chapter

B

VOCABULARY TOPICS

1	Functional Words	12	Social Issues
2	Where? — Position & Movement	13	Religion
		14	Business & Economics
3	When? — Expressions of Time	15	Communicating with Others
4	How Much? — Expressions of Quantity	16	Leisure & Sport
		17	The Arts
		18	The Media
5	What Sort Of? — Descriptions & Judgments	19	Travel
		20	Vacation / Holidays
		21	Language
6	The Human Mind & Character	22	Education
		23	Science: The Changing World
7	Human Life & Relationships	24	The Environment: The Natural World
8	Daily Life		
9	Shopping	25	Government & Politics
10	Food & Drink	26	Crime & Justice
11	Health & Illness	27	War & Peace

Functional Words

Articles

a **un, una**
the **el, la, los, las**
some **unos, unas**
   algunos, algunas

Demonstrative
   adjectives / pronouns*

this **este, esta**
that **ese, esa, aquel, aquella**
these **estos, estas**
those **esos, esas, aquellos,
   aquellas**
this one **éste, ésta**
that one **ése, ésa**
these **éstos, éstas**
those **ésos, ésas, aquéllos,
   aquéllas**

Emphatic subject pronouns*

I **yo**
you *(fam sing)* **tú**
   (fam pl) **vosotros / as, [ustedes]**
   (formal sing) **usted**
   (formal pl) **ustedes**
he **él**
she **ella**
it **ello**
we **nosotros / as**
they **ellos / as**

Personal object pronouns
   (accusative & dative)

me **me**
you *(fam sing)* **te**
   (fam pl) **os, [les]**
   (formal sing) **lo, la, le**
   (formal pl) **los, las, les**
him **lo, le**
her **la, le**
it **lo, la, le**

us **nos**
them **los, las, les**
one **lo, la, le**

Reflexive pronouns

myself **me**
yourself *(fam sing)* **te**
   (fam pl) **os, [les]**
   (formal sing / pl) **se**
him / herself **se**
itself **se**
ourselves **nos**
themselves **se**
oneself **se**
each other **se**

Prepositional pronouns*

me **mí**
you *(fam sing)* **ti**
   (fam pl) **vosotros / as, [ustedes]**
   (formal sing) **usted**
   (formal pl) **ustedes**
him **él**
her **ella**
it **ello**
. . . self, . . . selves **sí** *(reflexive)*
us **nosotros / as**
them **ellos / as**
one **uno**

Possessive adjectives*

my **mi, mis**
your *(fam sing)* **tu, tus**
   (fam pl) **vuestro / a / os / as, [su,
   sus]**
   (formal sing / pl) **su, sus**
his **su, sus**
her **su, sus**
its **su, sus**
our **nuestro / a / os / as**
their **su, sus**

one's   **su, sus**

Possessive pronouns*

mine **el mío, la mía, los míos, las mías**
yours *(fam sing)* **el tuyo,** etc.
   (fam pl) **el vuestro,** etc., **[el suyo,** etc.]
   (formal sing/pl) **el suyo,** etc.
his/hers **el suyo,** etc.
ours **el nuestro,** etc.
theirs **el suyo,** etc.
this is mine **este/a es mío/a**
mine is better **el mío/la mía es mejor**

Relative pronouns*

who **que**
   quien, quienes
   el/la que, los/las que
   el/la cual, los/las cuales
which **que**
   el/la que, los/las que
   el/la cual, los/las cuales
that **que**
   quien, quienes
   el/la que, los/las que
   el/la cual, los/las cuales
what **lo que, lo cual**
what you say is true **lo que dices es verdad**

Indefinite pronouns

somebody/one **alguien**
no one **nadie**
anybody/one(s) **cualquiera;** (pl)
   cualesquiera
nobody **nadie**
each **cada (uno/a)**
everybody/one **todos/as**
something **algo**
anything **algo, alguna cosa,**
   cualquier cosa
   (after negative) **nada**
nothing **nada**
everything **todo**

all (of them) **todos/as**
both (of them) **los/las dos,**
   ambos/as
some (of them) **algunos/as**

Questions

when? **¿cuándo?**
where? **¿dónde?**
how? **¿cómo?**
how much? **¿cuánto/a?**
how many? **¿cuántos/as?**
how far? **¿a qué distancia?,**
   [¿qué tan lejos?]
how long? **¿durante cuánto tiempo?**
how hot? **¿qué temperatura?**
why? **¿por qué?**
who? **¿quién(es)?**
whom? **¿a quién(es)?**
to whom? **¿a quién(es)?**
whose? **¿de quién(es)?**
what? **¿qué?**
what...? **¿qué ...?, ¿cuál(es) ...?**
which (one)? **¿cuál?**

Common prepositions and conjunctions

about **a eso de, acerca de**
also **también**
although **aunque**
and **y**
as *(since)* **puesto que**
because **porque**
but **pero**
if **si**
in **en**
in order that/so that **para que**
on **en, sobre**
only **sólo, solamente**
or **o**
since **puesto que**
so **pues**
too **también**
until **hasta (que)**
with **con**
without **sin**

2 Where? — Position & Movement

2a Position

about **alrededor de**
  about *(adv)* **por todas partes**
above **encima de**
across **a través (de)**
after **después (de)**
against **contra**
ahead **delante, [adelante]**
ahead of **delante de**
along **a lo largo de**
among **entre**
anywhere **en cualquier sitio**
around *(adv)* **alrededor de, por**
  around the garden **por el jardín**
as far as **hasta**
at **en**
  at home **en casa**
  at school **en el colegio**
  at work **en el trabajo**
back **detrás, atrás**
  at the back (of) **detrás (de), a la espalda (de), [atrás, en la parte trasera]**
  to the back **hacia atrás**
backwards **hacia atrás**
behind **detrás (de)**
below **debajo (de)**
  below **debajo, [abajo]**
beside **al lado de, [junto a]**
between **entre**
beyond **más allá (de)**
bottom **el fondo**
  at the bottom (of) **al fondo (de)**
center / centre **el centro**
  in the center / centre **en el centro (de)**
direction **la dirección**
  in the direction of Murcia **en la dirección de Murcia**
distance **la distancia**

in the distance **a la distancia**
distant **distante, distanciado, lejano**
down there **allí abajo**
downstairs **abajo**
edge **el borde**
  at the edge **al borde (de)**
end **el final**
  at the end **al final (de)**
everywhere **en todas partes, por todas partes, en todos los sitios**
far **lejos**
  far away (from) **lejos (de)**
first **primero**
  first (of all) **primero (de todo)**
  I am first **estoy primero**
from **de, desde**
front **el frente**
  at the front **al frente**
  I am in front **estoy al frente**
  in front of **delante de, al frente de**
  to the front **hacia delante, al frente**
here **aquí**
  here and there **aquí y allí**
in **en**
  in there **allí dentro**
inside **dentro**
  inside **adentro**
into **dentro**
last **último**
  last of all **por último**
  last of all *(adv)* **últimamente**
  I am last **soy el último**
left **izquierda**
  on the left **a la izquierda**
  to the left **hacia la izquierda**

middle **medio**
    in the middle (of) **en (el) medio (de)**
I move **me muevo**
movement **el movimiento**
near **cerca**
near(by) **cercano**
neighborhood / neigbourhood **el vecindario, las cercanías**
    in the neighborhood / neigbourhood of **en las cercanías (de)**
next **próximo, al lado**
    next *(adv)* **próximamente**
    next to **al lado de**
nowhere **en ningún sitio**
on **en, sobre**
onto **en**
opposite **opuesto (a), en frente (de)**
out of **fuera de**
    out there **allí fuera, [allá afuera]**
outside **fuera**
    outside **afuera**
over **encima**
    over there **allí, [allá]**
past **pasado**

right **derecho**
    the right **la derecha**
    to the right **a la derecha**
round / around **alrededor (de)**
    round / around the tree **alrededor del árbol**
side **lado**
    at the side **al lado**
    at both sides of **a ambos lados de**
somewhere **en alguna parte, en algún sitio**
there **allí**
to **a, hacia**
top **arriba, encima**
    top *(of mountain)* **la cima**
    at the top **encima**
    on top **encima**
towards **hacia**
under **debajo (de), bajo**
up there **allí arriba**
upstairs **arriba**
where? **¿dónde?**
where from? **¿de dónde?**
where to? **¿hacia dónde?, ¿adónde?**
with **con**

Over there in the distance is the river. It's not far — about 1 km from our house.
Opposite the houses is the church, and nearby are the shops / stores.

At the top of the hill is a farm, and in the middle of the village is the bank.
The first house on the main / high street is near the river. Our house is the last one. The next village is about five kilometers / kilometres away.

Allá a lo lejos está el río. No es lejos — a un kilómetro más o menos de nuestra casa.
Enfrente de la casa está la iglesia, y las tiendas están cerca.
En lo alto de la colina hay una granja, y en el centro del pueblo está el banco.
La primera casa de la calle principal está cerca del río. Nuestra casa es la última. El pueblo más cercano está a unos cinco kilómetros.

WHERE? — POSITION & MOVEMENT

2b Directions & Location

Points of the compass

atlas   **el atlas**
east   **el este, [el oriente]**
   east *(adj)*   **del este, oriental**
   in the east   **en el este**
   to the east   **al este**
compass   **la brújula**
latitude   **la latitud**
location   **la situación, la posición, la ubicación**
longitude   **la longitud**
map   **el mapa**
north   **el norte**
   north *(adj)*   **del norte, nórdico**
   in the north   **en el norte**
   to the north (of)   **al norte (de)**

northeast   **el nordeste**
northnortheast   **el nornordeste**
northwest   **el noroeste, el noruese**
northnorthwest   **el nornoroeste, el nornorueste**
point of the compass   **la cuarta**
south   **el sur**
   south *(adj)*   **del sur, sureño**
   in the south   **en el sur**
   to the south   **al sur**
southeast   **el sudeste, el sureste**

Santiago is south of La Coruña.
Right in the south is Pontevedra.
I prefer the south of Galicia to the north.

Santiago está al sur de La Coruña. Precisamente en el sur está Pontevedra. Prefiero el sur de Galicia al norte.

Look on the map. You go north(wards).

Mire el mapa. Usted sigue hacia el norte.

To the south of the woods you can see the church spire.

Hacia el sur del bosque se puede ver la aguja de la iglesia.

"How do I get to Pamplona?"
"Go straight on to the second intersection / crossroads.
Turn right at the lights and take the road to Vitoria. It's twenty-five kilometers / kilometres from here."

—¿Cómo se va a Pamplona?
—Siga todo derecho hasta el segundo cruce.
Doble a la derecha en el semáforo y tome la carretera para Vitoria. Está a veinte y cinco kilómetros de aquí.

"Is there a bank nearby?"
"It's behind the supermarket."
"Where is the tourist office?"

—¿Hay un banco cerca de aquí?
—Está detrás del supermercado.
—¿Dónde está la oficina de turismo?

"Opposite the town hall."

—En frente del ayuntamiento.

16 ➤ CONTINENTS & REGIONS, COUNTRIES App. 20a; GEOGRAPHY 24a

southsoutheast **el sudsudeste**
southwest **el sudoeste, el suroeste**
southsouthwest **el sudsudoeste**
west **el oeste, [el occidente]**
  west *(adj)* **del oeste, occidental**
  in the west **en el oeste, [al occidente]**
  to the west (of) **al oeste (de), [al occidente de]**

Location & existence

I am **soy, estoy**
  there is, there are **hay**
  there isn't (any), there aren't (any) **no hay (ninguno)**

it is ready **está listo, está preparado**
it amounts to **hace, [asciende a]**
I become **llego a ser**
I exist **existo**
existence **la existencia**
I have got / I have **tengo**
it lies **está situado**
I possess **poseo**
possession **la posesión**
present **el presente**
  I am present **estoy presente**
  I am present at **estoy presente en**
I am situated **estoy situado**

The town lies at a longitude of 32°.	**La ciudad está en la longitud de 32°.**
"Are you lost?"	**— ¿Se ha perdido usted?**
"Yes. Can you tell me the quickest way to the post office?"	**— Sí. ¿Me puede decir el camino más corto para ir al correo [a la oficina de correos]?**
"It's down there on the left."	**— Está allí abajo a la izquierda.**
How do you get to the other side?	**¿Cómo se va al otro lado?**
"Who's that?"	**— ¿Quién es?**
"It's me."	**— Soy yo.**
"How many children are present?"	**— ¿Cuántos niños asisten?**
"There are twenty-five. Five of them are at home."	**— Hay veinte y cinco. Cinco de ellos están en casa.**
"Is there any cake? Are there still any cookies / biscuits?"	**— ¿Hay torta / pastel? ¿Quedan galletas?**
"I am sorry, there is no cake, but there are some sandwiches."	**— Lo siento, no hay pastel, pero sí hay unos bocadillos [emparedados / sándwiches].**
I have been to Madrid. I was at a concert.	**He estado en Madrid. Fui a un concierto.**

2c Movement

I arrive **llego**	I go out **salgo, voy fuera**
I bring **traigo**	I go round **doy vueltas, doy la vuelta a**
by car **en coche**	
I carry **llevo**	I go up **subo, voy arriba**
I climb **escalo, subo**	I hike **hago auto(e)stop**
I come **voy, vengo**	I hurry **me apresuro**
I come down **bajo, voy abajo**	I hurry up **me doy prisa**
I come in **entro**	I jump **salto**
I come out **salgo**	I leave **salgo**
I come up **subo, voy arriba**	I leave (something) **dejo (algo)**
I creep **ando a gatas, [gateo]**	I lie down **me echo, me acuesto**
I drive **conduzco**	I march **desfilo**
I drive on the right **conduzco por la derecha**	I move **me muevo, me cambio**
	on foot **a pie**
I fall **caigo**	I pass **paso**
I fall down **me caigo**	I pass (in car) **paso en coche, [rebaso en carro]**
I follow **sigo**	
I get in **subo en / a**	I pull **tiro**
I get out **bajo de, salgo de**	I push **empujo**
I get up **me levanto**	I put **pongo**
I go **voy**	I ride a horse **monto a caballo**
I go down **bajo, voy abajo**	I run **corro**
I go for a walk **voy a pasear**	I run away **echo a correr**
I go in **entro, voy dentro**	I rush **voy de prisa**

Put the picnic lunch in the car! Don't forget to bring your umbrella.	**Pon (la comida d)el picnic en el coche [el carro]! No te olvides de traer el paraguas.**
I will take you as far as the river. Then you must get out and walk.	**Te llevaré hasta el río. Luego tendrás que bajar y continuar a pie.**
Keep to the left. Be careful not to fall into the river.	**Anda a la izquierda. Ten cuidado de no caerte al río.**
We go down the hill, along the river, and then turn left towards the woods.	**Bajamos la cuesta, seguimos al lado del río, y luego torcemos a la izquierda hacia el bosque.**
You pass a farm.	**Se pasa delante de una granja.**

I sit down **me siento**
I sit up **me levanto**
I slip **resbalo**
I am standing **estoy de pie**
  I stand still **(me) estoy quieto**
I stop **paro**
straight **derecho, seguido, recto**
  straight ahead **todo derecho, todo seguido, todo recto, [derecho]**
I stroll **me paseo**
I take **cojo**
I turn **tuerzo**
  I turn left **tuerzo a la izquierda**
  I turn off **me desvío**
  I turn round **me vuelvo, doy la vuelta**
walk **el paseo**
I walk **ando, camino**
I wander **voy sin rumbo**
way **el camino**

Here and there

Come here! **¡Ven aquí!**
I go there **voy allí**

I rush there **voy allí de prisa**
I travel there **viajo allí**

Up and down

Stand up! **¡Levántate!**
I climb the mountain **subo la montaña**
I climb the stairs **subo las escaleras**
I climb the wall **subo por la pared**
I fall down **me caigo**
I lie down **me echo, me acuesto**
Do sit down! **¡Siéntate!, ¡Siéntese!**
I go down the path **bajo por el camino**

Round

I go round the town **me paseo por la ciudad**
I run round in the garden **corro alrededor del jardín**
I run around **corro alrededor**
I turn round **doy la vuelta**

"Where are you going?"
"To town. Are you coming?"

"No, I am going to my mother's."
"Which direction is that?"
"I take the first road on the left, then straight ahead up to the marketplace, then I turn right."

"I will follow you as far as the market."
I am going by car but some of us will go on foot. John is going by bike.

— ¿Adónde vas / va usted?
— Al pueblo. ¿Vienes / Viene usted?

— No, voy a casa de mi madre.
— ¿En qué dirección es eso?
— Tomo la primera calle a la izquierda, luego sigo todo recto hacia la plaza del mercado, luego tuerzo a la derecha.
— Te / le seguiré hasta el mercado.
Voy en coche, pero algunos iremos a pie. John irá en bicicleta.

19

When? — Expressions of Time

3a Past, Present & Future

about **alrededor de**
after **después**
  after *(conj)* **después (de) que**
  afterwards **después, más tarde**
again **otra vez**
  again and again **una y otra vez**
ago **hace**
  a short time ago **hace poco tiempo**
already **ya**
always **siempre**
anniversary **el aniversario**
annual **anual**
as long as *(conj)* **siempre que, siempre cuando**
as soon as *(conj)* **tan pronto como**
at once **inmediatamente, ahora mismo**
before **antes (de)**
  before, beforehand **de antemano**
I begin **empiezo, comienzo**
beginning **el principio, el comienzo**

birthday **el cumpleaños**
brief **breve, corto**
briefly **brevemente**
by (next month) **al (mes próximo)**
calendar **el calendario, el almanaque**
centenary **el centenario**
century **el siglo**
  in the twentieth century **en el siglo veinte**
continuous **continuo**
daily **diariamente**
date **la fecha**
dawn **el amanecer**
  at dawn **al amanecer**
day **el día**
  by day **por día**
  every day **todos los días, cada día**
  one day (when) **un día (cuando)**
  the days of the week **los días de la semana**
decade **la década**

"Last Friday the train was late and you didn't get there till a quarter to three."
"I'll make it by three at the latest. If I'm late, you can have a coffee till I get there."

"I don't want to spend all afternoon drinking coffee. Then there will be no time left for shopping."

— **El viernes pasado el tren llevaba un retraso y no llegaste antes de las tres menos cuarto.**
— **Llegaré a las tres como más tarde [a más tardar]. Si llego tarde, puedes tomar un café mientras esperas mi llegada.**

— **No quiero pasar toda la tarde bebiendo café. Luego no quedará tiempo para hacer las compras.**

delay **el retraso, la posposición**
  delayed **retrasado, aplazado**
during **durante**
early **temprano, pronto**
  I am early **llego pronto**
end **el fin, el final**
  I end (something) **termino, finalizo**
  it ends **termina, finaliza**
ever **siempre**
every **todo, cada**
  every time **todas las veces, cada vez**
exactly **exactamente**
fast **rápido, adelantado**
  my watch is fast **mi reloj va adelantado**
finally **finalmente**
I finish **termino, finalizo**
first **el primero, primero**
  at first **primero, al principio**
  in the first place **primeramente, en primer lugar**
for **para, a, por**
for a day (duration) **por (un) día**
forever / for good **para siempre, por siempre**
formerly **anteriormente**
frequent **frecuente**
frequently **frecuentemente**

from **de, desde**
  as of / from (today) **de (hoy) en adelante**
  from now on **de ahora en adelante, desde ahora**
I go on **continúo**
half **la mitad**
  half **medio, media**
  one and a half **uno y medio, una y media**
it happens **sucede, ocurre**
hurry **la prisa, [el afán]**
  I hurry up **me apresuro, me doy prisa**
  I am in a hurry **tengo prisa [afán]**
instant **el instante**
just **justo**
  just now **justo ahora**
last / final **el último, el pasado**
  last night **anoche**
  last / previous **el último**
  it lasts a long / short time **dura mucho / poco tiempo**
late **tarde**
  I am late **llego tarde**
  lately **últimamente**
  later (on) **más tarde, después**
long **largo**
  in the long term **a largo plazo**

"You're sometimes late, too." — **A veces tú también llegas tarde.**

"Only in winter or in bad weather." — **Sólo en invierno o con (el) mal tiempo.**

"Last month I had to wait for twenty minutes." — **El mes pasado tuve que esperar veinte minutos.**

"Perhaps it would be better to meet another time. I'll call next week." — **Quizás sería mejor reunirnos en otra ocasión. Llamaré la semana que viene.**

WHEN? — EXPRESSIONS OF TIME

many **muchos, muchas**
   many times **muchas veces**
meanwhile **mientras tanto**
   in the meanwhile **mientras tanto**
middle **medio**
moment **el momento**
   at the moment **al momento**
   at this moment *(right now)* **en este momento**
   at that moment **en aquel momento**
   in a moment **en un momento**
month **el mes**
   monthly **mensualmente**
much **mucho/a**
never **nunca**
next *(adj)* **próximo**
   next *(adv)* **próximamente**
not till / until **no hasta**
now **ahora**
nowadays **hoy en día**
occasionally **a veces, ocasionalmente**
often **a menudo, con frecuencia**
on and off **de vez en cuando**
once **una vez**
   once upon a time **érase una vez, en tiempos de**
   once in a while **de vez en cuando**
   once a day **una vez al día**

one day **un día**
only **sólo**
past **el pasado**
per (day) **por (día)**
present **el presente**
   present *(adj)* **presente, actual**
   presently **en el momento presente**
   at present **en este momento**
previous(ly) **anterior(mente)**
prompt **pronto, con prontitud, sin dilación**
   promptly at (two) **a (las dos) en punto**
rarely **raramente**
recent **reciente**
recently **recientemente**
I remain **me quedo**
right away **en seguida, ahora mismo**
saint's day **el santo, el día del santo, la fiesta del santo**
season **la estación**
   in season *(fruit)* **en sazón**
seldom **rara vez, raramente**
several **algunos, varios**
   several times **algunas veces, varias veces**
short **corto**
   (in the) short term **(a) corto plazo**
   shortly **dentro de poco**

"Hello, John, Peter speaking / here. Thank you for yesterday's call. Sorry I couldn't call then. I had only gotten back from Madrid a quarter of an hour before."

—Hola, John, soy Peter. Gracias por haber llamado ayer. Siento que no pude llamar entonces. Sólo había llegado un cuarto de hora antes de Madrid.

After getting back I spent a long time with Anna; she thinks the project will take all month.

Después de volver pasé mucho tiempo con Ana; ella cree que hará falta todo el mes para terminar el proyecto.

since **desde**
slow **lento**
> my watch is slow **mi reloj va retrasado [está atrasado]**

sometimes **algunas veces**
soon **pronto**
> sooner or later **más tarde o más temprano, antes o después**
> the sooner the better **cuanto antes mejor**

I stay **me quedo**
still **todavía**
I stop (doing) **dejo (de hacer)**
suddenly **de repente**
sunrise **la salida del sol, el amanecer**
sunset **la puesta del sol**
I take (an hour) **me lleva, [gasto] (una hora)**
> it takes (an hour) **lleva (una hora)**

then *(next)* **luego, después**
> then *(at that time)* **entonces**

(one) thousand years **mil años**
till **hasta**
time *(in general)* **el tiempo**
time *(occasion)* **la vez**
> at any time **en cualquier momento**
> at the same time **al mismo tiempo**
> from time to time **de vez en cuando**
> for a long time **durante mucho tiempo**
> in good time **a tiempo**
> a long time ago **hace mucho tiempo**
> the whole time **todo el tiempo**

time zone **el huso horario**
twice **dos veces**
two weeks / fortnight **la quincena**
until **hasta**
usually **generalmente, usualmente**
vacation / holiday **las vacaciones**
I wait **espero**
week **la semana**
> weekly **semanalmente, por semana**
> weekday **el día de entre semana, el día laboral**
> weekend **el fin de semana**

when **cuando**
whenever **siempre que, cuandoquiera que**
while *(conj)* **mientras**
year **el año**
> yearly **anualmente**
yet **aún, todavía**
> not yet **todavía**

We should start on the work at the beginning of June, before the summer vacations / holidays start. We can then get it done in good time.
"Hello Peter, John Brown speaking/ here. I have been working on the project for a few days. Have you finished yours yet? Call me this afternoon. We must meet sometime."

Deberíamos empezar el trabajo a principios de junio, antes del comienzo de las vacaciones de verano. Entonces podremos terminarlo a tiempo.
—Hola Peter, soy John Brown. Llevo varios días trabajando en el proyecto. ¿Ya has terminado el tuyo? Llámame esta tarde. Deberíamos reunirnos alguna vez.

WHEN? — EXPRESSIONS OF TIME

3b The Time, Days & Dates

Time of day

a.m.   **de la mañana**
morning   **la mañana**
   in the morning(s)   **por la(s) mañana(s)**
noon   **el mediodía**
at noon   **al mediodía**
afternoon   **la tarde**
   in the afternoon(s)   **por la(s) tarde(s)**
p.m.   **de la tarde**
evening   **la tarde, la noche**
   in the evening(s)   **por la(s) tarde(s), por la(s) noche(s)**
night   **la noche**
   at night   **por la noche**
midnight   **las doce de la noche, medianoche**
   at midnight   **a las doce de la noche, a medianoche**
today   **hoy**
   in a week   **dentro de una semana**
   tomorrow   **mañana**
   tomorrow morning   **mañana por la mañana**
   tomorrow afternoon   **mañana por la tarde**
   tomorrow evening   **mañana por la tarde, mañana por la noche**

the day after tomorrow   **pasado mañana**
tonight   **esta noche**
yesterday   **ayer**
   yesterday afternoon   **ayer por la tarde**
   yesterday morning   **ayer por la mañana**
   yesterday evening   **ayer por la tarde, ayer por la noche**
   the day before yesterday   **anteayer**

Telling time

second   **el segundo**
minute   **el minuto**
hour   **la hora**
   half an hour   **media hora**
   in an hour's time   **dentro de una hora**
   hourly   **cada hora**
quarter   **un cuarto**
   quarter of an hour   **un cuarto de hora**
   three quarters of an hour   **tres cuartos de hora**
   quarter past / after (two)   **(dos) y cuarto**
   quarter to / of (two)   **(dos) menos cuarto**

"What's the date today?"	—¿A cuántos estamos? [¿Qué fecha es hoy?]
"The twenty-first of January."	—Estamos a veintiuno de enero.
"And what's the time, please?"	—¿Y qué hora es por favor?
"Ten past ten."	—Son las diez y diez.
"What time does the movie / film start this evening?"	—¿A qué hora empieza la película esta tarde / noche?
"20:00 hours."	—A las veinte horas.
"How long does it last?"	—¿Cuánto dura?
"One and a half hours."	—Dura una hora y media.

half past (two) **(dos) y media**
17:45 **las seis menos cuarto, las
cinco y cuarenta y cinco**
five past / after six **las seis y cinco**
five to / of six **las seis menos cinco**
12:00 noon **las doce del
mediodía, el mediodía**
12:00 midnight **las doce de la
noche, la medianoche**

The days of the week

Monday **el lunes**
Tuesday **el martes**
Wednesday **el miércoles**
Thursday **el jueves**
Friday **el viernes**
Saturday **el sábado**
Sunday **el domingo**

The months *

January **enero**
February **febrero**
March **marzo**
April **abril**
May **mayo**
June **junio**
July **julio**
August **agosto**
September **septiembre / setiembre**
October **octubre**
November **noviembre**
December **diciembre**

The seasons

spring **la primavera**
summer **el verano**
autumn / fall **el otoño**
winter **el invierno**

The date

last Friday **el viernes pasado**
on Tuesday **el martes**
on Tuesdays **los martes**
by Friday **para el viernes**
the first of January **el uno de
enero, [el primero de enero]**
on the third of January **el tres de
enero**
in 2000 **en el año dos mil**
January 1st / 1st January, 1998 **el
uno de enero de 1998**
at the end of 1999 **a finales de
1999**
by the end of 1999 **para finales de
1999**
at the beginning (of July) **a
primeros de (julio)**
by the beginning (of July) **para
primeros de (julio)**
in December **en diciembre**
in mid / the middle of January **a
mediados de enero**
at the end of March **al final de
marzo**
in spring **en primavera**

"I am going shopping tomorrow
morning. Would you like to come
too?"
"I'd prefer to go in the afternoon.
And let's go on Tuesday. I always
have so much to do on Mondays."

"All right, I'll leave home at two
o'clock and meet you at half-past
two at the station."

— **Voy de compras mañana por
la mañana. ¿Te gustaría ir
conmigo?**
— **Preferiría ir por la tarde.
Y vayamos el martes. Siempre
tengo mucho que hacer los
lunes.**

— **Vale, saldré de casa a las dos
y te veré a las dos y media en la
estación.**

➤ All months in Spanish are masculine.

How Much? — Expressions of Quantity

4a Length & Shape

angle	**el ángulo**
area	**el área, la superficie**
big	**grande**
center / centre	**el centro**
concave	**cóncavo**
convex	**convexo**
curved	**curvo**
deep	**profundo, hondo**
degree	**el grado**
depth	**la profundidad**
diagonal	**diagonal**
distance	**la distancia**
I draw	**dibujo**
height	**la altura**
high	**alto**
horizontal	**horizontal**
large	**grande**
length	**la longitud**
line	**la línea**
long	**largo**
low	**bajo**
it measures	**mide**
narrow	**estrecho**
parallel	**paralelo**

perpendicular	**perpendicular**
point	**el punto**
room (space)	**el espacio, el sitio**
round	**redondo**
ruler	**la regla**
shape	**la forma, la figura**
short	**corto**
size	**el tamaño, la talla, la medida**
small	**pequeño**
space	**el espacio**
straight	**derecho**
tall	**alto**
thick	**grueso, espeso**
thin	**fino, delgado**
wide	**ancho**
width	**la anchura**

Shapes

circle	**el círculo**
circular	**circular**
cube	**el cubo**
cubic	**cúbico**
cylinder	**el cilindro**
hectare	**la hectárea**

You need a ruler and pencil. Measure the space and then draw a plan.	**Necesita una regla y un lápiz. Mida el espacio, luego dibuje un plano.**
Leave room for the vegetable garden. The distance from the house to the fence is twelve meters / metres. The garden is not wide enough for a pool.	**Deja sitio para el huerto. La distancia entre la casa y la tapia es doce metros. El jardín no es bastante ancho para un estanque.**
"How high is the tree?" "About five meters / metres."	**— ¿Qué altura tiene el árbol? — Unos cinco metros.**

pyramid **la pirámide**
rectangle **el rectángulo**
   rectangular **rectangular**
sphere **la esfera**
   spherical **esférico**
square **el cuadrado**
   square **cuadrado**
triangle **el triángulo**
   triangular **triangular**

Units of length

centimeter / centimetre **el centímetro**
foot **el pie**
inch **la pulgada**
kilometer / kilometre **el kilómetro**
meter / metre **el metro**
mile **la milla**
millimeter / millimetre **el milímetro**
yard **la vara, la yarda**

Expressions of quantity

about **alrededor, aproximadamente**
almost **casi**
approximate **aproximado**
approximately **aproximadamente**
as much as **tanto como**
at least **al menos**
capacity **la capacidad, el volumen**

it contains **contiene**
cubic capacity **la capacidad cúbica**
it decreases **disminuye**
difference **la diferencia**
empty **vacío**
I empty **vacío**
enough **bastante, suficiente**
I fill **lleno**
full (of) **lleno (de)**
growth **el aumento**
hardly **difícilmente, casi**
increase **el aumento**
it increases **aumenta**
little **pequeño**
   a little **un poco**
a lot (of) **mucho (de)**
I measure **mido**
measuring tape **la cinta métrica, [el metro]**
more **más**
nearly **casi**
number **el número**
part **la parte**
quantity **la cantidad**
sufficient **suficiente**
too much **demasiado**
volume **el volumen**
whole **la totalidad, el todo**
   whole *(adj)* **todo**

The shed will be at an angle of about forty degrees to the house, diagonally across from the gate.

El cobertizo estará a un ángulo de unos cuarenta grados con relación a la casa, en sentido diagonal con relación a la puerta.

The area of our garden is one hundred square meters / metres. It is ten meters / metres long and ten wide.

El área de nuestro jardín es cien metros cuadrados. Tiene diez metros de largo y diez metros de ancho.

We put in a round pond, only eighty to one hundred centimeters / centimetres deep.

Introdujimos un estanque redondo, de una profundidad de ochenta a cien centímetros.

HOW MUCH? — EXPRESSIONS OF QUANTITY

4b Measuring

Expressions of volume

bag   **el saco, la bolsa**
bar   **la barra**
bottle   **la botella**
box   **la caja**
container   **el recipiente, [el contáiner]**
cup   **la copa, la taza**
gallon   **el galón**
glass   **el vaso**
liter / litre   **el litro**
   centiliter / centilitre   **el centilitro**

milliliter / millimetre   **el mililitro**
pack   **el paquete, la cajetilla**
pair   **el par, la pareja**
piece   **la pieza**
   a piece of cake   **una porción de tarta**
pint   **la pinta**
portion   **la porción**
pot   **la olla**
sack   **el saco, [el costal]**
tube   **el tubo**

"How many centiliters / centilitres are there in the bottle?"
"Seventy-five, but you can also get it in liter / litre bottles."

— **¿Cuántos centílitros hay en la botella?**
— **Setenta y cinco, pero también se puede obtener en botellas de litro.**

"Would you like a cup of tea?"
"No, I would prefer a glass of water."

— **¿Desea una taza de té?**
— **No, preferiría un vaso de agua.**

May I have two packets of tissues and a packet of aspirin please?

Quisiera dos paquetes de pañuelos de papel y un paquete de aspirina, por favor.

"How much wood do you want?"
"Enough for the whole fence.
I must not buy too much. Yes, that should be sufficient. Give me a bag of cement too."

— **¿Cuánta madera desea?**
— **Lo suficiente para toda la valla. No debería comprar demasiado. Sí, eso será suficiente. Deme también un saco de cemento.**

"How many cubic meters of concrete do you need?"
"About two."

— **¿Cuántos metros cúbicos de hormigón necesita?**
— **Dos, más o menos.**

Temperature

it boils	**hierve**
I chill	**enfrío**
cold	**el frío**
cold *(adj)*	**frío**
cool	**fresco**
I cool it down	**lo enfrío**
degree	**el grado**
I freeze	**congelo**
heat	**el calor**
I heat	**caliento**
hot	**caliente**
temperature	**la temperatura**
I warm it (up)	**lo caliento**
warmth	**el calor**

Weight and density

balance / scales	**el peso, la balanza**
dense	**denso**
density	**la densidad**
gram / gramme	**el gramo**
heavy	**pesado**
kilo	**el kilo**
light	**ligero**
mass	**la masa**
ounce	**la onza**
pound *(lb)*	**la libra**
ton(ne)	**la tonelada**
I weigh	**peso**
weight	**el peso**

It's so hot! What's the temperature? It must be nearly thirty centigrades. I am too hot.

¡Qué calor hace! ¿Cuál es la temperatura? Serán unos treinta centígrados. Tengo demasiado calor.

In winter it's cold here. We all freeze in this house and have to put on the heating in September.

En el invierno hace frío aquí. Todos pasamos frío en esta casa y tenemos que poner la calefacción en setiembre.

When the temperature reaches zero we have to light two fires.

Cuando la temperatura baja a cero grados, tenemos que encender dos fuegos.

"Would you weigh the ingredients?" "How many grams of sugar do we need?" "I want a pound—that must be about five hundred grams / grammes. I need a little flour and a lot of sugar. Give me a piece of butter. About one hundred grams / grammes. I will need several eggs."

— ¿Podría pesar los ingredientes? — ¿Cuántos gramos de azúcar necesitamos? — Quiero una libra—que serán unos quinientos gramos. Necesito un poco de harina y mucho azúcar. Póngame un trozo de mantequilla. Unos cien gramos. Necesitaré unos huevos.

"That's too little. We need even more cakes. Make a bit more."

— No basta así. Vamos a necesitar más pasteles aun. Haz un poco más.

HOW MUCH? — EXPRESSIONS OF QUANTITY

4c Numbers

Cardinal numbers

zero **cero**
one **uno**
two **dos**
three **tres**
four **cuatro**
five **cinco**
six **seis**
seven **siete**
eight **ocho**
nine **nueve**
ten **diez**
eleven **once**
twelve **doce**
thirteen **trece**
fourteen **catorce**
fifteen **quince**
sixteen **dieciséis**
seventeen **diecisiete**
eighteen **dieciocho**
nineteen **diecinueve**

twenty **veinte**
twenty-one **veintiuno**
twenty-two **veintidós**
twenty-nine **veintinueve**
thirty **treinta**
thirty-one **treinta y uno**
forty **cuarenta**
fifty **cincuenta**
sixty **sesenta**
seventy **setenta**
eighty **ochenta**
ninety **noventa**
a hundred **cien, ciento**
a hundred and one **ciento uno**
two hundred **doscientos**
a thousand **mil**
two thousand **dos mil**
million **el millón**
two million **dos millones**
billion **el billón**
billion / milliard **mil millones**

Half of the house belongs to my brother. We divided it between us. However, he only pays a quarter of the costs as I rent my half out in summer.

La mitad de la casa pertenece a mi hermano. La dividimos entre los dos. Sin embargo, sólo paga la cuarta parte de los gastos, pues yo dejo mi mitad en alquiler durante el verano.

"What is the volume of water in the swimming pool?"
"Ten thousand gallons, that is about forty-five thousand liters / litres."

— ¿ Cuánta agua hay en la piscina?
— Diez mil galones, es decir unos cuarenta y cinco mil litros.

Ordinal numbers

first	**el primero**
second	**el segundo**
third	**el tercero**
fourth	**el cuarto**
nineteenth	**el décimonoveno**
twentieth	**el vigésimo**
twenty-first	**el vigésimo primero**
hundredth	**el centésimo**

Nouns

one   **el uno**
  unit   **la unidad**
a pair / couple of   **un par (de)**
ten   **el diez**
  about ten (of)   **una decena (de)**
  tens   **las decenas**
dozen   **la docena**
about twenty   **una veintena (de)**
hundred   **el cien**
  hundreds of   **cientos de**
about a thousand   **un millar**
  thousands (of)   **millares / miles (de)**
million   **el millón**
  millions of   **millones de**

Writing numerals

1,000	**1.000**
1,500	**1.500**
1st	**1°**
2nd	**2°**
1.56	**1,56 (uno coma cincuenta y seis)**
.05	**,05 (coma cero cinco)**

Fractions

half   **la mitad, el medio**
  a half   **una mitad, un medio**
  one and a half   **uno y medio**
  two and a half   **dos y medio**
quarter   **el cuarto**
a quarter   **un cuarto**
three quarters   **tres cuartos**
third   **el tercio**
fifth   **el quinto**
five and five sixths   **cinco y cinco sextos**
tenth   **el décimo**
sixth   **el sexto**
hundredth   **el centésimo**
thousandth   **el milésimo**
millionth   **el millonésimo**

"You cannot all have half a bar of chocolate.	**—No todos podéis tener media tableta de chocolate.**
There is only enough for a quarter each.	**Sólo hay suficiente para una cuarta parte para cada uno.**
And a quarter of a liter / litre of apple juice."	**Y un cuarto de litro de zumo de manzana.**
"I don't want a quarter, I want a half."	**—No quiero una cuarta parte, quiero una mitad.**

HOW MUCH? — EXPRESSIONS OF QUANTITY

4d Calculations

addition **la suma, la adición**
  I add **sumo, adiciono**
average **la media, el medio, el promedio**
  I average out **saco la media**
  on average **como media**
I calculate **calculo**
  calculation **el cálculo**
  calculator **la calculadora**
I correct **corrijo**
I count **cuento**
data **el dato, los datos**
  piece of data **el dato**
decimal **el decimal**
  decimal point **el punto decimal**
diameter **el diámetro**
digit **el dígito, la cifra**
  two digit **de dos dígitos**
I double **multiplico por dos, doblo**
division **la división**

I divide by **divido entre / por**
six divided by two **seis dividido entre / por dos**
it equals **es igual a**
equation **la ecuación**
it is equivalent to **es equivalente a**
I estimate **estimo**
even **el par**
figure **la cifra**
graph **el gráfico**
is greater than **es mayor que**
is less than **es menor que**
maximum **el máximo**
  maximum **máximo**
  up to a maximum of **hasta un máximo de**
medium **la media**
  medium (adj) **medio**
minimum **el mínimo**
  minimum (adj) **mínimo**
minus **menos**

An inch is the same as 2.54 cm, and there are twelve inches in a foot, thirty-six in a yard. A mile is 1760 yards. A kilometer / kilometre is 1000 meters / metres.

Una pulgada equivale a 2,54 centímetros, y hay doce pulgadas en un pie, treinta y seis en una vara. Una milla tiene 1.760 varas. Un kilómetro tiene 1.000 metros.

What is fourteen plus eight? It equals twenty-two. Did you get the right result?

¿Cuántos son catorce más ocho? Son veinte y dos. ¿Obtuviste el resultado correcto?

Twenty minus five is fifteen, twenty divided by five equals four.

Veinte menos cinco son quince, veinte dividido por cinco son cuatro.

Work out twelve times twenty-two. That is an easy sum.

Calcula doce por veinte y dos. Es un cálculo fácil.

Two to the power of three is eight. Three squared equals nine.

Dos a la potencia de tres son ocho [dos al cubo son ocho]. Tres al cuadrado son nueve.

mistake / error **el error**

multiplication **la multiplicación**

   I multiply **multiplico**

   three times two **tres por dos**

negative **el negativo**

number **el número**

   cardinal / ordinal numbers **los números cardinales / ordinales**

numeral **el numeral**

odd **el impar**

percent **el por ciento**

   ten percent **el diez por ciento**

percentage **el porcentaje**

plus **más**

   two plus two **dos más dos**

positive **el positivo**

power **la potencia**

   to the power of five **a la quinta potencia**

problem **el problema**

quantity **la cantidad**

ratio **la proporción**

   a ratio of 100:1 **una proporción de cien a uno**

result **el resultado**

similar **similar**

solution **la solución**

   I solve **resuelvo**

square **el cuadrado**

square root **la raíz cuadrada**

   three squared **la raíz cúbica**

statistic **la estadística**

statistics **las estadísticas**

statistical **estadístico**

sum **la suma**

subtraction **la resta, la sustracción**

   I subtract **resto, sustraigo**

symbol **el símbolo**

I take away **resto**

total **el total**

   in total **en total**

I treble **triplico**

triple **el triple**

I work out **saco, calculo**

wrong **mal, equivocado**

"I estimate that we have about five hundred visitors a year."

"What percentage of visitors are local?"

"Twenty percent."

—**Calculo que recibimos a unos quinientos visitantes al año.**

—**¿Qué porcentaje de los visitantes son de esta misma región?**

—**Veinte por ciento.**

Have you got any statistics about it?

—**¿Tiene estadísticas sobre ello?**

A snail travels at an average speed of 0.041 kilometers / kilometres per hour.

Un caracol viaja a una velocidad de 0,041 kilómetros por hora.

"In this game you add up your score over the week."

"What was the total score?"

"I have a total of five hundred points."

—**En este juego, se hace la puntuación total de la semana.**

—**¿Cuál fue la puntuación final?**

—**Tengo un total de quinientos puntos.**

To calculate the average you add up the totals and divide by the number of games.

Para calcular el promedio, sumas los totales y lo divides por el número de juegos.

What Sort Of? — Descriptions & Judgments

5a Describing People

appearance **la apariencia**	fat **gordo**
attractive **atractivo**	feature **la facción, el rasgo**
average **medio**	female **la mujer**
he is bald **es calvo**	feminine **femenino**
beard **la barba**	figure **la figura, el tipo**
bearded **con barba**	fit **en forma**
beautiful **guapo, bello**	I frown **frunzo el ceño**
beauty **la belleza**	glasses **las gafas**
beauty mark **el lunar**	good-looking **guapo**
with beauty marks **con lunares**	I grow **crezco**
blond **rubio**	hair **el pelo, el cabello**
broad **ancho**	hairstyle **el peinado**
build **la constitución**	handsome **hermoso, bello,**
chic **chic, de moda**	**distinguido**
cleanshaven **afeitado**	heavy **pesado, grueso**
clumsy **torpe**	height **la altura**
complexion **la constitución**	large **grande**
curly **rizado, crespo**	I laugh **río, me río**
dark **oscuro, moreno**	laugh **la risa**
I describe **describo**	I am left-handed **soy zurdo**
description **la descripción**	light **claro**
different (from) **diferente de,**	I look like **soy, mi apariencia es**
distinto de	I look good **soy guapo**
elegant **elegante**	male **el varón, el hombre**
energy **la energía, el vigor**	masculine **masculino**
expression **la expresión**	mustache **el bigote**
farsighted / longsighted **présbite,**	nearsighted / shortsighted **miope**
hipermétrope	neat **limpio, acicalado, pulcro**

adolescence **la adolescencia**	older / elder **mayor**
adolescent **el / la adolescente**	teenager **el adolescente**
age **la edad**	young **joven**
elderly **viejo, mayor, anciano**	young person **el joven, la**
grown up **el adulto**	**persona joven**
grown up **adulto**	young people **los jóvenes**
middle-aged **de mediana edad**	youth **la juventud**
old **viejo, mayor**	youthful **lleno de juventud**

neatness **la limpieza, el aseo**
obese **obeso**
overweight **el sobrepeso, el exceso de peso**
part of body **la parte del cuerpo**
paunch **la barriga, la panza**
physical **físico**
pimple **el grano**
   pimply **con granos**
plump **rechoncho**
pretty **guapo, bonito**
red-haired **pelirrojo**
I am right-handed **soy diestro**
I scowl **pongo mal gesto, frunzo el ceño, hago mala cara**
sex / gender **el sexo, el género**
short **bajo, corto**
similar (to) **parecido a, similar a**
similarity **la similaridad**
size **el tamaño, la talla**

slim / slender **delgado, esbelto**
small **pequeño, bajo**
I smile **sonrío**
smile **la sonrisa**
stocky **rechoncho, bajo pero fuerte**
strength **la fuerza**
striking **impresionante, imponente**
strong **fuerte, robusto**
tall **alto**
thin **delgado, flaco**
tiny **pequeño**
trendy **moderno**
ugliness **la fealdad**
ugly **feo**
walk **el andar, el paso**
wavy **ondulado**
I weigh **peso**
weight **el peso**

"What's your uncle like? Can you describe him?"
"He looks a lot like my father, but he wears glasses. Look, who's that tall fellow?"
"That's my brother, with the beard. He's mad about keeping fit."

"What a pretty girl! Is that your cousin?"
"Yes, she's blonde with blue eyes. She's very slim, with a good figure and a beautiful smile."
"Little Ben now has dark hair and is about one meter / metre tall.

He looks very well, but he's very thin."
"Yes, he only weighs sixteen kilos."

— ¿Cómo es tu tío? ¿Puedes describirlo?
— Se parece mucho a mi padre, pero lleva gafas. Mira, ¿quién es ese tipo alto?
— Es mi hermano con la barba. Es muy aficionado a mantenerse en forma.

— ¡Qué chica más bonita! ¿Es tu prima?
— Sí, es rubia con ojos azules. Es muy esbelta, con un buen físico y una sonrisa hermosa.
— Ahora el pequeño Ben tiene el pelo oscuro y mide aproximadamente un metro. Tiene buena cara, pero es muy delgado.
— Sí, sólo pesa diez y seis kilos.

5b The Senses

bitter	**amargo**
bright	**claro, luminoso**
bright *(harsh)*	**brillante**
cold	**el frío**
cold	**frío**
color / colour	**el color**
colorful / colourful	**lleno de color**
dark	**oscuro**
darkness	**la oscuridad**
delicious	**delicioso**
disgusting	**desagradable**
dull	**apagado, sombrío**
I feel . . .	**siento**
it feels	**es**
I hear	**oigo**
hot	**caliente**
light *(color / colour)*	**claro, pálido**
I listen	**oigo, escucho**
I look	**miro, veo**
I look at	**miro**
loud	**alto, ruidoso**
noise	**el ruido**
noisy	**ruidoso**
odor / odour	**el olor**
opaque	**opaco**
perfume	**el perfume**
perfumed	**perfumado**

quiet	**quieto, tranquilo, callado**
rough	**rugoso, áspero**
salty	**salado**
I see	**veo**
sense	**el sentido**
silence	**el silencio**
silent	**silencioso**
I am silent	**estoy silencioso, estoy en silencio**
smell	**el olor**
I smell	**huelo**
it smells (of)	**huele a**
smelly	**oloroso, apestoso**
soft *(sound)*	**bajo, flojo, suave**
soft *(texture)*	**suave**
sound	**el sonido**
it sounds	**suena**
it sounds like	**suena como**
sour	**agrio**
sticky	**pegajoso**
it is sticky	**es pegajoso**
sweet	**dulce**
taste	**el sabor**
I taste	**saboreo**
it tastes (of)	**sabe a**
tepid	**tibio**
I touch	**toco**

"What color / colour is your new coat?"
"Well, it's sort of red."
"Dark or light red?"
"It is more maroon."

—¿De qué color es tu abrigo nuevo?
—Bueno, es una especie de rojo.
—¿Rojo oscuro o claro?
—Es más bien rojo oscuro.

The jam tastes of fruit but is very bitter.

La mermelada sabe a fruta, pero está muy amarga.

Don't touch that book, your hands are all sticky.

No toques ese libro, tienes las manos todas pegajosas.

transparent **transparente**
visible (in-) **(in)visible**
warm **caliente**
warmth **el calor**

Common parts of the body

arm **el brazo**
back **la espalda**
body **el cuerpo**
   part of the body **la parte del**
   cuerpo
chest **el pecho**
ear **la oreja**

eye **el ojo**
face **la cara**
hand **la mano**
head **la cabeza**
leg **la pierna**
mouth **la boca**
neck **el cuello**
neck (back of) **la nuca**
nose **la nariz**
shoulder **el hombro**
stomach **el estómago**
tooth **el diente**

Colors / Colours

beige **beige**
black **negro**
blue **azul**
brown **marrón, café**
brownish **amarronado**
cream **crema**
gold *(metal)* **el oro**
   gold *(adj)* **de oro, dorado**
green **verde**
gray / grey **gris**
maroon **rojo oscuro**
orange *(fruit)* **la naranja**

orange *(adj)* **anaranjado**
pink **rosa, rosado**
purple **purpúreo, [morado]**
red **rojo**
scarlet **escarlata** *(invar)*
silver *(metal)* **la plata**
   silver *(adj)* **plateado**
turquoise **la turquesa**
   turquoise *(adj)* **aturquesado**
violet **violeta** *(invar)*
white **blanco**
yellow **amarillo**

"What's in that bag? It feels hard."

"Let me feel — it's a bottle. What's in it?"

"I don't know. It looks like orange juice."

"I'll taste it . . . It's disgusting. It tastes of oranges, but it's too sweet."

"What a beautiful smell."
"Yes, that's the flowers; they are so bright and colorful."

— ¿Qué hay en esta bolsa? Parece ser algo duro.

— Déjame palparlo — es una botella. ¿Qué tiene dentro?

— No sé. Se parece a zumo de naranja.

— Lo voy a probar ... Es asqueroso. Sabe a naranjas, pero es demasiado dulce.

— ¡Qué olor más agradable!
— Sí, son las flores; están tan llenas de colores vivos.

5c Describing Things

appearance **la apariencia**
big **grande**
broad **ancho**
broken **roto**
clean **limpio**
closed **cerrado**
color / colour **el color**
   colored / coloured **de color**
   colorful / colourful **de muchos colores**
damp **húmedo**
deep **hondo, profundo**
   depth **la hondura, la profundidad**

dirt **la suciedad**
dirty **sucio**
dry **seco**
empty **vacío**
enormous **enorme**
fashionable **de moda**
fat **gordo**
firm **firme**
flat **plano**
flexible **flexible, elástico**
fresh **fresco**
full (of) **lleno (de)**
genuine / real **genuino, auténtico**
hard **duro**

Ten questions

What's that thingamajig? **¿Qué es ese chisme?, [¿Qué es esa cosa?]**
What's it for? **¿Para qué sirve?**
What do you use it for? **¿Para qué lo utilizas?**
Can you see it? **¿Lo ves?**
What's it like? **¿Cómo es?**

What does it look like? **¿A qué se parece?**
What does it sound like? **¿A qué suena?**
What does it smell of? **¿A qué huele?**
What color / colour is it? **¿De qué color es?**
What kind of thing is it? **¿Qué tipo de cosa es?**

"What's that over there?"
"That thing there? It's a new kind of bottle opener."
"Does it work?"
"Yes, indeed. It's the best there is."

— **¿Qué es aquello que está allí?**
— **¿Aquello allí? Es un nuevo tipo de abrebotellas.**
— **¿Funciona?**
— **Claro. Es el mejor que existe.**

This is a genuine natural material, soft and thick. That is a synthetic material, it's smooth, but the colors / colours are harsh.

Éste es un tejido genuinamente natural, blando y espeso. Aquel es un tejido sintético, es liso, pero los colores son chillones.

height **la altura**	shallow **poco profundo**
it looks like **se parece a**	shiny **brillante**
it matches **hace juego con**	short **corto**
kind **agradable**	shut **cerrado**
large **grande**	small **pequeño**
liquid **líquido**	smooth **liso**
little **pequeño**	soft *(texture)* **suave**
long **largo**	solid **sólido, compacto**
low **bajo**	soluble **soluble**
main **principal, importante**	sort **la clase, el tipo**
material **material**	spot **el lunar, la mota**
matter **la materia**	spotted **a lunares, moteado**
moist **mojado, húmedo**	stain **la mancha**
moldy / mouldy **mohoso, enmohecido**	stained **manchado**
narrow **estrecho**	stripe **la raya**
natural **natural**	striped **a rayas, rayado**
new **nuevo**	subsidiary **secundario**
open **abierto**	substance **la substancia**
out-of-date **pasado de moda**	synthetic **sintético**
painted **pintado**	thick **espeso**
pale **pálido, claro**	thing **la cosa, el objeto**
pattern **el diseño**	thingamajig **la cosa**
patterned **modelado**	tint **el tinte**
plump **lleno, rechoncho**	varied **variado**
resistant **resistente**	waterproof **a prueba de agua**
rotten **podrido**	wet **mojado**
shade **el tono, el matiz**	wide **ancho**

"I'm looking for something big to stand on."	—Busco algo grande en que subirme.
"Will anything do?"	—¿Bastará cualquier cosa?
"Well, it must be something solid."	—Bueno, tiene que ser algo sólido.
"What about this?"	—¿Qué te parece esto?
"Is there nothing bigger?"	—¿No hay nada más grande?
"Stand on the chair."	—Levántate en la silla.
"It's too soft."	—Es demasiado blanda.
"All the other chairs are too low."	—Todas las demás sillas son demasiado bajas.
"Both the cupboards are too high."	—Ambos armarios son demasiado altos.

5d Evaluating Things

abnormal **anormal, raro**	I enjoy **disfruto**
I adore **adoro**	easy **fácil**
all right **muy bien, bueno**	essential (un-) **(no) esencial**
it is all right **está bien**	excellent **excelente**
appalling **espantoso, horroroso**	expensive **caro, costoso**
bad **malo**	I fail **fallo, fracaso**
beautiful **bonito**	failure **el fallo, el fracaso**
better / best **mejor, el mejor**	false **falso**
cheap **barato**	fine **bueno, fino, delicado**
correct **correcto**	good **bueno**
it costs **cuesta**	good value **buen precio**
delicious **delicioso**	great / terrific **magnífico,**
I detest **detesto**	**estupendo, tremendo**
difficulty **la dificultad**	I hate **odio, detesto**
difficult / hard **difícil, duro**	high **alto, bueno**
disgusting **repugnante,**	important (un-) **(no) importante**
asqueroso	incorrect **incorrecto**
I dislike **no me gusta**	interesting (un-) **(no) interesante**

a bit **un poco**	not at all **nada en absoluto**
enough **bastante, suficiente**	particularly **particularmente,**
extremely **extremadamente**	**especialmente**
fairly **bastante**	quite **bastante**
hardly … at all **difícilmente**	rather **muy, bastante**
little **pequeño, poco**	really **realmente**
a little **un poco**	so **así, de esta manera**
a lot **mucho**	too (good) **demasiado (bueno)**
much (better) **mucho mejor**	very **muy**

How do you like our neighbor's / neighbour's garden / yard? We do not like it at all.	¿Qué te parece el jardín de nuestro vecino? A nosotros no nos gusta nada.
I wish he would throw away that broken seat.	Me gustaría que tirara [botara] aquella silla rota.
It is only plastic anyway. We always buy the best! Our garden furniture is made of wood.	Sólo es de plástico. ¡Siempre compramos lo mejor! Nuestros muebles de jardín son de madera.
And his lawn mower is out of order.	Y su cortacésped no funciona.

I like **me gusta**
mediocre **mediocre**
necessary (un-) **(in)necesario**
normal **normal, común**
order **el orden**
   in order **en orden**
   out of order **sin orden**
out-of-date **fuera de fecha, caducado**
ordinary **ordinario, normal, común**
pleasant **agradable**
poor **pobre**
practical (im-) **(no) práctico**
I prefer **prefiero**
quality **la calidad**
   top quality **la mejor calidad, la alta calidad**
   poor quality **la mala calidad, la baja calidad**

right **bueno**
strange **extraño, raro**
I succeed **consigo**
success **el éxito, la consecución**
successful **exitoso**
true **verdadero**
I try **intento, pruebo**
ugly **feo**
unpleasant **desagradable**
unsuccessful **sin éxito, fracasado**
I use **uso, utilizo**
use **el uso, la utilización**
useful **útil**
well **bien**
worse / worst **peor, el peor**
I would rather **prefiero, preferiría**
wrong **equivocado**

He never puts it away, and now he'll have to get it fixed / mended.
I fear he's not a very successful gardener. His vegetables are a complete failure.

Nunca la guarda, y ahora tendrá que hacerla reparar.
Por desgracia no tiene mucho éxito como jardinero. Sus legumbres han fallado [se perdieron] por completo.

I do like to keep the garden / yard tidy / neat.
People always say our garden / yard is the best on the street.

Me gusta mucho mantener el jardín en buen estado.
La gente siempre dice que nuestro jardín es el mejor de la calle.

I tried to call / ring you yesterday, but the telephones were out of order.

Traté de llamarte ayer pero no funcionaban los teléfonos.

"Would you like to try this wine?"
"Thank you, it is quite delicious."

—¿Te gustaría probar este vino?
—Gracias, está muy delicioso.

"Do you enjoy going to the movies / cinema?"
"Yes, I particularly enjoyed last week's movie / film."

—¿Te gusta ir al cine?
—Sí, me gustó sobre todo la película de la semana pasada.

5e Comparisons

*Regular comparatives & superlatives**

easy **fácil**
    easier **más fácil**
    easiest **el más fácil**

*Irregular comparatives and superlatives**

bad **malo**
    worse **peor**
    worst **el peor**

big **grande**
    bigger **mayor, más grande**
    biggest **el mayor, el más grande**
good **bueno**
    better **mejor**
    best **el mejor**
small **pequeño**
    smaller **menor, más pequeño**
    smallest **el menor, el más pequeño**

Look at the children! Peter, our eldest son, is now the tallest. He's best at soccer, too. That's what he enjoys best.	¡Mira a los niños! Pedro, nuestro hijo mayor, ya es el más alto. Es el que juega mejor al fútbol también. Es lo que a él le gusta más hacer.
John is now fairly large, almost as tall as Peter, and he really is too fat. He prefers to swim.	Juan ya es bastante grande, casi tan alto como Pedro, y la verdad es que es demasiado gordo. Prefiere nadar.
The smallish boy over there is David. He is quite small compared to the others, but on the other hand very confident. He behaves less well than his brother.	El chico pequeño que está allá es David. Es bastante pequeño en comparación con los demás, pero por otra parte está muy seguro de sí mismo. Se comporta menos bien que su hermano.
John has eaten the largest cake. He gets larger and larger.	Juan ha comido el pastel más grande. Se pone cada vez más grande.

5f Materials

acrylic **el acrílico**
brick **el ladrillo**
cashmere **la cachemira, el cachemir**
cement **el cemento**
china **la porcelana**
concrete **el hormigón**
cotton **el algodón**
Dacron / Terylene **el dacrón, el terilene**
denim **el dril, la tela vaquera**
gas **el gas**
glass **el vidrio, el cristal**
gold **el oro**
iron **el hierro**
leather **la piel, el cuero**
linen **el lino, el lienzo, [el hilo]**
metal **el metal**
mineral **el mineral**
nylon **el nilón, el nailon**

oil **el aceite, el petróleo**
paper **el papel**
plastic **el plástico**
polyester **el poliéster**
pottery **la cerámica**
satin **el raso**
silk **la seda**
silky **sedoso**
silver **la plata**
steel **el acero**
steel *(adj)* **de acero, acerado**
stone **la piedra**
stone *(adj)* **de piedra**
velvet **el terciopelo**
viscose **la viscosa**
wood **la madera**
wooden **de madera**
wool **la lana**
woolen / woollen **de lana**

Have you seen our latest products? They are just as cheap as the competition.

¿Ha visto usted nuestros últimos productos? Son tan baratos como los de la competencia.

We cannot ask a higher price, as the greatest demand is for the cheaper product.

No podemos pedir un precio más alto, pues la demanda más grande es la del producto más barato.

Which dress would you like? Silk is softer than wool, but it costs a lot. Nylon is cheapest.

¿Qué vestido preferirías? La seda es más suave que la lana, pero cuesta mucho dinero. El nilón es el más barato.

The most beautiful dress is the one made of cotton.
The colors / colours are brighter and I think the cut is better, although it is not as warm as the woolen / woollen dress.
It is not at all expensive. I prefer it to the others.

El vestido más bello es el que está hecho de algodón.
Los colores son más vivos y creo que el corte es mejor, aunque no es tan abrigado como el vestido de lana.
No es caro de ninguna manera.
Lo prefiero a los demás.

▶ CLOTHING 9c; COMPOUNDS & ALLOYS, CHEMICAL ELEMENTS App. 23b

The Human Mind & Character

6a Human Character

active **activo**
I adapt **me adapto**
amusing **divertido**
I annoy **molesto, importuno**
bad **malo**
bad-tempered **de mal temperamento / genio**
I behave **me comporto, me porto**
behavior / behaviour **la conducta, el comportamiento**
I boast **presumo, fanfarroneo**
calm **tranquilo, calmado**
care **el cuidado**
careful **cuidadoso**
careless **descuidado**
character **el carácter**
characteristic **la característica**
characteristic *(adj)* **característico**
charming **encantador, atractivo**
cheerful **alegre**
clever **listo, despierto**
confident **seguro de sí mismo**
discipline **la disciplina, el orden**
dreadful **terrible, espantoso, horrible**

evil **el mal**
evil *(adj)* **maligno**
foolish **tonto**
forgetful **olvidadizo**
friendly (un-) **(poco) amistoso**
fussy **quisquilloso, exigente**
generous **generoso**
I get on with **me llevo bien con, [me entiendo con]**
gifted **con talento, dotado**
good **bueno**
good-tempered **amistoso, afable**
habit **la costumbre, el hábito**
hard-working **trabajador, laborioso**
I help **ayudo**
helpful **atento, servicial**
honest (dis-) **(des)honesto**
humor / humour **el humor, el estado de ánimo**
humorous **humorístico**
immorality **la inmoralidad**
innocent **inocente**
intelligence **la inteligencia**
intelligent **inteligente**
kind (un-) **(poco) amable**

Don't be so suspicious. Please trust me.

No seas tan desconfiado. Por favor, fíate de mí [confía en mí].

Our neighbor / neighbour is a lazy fellow, but very gifted. He has a good sense of humor but is very pretentious.
His wife is very pleasant and helpful.
The children are lively characters. They never obey their mother.

Nuestro vecino es un tipo perezoso, pero tiene mucho talento. Tiene un buen sentido de humor, pero es muy presumido. Su esposa es muy simpática y amable. Los niños son muy enérgicos. Nunca le obedecen a su madre.

kindness **la amabilidad**
lazy **perezoso, holgazán**
laziness **la pereza, la holgazanería**
lively **animado, alegre, vivo**
mad **loco**
manners **los modales, las maneras**
mental(ly) **mental(mente)**
moral (im-) **(in)moral**
morality **la moralidad**
nervous **nervioso, agitado**
nice **agradable, bonito**
I obey (dis-) **(des)obedezco**
optimistic **optimista**
patient (im-) **(im)paciente**
personality **la personalidad**
pessimistic **pesimista**
pleasant **agradable, placentero**
polite (im-) **(mal) educado, (des)cortés**
popular **popular**
quality **la calidad**
reasonable (un-) **(ir)razonable**
respect **el respeto**
I respect **respeto**
rude **grosero, descortés**
sad **triste**
self-confident **seguro de sí mismo**
self-esteem **la autoestima**
sense **el sentido**
   common sense **el sentido común**
   good sense **el buen sentido**

sensible **sensato, prudente**
serious **serio, formal**
shy **tímido, retraído**
skill **la habilidad**
skillful **habilidoso**
sociable (un-) **(in)sociable**
strange **extraño, raro**
stupid **tonto, estúpido**
stupidity **la estupidez**
suspicious **suspicaz, desconfiado**
sympathetic **comprensivo, compasivo**
sympathy **la simpatía, la solidaridad, la comprensión**
tactful **discreto, con tacto**
tactless **indiscreto, sin tacto**
talented **con talento, dotado**
temperament **el temperamento, el carácter**
temperamental **temperamental, con mucho temperamento**
I trust **confío, me fío de**
trusting **confiado**
warm **cálido, efusivo**
well-known **conocido, sabido**
wise **prudente, cauteloso**
wit **el ingenio, la agudeza mental**
witty **ingenioso, agudo, ocurrente**

The pupils here are hardworking and well-behaved. | **Los alumnos de aquí son muy trabajadores y formales.**
We encourage self-confidence and discipline. | **Fomentamos la confianza en sí mismo y la disciplina.**
Bad behavior/behaviour and laziness are punished. | **Castigamos a los que se comportan mal y a los perezosos.**

Mr. B is a serious person, but rather pessimistic. | **El señor B es un hombre muy serio, pero bastante pesimista.**

▶ THOUGHT PROCESSES 6c; EXPRESSING VIEWS 6d

6b Feelings & Emotions

I am afraid (of)   **tengo miedo (de)**

I am amazed   **estoy asombrado**

amazement   **el asombro, la sorpresa, la estupefacción**

I amuse   **divierto, entretengo**

   I am amused by   **me divierte, me hace gracia**

amusement   **la diversión**

anger   **la furia, la ira, la cólera**

angry   **enfadado, furioso**

I am annoyed (at / about)   **estoy molesto (por / con)**

anxiety   **la ansiedad**

anxious   **ansioso**

I approve (of)   **apruebo, tengo buen concepto (de)**

I am ashamed (of)   **estoy avergonzado (de)**

I am bored   **estoy aburrido**

boredom   **el aburrimiento**

content (with)   **contento (con), satisfecho (de)**

cross (with)   **enfadado (con)**

delighted (about)   **encantado (con)**

I dislike   **no me gusta**

dissatisfaction   **el descontento, la insatisfacción**

dissatisfied (with)   **descontento (con), insatisfecho (de)**

embarrassed (about)   **desconcertado (con), avergonzado (por)**

embarrassment   **el desconcierto, la turbación, la vergüenza**

emotion   **la emoción**

emotional(ly)   **emocional(mente)**

I enjoy   **disfruto**

envy   **la envidia**

envious (of)   **envidioso (de)**

fear   **el miedo**

I feel   **siento**

I forgive   **perdono**

forgiveness   **el perdón**

I am frightened (of)   **estoy asustado (de), tengo miedo (a)**

furious (about)   **furioso (acerca de)**

fussy   **quisquilloso, exigente**

grateful (to)   **agradecido (a)**

gratitude   **la gratitud**

guilty   **culpable**

I like our neighbor / neighbour a lot but worry about his wife. She cares for her old mother, who has not adapted to life in the city. She is often in a bad temper and very fussy.

Me gusta mucho nuestro vecino, pero me preocupa su esposa. Cuida a su madre anciana quien no se ha adaptado a la vida de la ciudad. Muchas veces tiene [está de mal] genio y es muy quisquillosa.

"I am really ashamed of my behavior / behaviour yesterday. I was so upset and worried."
"It really doesn't matter. I am thankful that you feel better."

—De verdad estoy avergonzado de mi comportamiento de ayer. Quedé tan trastornado y preocupado.
—La verdad es que no importa. Estoy agradecido de que te sientas mejor.

happiness **la alegría, la felicidad**
happy (about) **contento (con)**
hate **el odio**
I hate **odio, detesto**
I have a grudge against him **le tengo rencor, le tengo inquina**
hope **la esperanza**
I hope **espero**
hopeful **optimista, esperanzado**
idealism **el idealismo**
indifference **la indiferencia**
indifferent (to) **indiferente (a)**
I am indifferent (to) **soy indiferente (a)**
interest **el interés**
I am interested (in) **me interesa, estoy interesado (en)**
jealous **celoso**
jealousy **los celos**
joy **la alegría, el júbilo, el gozo**
joyful **alegre, jubiloso**
I like **me gusta**
I would like **quisiera**
love **el amor**
I love **amo**
miserable (about) **triste (por)**
misery **el sufrimiento, la tristeza, la aflicción**

mood **el humor, el estado de ánimo**
in a good / bad mood **de buen / mal humor**
I'm pleased / glad that **estoy contento / satisfecho que**
I prefer **prefiero**
I regret **me arrepiento de, lamento**
satisfaction **la satisfacción**
satisfied (with) **satisfecho (de)**
surprise **la sorpresa**
I am surprised (at) **estoy sorprendido (de)**
thankful **agradecido**
unhappy **infeliz, desdichado**
unhappiness **la infelicidad, la desdicha**
upset (about) **desconcertado, perturbado, molesto (por)**
I wonder (at) **me pregunto**
I wonder if **me pregunto si**
worried (about) **preocupado (por)**
worry **la preocupación**
I worry (about) **me preocupo (por)**
it worries me **me preocupa**

I am so glad you are not angry with me.

Me alegro / Me alegra tanto que no estés enfadado conmigo.

We are very fond of our uncle. He has many good qualities. However, he is often somewhat temperamental. He hates it when we thank him. It makes him embarrassed.

Le tenemos mucho cariño a nuestro tío. Tiene muchas buenas cualidades. Sin embargo, a menudo es algo caprichoso. Lo odia cuando le expresamos nuestra gratitud. Le hace sentirse desconcertado.

The boss is in a bad mood. He is cross with his secretary. She is bored with the work and indifferent to his annoyance.

El jefe está de mal humor. Está enfadado con su secretaria. A ella le aburre su trabajo, y no le importa nada el enojo de él.

6c Thought Processes

against **en contra de**
I am against it **estoy en contra de ello**
I analyze **analizo, estudio**
analysis **el análisis, el estudio**
I assume **asumo, me hago cargo de**
assuming that . . . **asumiendo que, suponiendo que**
attention **la atención**
aware of (un-) **enterado de, (in)consciente de**
I base **baso**
basic **básico**
basically **básicamente**
basis **la base**
belief **la creencia**
I believe **creo, pienso**
I believe in **creo en**
certainty **la seguridad, la certeza**
certain, sure **cierto, seguro**
coherent (in-) **(in)coherente**
complex **el complejo**
inferiority complex **el complejo de inferioridad**
I comprehend **entiendo**
comprehensible **comprensible**
I concentrate **concentro**
I concentrate on **me concentro en**
I conclude (that) **concluyo (que)**
conscience **la conciencia**
with a clear conscience **con la conciencia limpia**
I consider . . . (to be) **considero**
consideration **la consideración**
I take into consideration **tengo en consideración / cuenta, tomo en consideración**
taking everything into consideration **considerándolo todo**
I contemplate **pienso**
context **el contexto**

on the contrary **por el contrario**
controversial **controvertido, conflictivo**
I decide **decido**
decision **la decisión**
I deduce **deduzco que**
I delude myself **me engaño**
delusion **el engaño, la ilusión**
I determine **determino**
I disbelieve **no creo**
I distinguish **distingo**
doubt **la duda**
I doubt **dudo**
doubtful **dudoso**
doubtless / without a doubt **sin duda**
exception **la excepción**
evidence **la evidencia**
evidently **evidentemente**
fact **el hecho**
in fact **de hecho**
false **falso**
fantasy **la fantasía**
fiction **la ficción**
for **por, para**
I am for it **estoy por ello, [estoy a favor de ello]**
I forbid **prohibo**
I forget **olvido, no me acuerdo de**
genius (for) **el genio (para)**
I grasp **comprendo**
hypothesis **la hipótesis**
I imagine **imagino**
imagination **la imaginación**
implication **la implicación**
interesting **interesante**
I invent **invento**
invention **el invento, la invención**
issue **el asunto, la materia**
I judge **juzgo**
judgment **el juicio**
justice **la justicia**
I justify **justifico**
I know **sé, conozco**

knowledge   el conocimiento, el saber
logic   la lógica
logical   lógico
I go mad   me vuelvo loco
madness   la locura
meaning   el sentido
it means   quiere decir
I meditate (on)   medito
memory   la memoria
metaphysics   la metafísica
mind   la mente, la inteligencia
   a great mind   el sabio
I misunderstand   no entiendo
misunderstanding   el malentendido
motive   el motivo
philosophy   la filosofía
point of view   el punto de vista
I ponder   reflexiono, medito
premise   la premisa
I presume   presumo, supongo
principle   el principio
   in / on principle   en principio
problem   el problema
proof   la prueba
I prove   pruebo
psychology   la psicología
psychoanalysis   el psicoanálisis
rational (ir-) *(thinking)*   (ir)racional, (i)lógico
reality   la realidad
I realize   me doy cuenta
I reason   razono
   I reason *(conclude)*   concluyo

reason *(faculty)*   la razón
I recognize   reconozco
I reflect   reflexiono
relevant   pertinente, conexo, relacionado
I remember   me acuerdo
right   correcto, verdadero
   I am right   tengo razón
   it is right   es verdad, está bien
I see   veo
I solve   resuelvo
solution   la solución
I speculate   especulo
subconscious   el subconsciente
I suppose   supongo
theoretical   teórico
theory   la teoría
   in theory   en teoría
I think   pienso, creo
thought   el pensamiento
true   verdadero
truth   la verdad
I understand   entiendo, comprendo
understanding   el entendimiento, la comprensión
valid (in-)   (in)válido
view   la opinión
   in my view   en mi opinión
wrong   equivocado
   I am wrong   estoy equivocado
   it is wrong   está equivocado

He is partly right about the reasons for our difficulties, but there is probably much more behind it.

Even if he is right, there is virtually nothing we can do about it.

En parte tiene razón cuando se refiere a las causas de nuestras dificultades, pero habrá otras razones que no son tan obvias.

Aun si tiene razón, no hay casi nada que podamos hacer para remediarlo.

THE HUMAN MIND & CHARACTER

6d Expressing Views

I accept **acepto**
I agree (with / about) **estoy de acuerdo (con / sobre)**
I answer **contesto, respondo**
answer **la respuesta**
I argue **arguyo, discuto**
argument **el argumento, la discusión**
I ask (a question) **pregunto**
I contradict **contradigo**
I criticize **critico**
I define **defino**
definition **la definición**
I deny **niego**
I describe **describo**
description **la descripción**
I disagree (with / about) **no estoy de acuerdo (con / sobre)**
I discuss **discuto**
discussion **la discusión**
I maintain **mantengo, [sostengo]**
I mean **quiero decir**
opinion **la opinión**

in my opinion **en mi opinión, a mi modo de ver**
question **la cuestión, el caso**
a thorny question **una cuestión espinosa**
it is a question of **es una cuestión de**
I question **me cuestiono**
I say **digo**
I state **afirmo**
statement **la afirmación**
suggestion **la sugerencia**
I suggest **sugiero**
I summarize **resumo**
summary **el sumario, el resumen**
I think (of / about) **pienso (en)**
thought **el pensamiento**

Giving examples

as is known **como es sabido**
etc. / and so on **y así sucesivamente**
example **el ejemplo**

"In my opinion, he did not consider the basic problem. I would have liked to ask more questions."
"In principle, I agree with his views. On the one hand he proved the need for new housing. On the other hand he discussed the problems of finding a site."

"I suggest we try to analyze the problem carefully. Then we shall be able to judge the situation and come to a sound conclusion."

—**En mi opinión no consideró el problema básico. Querría haber preguntado algo más.**
—**En principio estoy de acuerdo con sus opiniones. Por una parte, ha demostrado la necesidad de construir casas nuevas. Por otra parte habló de los problemas de encontrar un solar [lote] apropiado.**
—**Sugiero que tratemos de analizar el problema con cuidado. Luego podremos juzgar la situación y llegar a una conclusión razonable.**

for example **por ejemplo**
i.e. **a saber**
namely **es decir**
I quote **cito**
such as **como**

Comparing and contrasting

advantage **la ventaja**
I compare **comparo**
comparison **la comparación**
  in comparison with **en comparación con**
it contrasts with **contrasta con**
contrast **el contraste**
  in contrast **en contraste**
I differ **difiero**
difference **la diferencia**
different (from) **diferente de, distinto de**
disadvantage **la desventaja**
dissimilar **distinto**
I distinguish **distingo**
pros and cons **los pros y los contras**
relatively **relativamente**

same **el mismo**
similar **similar, igual**

Expressing reservations

even if **aun cuando**
even so **aun así**
to some extent **en alguna medida**
at first sight **a primera vista**
hardly **con dificultad, difícilmente**
in general **en general**
in the main **en general, en su mayoría**
in part / partly **en parte**
perhaps **quizás**
presumably **posiblemente**
probably **probablemente**
relatively **relativamente**
reservation **la reserva, [la reservación]**
unfortunately **desafortunadamente**
virtually **virtualmente**
in a way **de algún modo**

beginning **el principio, el comienzo**
from the beginning **desde el principio, desde el comienzo**
I am brief **soy breve, soy lacónico**
  in brief **en resumen**
I conclude **concluyo**
conclusion **la conclusión**
  in conclusion **en conclusión**
final **final**
finally **finalmente**
first **el primer, el primero**
in the first place **en primer lugar**
furthermore **más aun**
on the one hand **por una parte, de una parte**

on the other hand **por otra parte**
initially **inicialmente**
last **el último**
lastly **útimamente**
  at last **por fin**
next **el próximo**
place **lugar**
  in the first place **en primer lugar**
  in the second place **en segundo lugar**
secondly **en segundo lugar**
in short **en breve, próximamente**
I sum up **resumo**

THE HUMAN MIND & CHARACTER

Arguing a point

admittedly **se reconoce que, es verdad que, [se sabe que]**
all the same **de cualquier manera**
although **aunque**
anyway **de todas formas, de cualquier modo**
apart from **aparte de**
as for **en cuanto a, en lo que concierne a, en lo que se refiere a**
as I see it **como yo lo veo**
as well **también**
despite this **a pesar de esto**
in effect **en efecto**
however **sin embargo**
incidentally **incidentalmente**
instead **en cambio**
instead of **en vez de, en lugar de**
just as important **tan importante**
likewise **asimismo, además**
no matter whether **sin que importe que**
that may be so **puede ser así**
nevertheless **sin embargo, no obstante**
otherwise **de otra manera**

in reality **en realidad**
in many respects **en muchos respectos**
in return **en cambio**
as a rule **como regla (general)**
so to speak **para decirlo así**
in spite of **a pesar de**
still . . . **aun así**
to tell the truth **para decir la verdad, [para ser franco]**
whereas **mientras, visto que**
on the whole **en general, por regla general**

Cause & effect

all the more (because) **tanto más (porque)**
as **como**
because **porque**
cause **la causa**
consequence **la consecuencia**
consequently **consecuentemente, por consecuencia**
effect **el efecto**
it follows that **se deduce que**
how? **¿cómo?**
if **si**

"How did he break his leg?"
"When he went to get the ladder, he did not notice that it was broken. So he fell off it."
"Why did he want the ladder?"

"Because he wanted to paint the house."

"What are the reasons for his behavior / behaviour?"
"Maybe he is cross with me and that is why he went away."

— ¿Cómo se rompió la pierna?
–– Al ir a buscar la escalera, no se fijó en que estaba rota. Por lo tanto se cayó de ella.
— ¿Por qué necesitaba la escalera?

— Porque quería pintar la casa.

— ¿Cuáles son las causas de su comportamiento?
— A lo mejor está enfadado conmigo y por eso se fue.

reason **la razón**
   for this reason **por esta razón**
result **el resultado, la**
   consecuencia
   as a result **como resultado**
provided that **suponiendo que**
since **desde que, en vista de que**
so long as **con tal que**
therefore, so **por lo tanto**
thus **de este modo, así es que**
whether **si**
why? **¿por qué?**

Emphasizing

above all **sobre todo**
in addition **además**
all the more **tanto más**
also **también**
certainly **desde luego, por**
   supuesto, naturalmente
clearly **claramente**
under no circumstances **bajo**
   ninguna circunstancia
completely **completamente**
especially **especialmente**
even (more) **aun**
without exception **sin excepción**

I emphasize **enfatizo**
extremely **extremadamente**
far and away **con mucho**
fortunately **afortunadamente**
honestly **honestamente,**
   honradamente
just when **sólo cuando**
mainly **principalmente**
moreover **más aun**
naturally **naturalmente**
not at all **para nada, de ninguna**
   manera
not in the least **en lo más mínimo**
both . . . and **tanto ... como**
obviously **obviamente**
in particular **en particular**
particularly **particularmente**
in every respect **en todos los**
   respectos
I stress **acentúo**
thanks to **gracias a**
undeniably **innegablemente**
very **muy**
and what is more **y lo que es más**

Honestly I'm extremely angry with him. Thanks to his carelessness we missed the plane.

De verdad, estoy muy enfadada con él. Gracias a su descuido perdimos el avión.

Fortunately, there was another, but we got to Chicago completely exhausted.

Afortunadamente hubo otro, pero llegamos completamente agotados a Chicago.

And what is more, he clearly didn't care at all.

Y lo que es más, no le preocupaba a él de ninguna manera.

Obviously, I shall tell his firm exactly what I think of him. Under no circumstances will I employ him again.

Claro que informaré a su compañía lo que pienso de él. No lo emplearé otra vez bajo ninguna circunstancia.

Human Life & Relationships

7a Family & Friends

Friendship

acquaintance **el conocido**
boyfriend **el amigo, el novio**
buddy / mate **el compañero, el camarada, [el compinche]**
classmate **el compañero de clase**
companion **el compañero**
friend (close) **el íntimo**
friend **el amigo**
friendship **la amistad**
gang **la pandilla, la cuadrilla**
we get on well together **nos llevamos bien**
we get together **nos reunimos**
I get to know **llego a conocer ..., concozco**
girlfriend **la amiga, la novia**
I introduce **presento a ...**
pal / chum **el compañero, el compinche**
pen pal / penfriend **el amigo por correspondencia**
relationship **la relación**
schoolfriend / pal **el amigo de clase**

The family and relatives

adopted **adoptivo**
ancestor **el antepasado**
aunt **la tía**
baby **el bebé, el nene, la nena, [el / la guagua]**
brother **el hermano**
brother-in-law **el cuñado, el hermano político**
brothers and sisters **los hermanos**
children **los niños, los hijos**
close relative **el pariente cercano**
common-law husband **el marido en una unión consensual**
common-law wife **la mujer en una unión consensual**
cousin **el primo**
dad **el papá, el papaíto, [el papito]**
daughter **la hija**
daughter-in-law **la nuera, la hija política**
distant relative **el pariente lejano**
elder **mayor**
family **la familia**
family tree **el árbol genealógico**

We are good friends. We get on well together. We do a lot together.

Somos buenos amigos. Nos llevamos bien. Hacemos muchas cosas juntos.

We are more open with one another. We settle conflicts.

Somos más sinceros el uno con el otro. Resolvemos los conflictos.

---

father **el padre**
father-in-law **el suegro, el padre político**
fiancé(e) **el novio, (la novia), el prometido, (la prometida)**
forebear **el antepasado**
foster (adj) **adoptivo**
foster mother **la madre adoptiva**
genealogy **la genealogía**
godchild / son **el ahijado**
goddaughter **la ahijada**
godfather **el padrino**
godmother **la madrina**
grandad / pa **el abuelito**
grandchildren **los nietos**
granddaughter **la nieta**
grandfather **el abuelo**
grandma / granny **la abuelita**
grandmother **la abuela**
grandparents **los abuelos**
grandson **el nieto**
great-aunt **la tía abuela**
great grandchild **el bisnieto**
great-grandfather **el bisabuelo**
great-grandmother **la bisabuela**
great-nephew **el sobrinonieto**
great-niece **la sobrinanieta**
great-uncle **el tío abuelo**
guardian **el tutor, la tutora**
half-brother **el medio hermano**
half-sister **la media hermana**
husband **el marido**

mom / mum **la mamá**
mother **la madre**
mother-in-law **la suegra, la madre política**
nephew **el sobrino**
niece **la sobrina**
only (child) **(el hijo) único**
parents **los padres**
partner **el cónyuge, la pareja, el compañero**
related **emparentado**
relation **el pariente**
relationship **el parentesco, la parentela, el trato, la relación**
relative **el pariente**
second cousin **el primo segundo**
sister **la hermana**
son **el hijo**
son-in-law **el yerno, el hijo político**
spouse **el cónyuge**
stepbrother **el hermanastro**
stepdaughter **la hijastra**
stepfather **el padrastro**
stepmother **la madrastra**
stepsister **la hermanastra**
stepson **el hijastro**
twin brother **el (hermano) gemelo**
twin sister **la (hermana) gemela**
uncle **el tío**
wife **la mujer, la esposa**
younger **menor**

I come from a large family. We just don't get on well.
There are family problems.

**Vengo de una familia grande. Es que no nos llevamos bien.
Hay problemas familiares.**

It runs in the family.

Viene de familia.

She's very difficult to get along with.
I fell out with her.

Es muy difícil llevarse bien con ella. Me reñí con ella.

▶ LOVE, MARRIAGE, CHILDREN 7b; GROWING UP, DEATH 7c

7b Love & Children

Love & marriage

affair la aventura amorosa, el amorío
bachelor el soltero
best man el padrino de boda
betrothal el noviazgo, los desposorios
betrothed prometido
bride la novia
bridegroom el novio
bridesmaid la dama de honor
couple la pareja
  married couple el matrimonio
I court cortejo, hago la corte a ...
courtship el cortejo, el noviazgo
divorce el divorcio
divorced divorciado
divorcé(e) el divorciado, la divorciada
engaged prometido
engagement el compromiso, el noviazgo
I fall for me enamoro de
I fall in love (with) me enamoro (de)
I get divorced (from) me divorcio (de)

I get engaged (to) me prometo, [me compremeto] (con)
I get married (to) me caso (con)
I go out with salgo con
honeymoon la luna de miel
lover el amante, la amante, el querido, la querida
marriage / matrimony el matrimonio
married casado
I marry me caso con
mistress la querida, la amante
newly married couple los recién casados
I separate from me separo de
separated separado
separation la separación
I have sex (with) tengo relaciones sexuales (con)
unmarried soltero
unmarried mother la madre soltera
wedding la boda, las bodas, el casamiento
widow la viuda
widower el viudo

We are madly in love. It was love at first sight.

Estamos enamorados perdidamente. Fue un flechazo [Fue amor a primera vista].

Are you married?

¿Estás casado?

She doesn't understand me. She is always nagging.

No me entiende. Siempre me importuna con sus quejas.

We have nothing to say to each other.

Ya no tenemos nada que decirnos.

Our relationship is breaking up.

Nuestras relaciones se están rompiendo.

Birth & children

abortion **el aborto**
I have an abortion **me hago un aborto**
I adopt **adopto**
adoption **la adopción**
au pair **la chica au pair, [la niñera]**
baby **el bebé, el nene/la nena, [el/la guagua]**
baby food **la comida para niños**
babysitter **el canguro, la niñera**
baptism **el bautizo, el bautismo**
bib **el babero, el babador**
birth **el nacimiento, el parto**
birthrate **(la tasa de) natalidad**
birthday **el cumpleaños**
I was born **nací**
boy **el niño, el muchacho, el chico, el joven, el mozo, el chaval, el zagal**
I breast feed **crío a los pechos, amamanto, doy el pecho**
I bring up a child **crío/educo a un niño**
caesarian section **la operación cesárea**
child, children **el niño, los niños**
childhood **la niñez, la infancia**
christening **el bautizo, el bautismo**
condom **el condón**
contraception **la contracepción, [la anticoncepción]**
contraction **la contracción**
crib **la cuna**
I deliver (a baby) **asisto en el nacimiento, parto**
I am expecting a baby **estoy encinta/embarazada**
feeding bottle **el biberón**
fertile (in-) **(in)fecundo (estéril)**

fertility **la fecundidad**
fetus **el feto**
I foster **crío**
fostering **el acogimiento familiar**
I get pregnant **quedo embarazada**
I give birth **doy a luz**
girl **la niña, la muchacha, la chica, la joven, la moza, la chavala, la zagala**
incubator **la incubadora**
infancy **la infancia**
infant **el niño, la criatura**
infantile **infantil**
I am in labor **estoy de parto**
live birth **el nacimiento vivo**
I have a miscarriage **malparo, aborto**
nanny **la niñera**
diaper **el pañal**
newborn child **el (bebé) recién nacido**
orphan **el huérfano**
pacifier **el chupete**
period **el período, la regla**
pill **la píldora**
pregnant **encinta, embarazada**
saint's day **el santo, el día del santo, la fiesta del santo**
sibling **el hermano, la hermana**
stillbirth **el nacimiento de un niño muerto**
stillborn **nacido muerto, mortinato**
stroller/perambulator **el cochecito de niño**
I take after **salgo a, me parezco a**
toddler **el pequeñito (que da sus primeros pasos)**
triplets **los trillizos**
twin **gemelo**

7c Life & Death

Growing up

adolescent **adolescente**
adult **el adulto, el mayor**
   adult *(adj)* **adulto, mayor**
age **la edad**
aged **viejo, anciano**
centenarian **el centenario**
he comes from **es de**
I come of age **llego a la mayoría de edad**
elderly **de edad, mayor, anciano, viejo**
eldest **el / la mayor**
female **la hembra**
   female *(adj)* **femenina**
foreigner **el extranjero**
generation **la generación**
generation gap **la barrera generacional**
life **la vida**
life insurance **el seguro de vida**
I look my age **represento los años que tengo**
male **el macho, el varón**
   male *(adj)* **masculino, macho**
man **el hombre**
manhood **la virilidad, la masculinidad**
manly **varonil, viril, masculino**
mature **maduro**
maturity **la madurez**
menopause **la menopausia**
middle age **de mediana edad**
name **el nombre**
nickname **el apodo, el mote**
octogenarian **el octogenario**
old **viejo, anciano**
old age **la vejez**
old man, woman **el viejo, la vieja, el anciano, la anciana**
old age home **el asilo de ancianos**
pension **la pensión**
pensioner **el jubilado, la jubilada, el pensionado, la pensionada, el / la pensionista**
people **la gente**
permissive society **la sociedad permisiva**
person **la persona**
present **el regalo**
I prosper **prospero**
responsible **responsable**
retired **jubilado**
single **soltero**
spinster **la soltera**

He respects his elders.	**Respeta a sus mayores.**
I learn from my own experience.	**Aprendo por mi propia experiencia.**
"How old are you?"	**— ¿Cuántos años tienes?**
"I'm twenty-five."	**— Tengo veinte y cinco años.**

stranger   el forastero
surname   el apellido
underage   menor de edad
woman   la mujer
womanhood   la feminidad
young   joven
young person   el / la joven
younger   más joven
youngest   el / la más joven
youth   la juventud
youth (persons)   el / la joven

Death

afterlife   la vida futura
angel   el ángel
ashes   las cenizas
autopsy   la autopsia, [la necropsia]
body   el cadáver
burial   el entierro
I bury   entierro
cemetery / graveyard   el cementerio
corpse   el cadáver
he is cremated   es incinerado
cremation   la incineración, la cremación
crematorium / crematory   el horno crematorio
dead   muerto
death   la muerte

death certificate   la partida de defunción
he dies   muere
epitaph   el epitafio
eulogy   el elogio, el encomio
funeral   el entierro, los funerales
he goes to heaven   sube al cielo
grave   la sepultura
heaven   el cielo
hell   el infierno
I inherit   heredo
inheritance   la herencia
last rites   las exequias
he lies in state   está expuesto en capilla ardiente
mortuary   el depósito de cadávares
I mourn   estoy de luto
mourning   la lamentación, el luto
I am in mourning for   llevo luto por
neonatal death rate   la (tasa de) mortalidad neonatal
obituary   la necrología
he passes away   fallece
remains   los restos
tomb   la tumba
tombstone / gravestone   la lápida
undertaker   el director de pompas fúnebres
will   el testamento

The baby was born in the early hours of the morning but died an hour later.

El nene nació por la madrugada pero murió una hora después.

Daily Life

8a The House

amenities **las comodidades, las conveniencias**

apartment / flat **el piso, el apartamento**

apartment house / block of flats **el bloque de pisos, [el edificio de apartamentos]**

(of) brick **de ladrillo**

I build **construyo**

building **el edificio**

building plot **el solar (para construcción), [el lote]**

building site **el solar (para construcción), la obra**

bungalow **el chalet, el bungalow**

caretaker **el conserje, el portero, el vigilante**

chalet **el chalet, el chalé**

detached house **la casa independiente, el chalet**

furnished apartment / flat **el piso / apartamento amueblado**

furnished house **la casa amueblada**

freehold **propiedad absoluta**

I have an extension built **hago construir un ensanche**

garbage / refuse collection **la recolección de basuras**

house **la casa**

housing **la vivienda**

landlord **el propietario, el dueño**

lease / leasehold **el arrendamiento**

leased / leasehold property **el inmueble arrendado**

lodger / roomer **el huésped**

I modernize **modernizo**

mortgage **la hipoteca**

mortgage rate **el tipo de interés hipotecario**

I move (house) **me mudo (de casa)**

I occupy **ocupo**

I own **poseo**

owner-occupied apartment / flat **el piso / apartamento ocupado por el propietario**

The whole house needs painting before we sell it. We are buying a new detached house.

Tenemos que pintar la casa entera antes de venderla. Compramos un nuevo chalet.

We are having a house built.

Hacemos construir una casa.

I live in a rented, furnished apartment.

Vivo en un apartamento amueblado, alquilado.

Her penthouse is for rent.

Su ático está disponible para alquilar.

owner-occupied house **la casa ocupada por el propietario**
penthouse **el ático, la casa de azotea**
partly furnished **amueblado en parte**
prefabricated house **la casa prefabricada**
premises **el local, la propiedad**
public housing **el piso de protección oficial, la casa protegida, [el apartamento estatal]**
rent **el alquiler, el arriendo**
I rent **alquilo**
semi-detached house **la casa semi-separada**
sewage disposal **la depuración de aguas residuales**
(of) stone **de piedra**
street light **el farol**
I take out a mortgage **obtengo una hipoteca**
tenancy **el inquilinato, la ocupación**
tenant **el inquilino, el arrendatario**
unfurnished **sin muebles**
unfurnished apartment / flat **el piso / apartamento desamueblado**

Rooms

attic **el ático, el desván, la buhardilla**
basement **el sótano**
backdoor **la puerta trasera**
bathroom / lavatory **el cuarto de baño, el retrete, el lavabo, el inodoro, el excusado, [el baño]**
bedroom **el dormitorio**
breakfast room **la habitación del desayuno**
cellar **el sótano, la bodega**
corridor **el pasillo, el corredor**
dining room **el comedor**
hall(way) **el hall, el vestíbulo, el pasillo**
landing **el descanso, el rellano**
kitchen **la cocina**
living room / sitting-room **el cuarto de estar, el living, el salón**
loft **el desván**
lounge **el cuarto de estar, el living, el salón**
restroom / W.C. **el retrete, el lavabo, el inodoro, el excusado, [el baño]**
shower **la ducha**
study **el despacho, el estudio**
utility room **la trascocina**
veranda **la veranda, la terraza, la galería**

My tenancy has two weeks to run. **Quedan dos semanas de mi arrendamiento.**

We moved two years ago. **Mudamos de casa hace dos años.**

The house has a fairly pleasant view: it grows on you after a while. **La casa tiene un panorama bastante agradable: después de un rato le gusta a uno cada vez más.**

DAILY LIFE

aerial **la antena**
backdoor **la puerta trasera**
balcony **el balcón**
baseboard **el rodapié, la cenefa**
blind **la persiana**
boiler **la caldera, el calentador**
burglar alarm **la alarma antirrobo**
carpet **la moqueta, la alfombra**
ceiling **el techo**
chimney / smokestack **la chimenea**
central heating **la calefacción**
clean **limpio**
comfortable **cómodo**
cozy **cómodo, acogedor**
curtain **la cortina**
desk **el escritorio, la mesa de trabajo**
dirty **sucio**
door **la puerta**
doorhandle **el tirador (de puerta), el puño, [el porno]**
doorknob **el tirador (de puerta), el pomo (de puerta)**
doormat **el felpudo, la estera, la alfombrilla, [el tapete]**
downstairs **abajo, en el piso de abajo**
electric **eléctrico**
electric plug **el enchufe,**
electric socket **el enchufe, la toma (de electricidad), el toma-corriente**

electricity **la electricidad, la luz**
elevator / lift **el ascensor**
extension cord **el cable, el cordón (de la luz)**
fire alarm **la alarma de incendio**
fire extinguisher **el extintor de incendio**
fireplace **el hogar, la chimenea**
floor **el suelo**
floor *(story / storey)* **el piso, la planta**
frontdoor **la puerta principal, la puerta de entrada**
furnished **amueblado**
furniture **los muebles**
item of furniture **el mueble**
garage **el garaje, la cochera**
gas **el gas**
glass *(material)* **el vidrio, el cristal**
ground floor **la planta baja, [el primer piso]**
handle **el puño**
(on jug, etc.) **el asa** *(f)*, **el asidero**
(drawer, etc.) **el tirador, la manija**
hearth **el hogar, la chimenea**
included **incluido**
key **la llave**
keyhole **el ojo de la cerradura**
lamp **la lámpara**
lampshade **la pantalla de lámpara**
letterbox **el buzón**

The bed has not been changed. **La cama no ha sido cambiada.**

I have just bought a compact disc player. **Acabo de comprar un reproductor de discos compactos.**

lever **la palanca**
light **la luz**
lightbulb **la bombilla**
lightswitch **el interruptor, el conmutor**
lock **la cerradura**
it looks onto **da a**
mantelpiece **el manto (de chimenea), la repisa de chimenea**
mat **la estera, la esterilla**
mezzanine floor **el entresuelo**
modern **moderno**
new **nuevo**
nice **bonito, ameno**
off *(switches, electrical appliance)* **desconectado, desenchufado, apagado**
off *(tap)* **cerrado**
old **viejo**
on *(switches, electrical appliance)* **conectado, enchufado, encendido, puesto**
on *(tap)* **abierto**
on the first floor **en el primer piso**
own **propio**
passage **el pasillo**
radiator **el radiador**
rent **el alquiler, el arriendo**
roof **el tejado, el techo**
room **la habitación, el cuarto**
shelf **el estante, la tabla, el anaquel, [la repisa]**
shutter **la contraventana**

situation **la situación, el emplazamiento**
skylight **el tragaluz, la claraboya**
small **pequeño**
spacious **espacioso, amplio**
staircase **la escalera**
stairs **la escalera**
step **el peldaño, el escalón, la grada**
terrace **la terraza**
tile *(floor)* **la baldosa**
roof tile **la teja**
toilet **el retrete, el inodoro, el lavabo, el wáter, el excusado, [el baño]**
trashcan / dustbin **el cubo de basura, [el balde], [la caneca]**
upper floor **el piso superior, el piso de arriba**
upstairs **arriba**
view **la vista, el panorama**
wall **el muro**
inside wall **la pared**
partition wall **el tabique**
garden wall **la tapia**
wastepaper basket / litter bin **la papelera**
water **el agua** *(f)*
window **la ventana**
windowsill **el alféizar, el antepecho**
wire **el alambre**
wiring **el alambrado**
with bath **con baño adjunto**
wood **la madera**

The washing machine doesn't work! Can you repair it? — **¡La lavadora no funciona! ¿Puede usted repararla?**

Come into the dining room. — **Pase al comedor.**

8c Furnishings

Lounge

armchair **la butaca, la silla**
ashtray **el cenicero**
bookcase **la librería, el estante**
bookshelf **el estante, la estantería**
bureau **el escritorio**
closet / cupboard **el armario**
coffee table **la mesita baja**
cushion **el cojín**
easy chair **la butaca, la silla**
ornament **el adorno, el ornamento**
picture **el cuadro, la pintura**
     picture *(portrait)* **el retrato**
photo **la foto**
poster **el cartel, el póster**
rocking chair **la mecedora**
rug **el tapete, la alfombrilla**
sofa / settee **el sofá**

Kitchen

bottle opener **el abrebotellas**
bowl **el plato, el tazón**
clothesline **la cuerda de tendedero, la tendedera**
clothespin **la pinza**
coffee machine **la máquina de café, la cafetera**
coffeepot **la cafetera**
colander **el colador, el escurridor**
crockery **la vajilla, los platos**
cup **la taza**
cupboard **el armario**
     wall cupboard **la alacena**
cutlery **los cubiertos, la cuchillería**
deepfreeze **el (ultra)congelador**
dish **el plato**
dishcloth **el trapo de fregar, el paño de cocina, el limpión**
dishwashing detergent **el detergente líquido, el lavavajillas**
draining board **el escurreplatos, la escurridera, el escurridor**

faucet / tap **el grifo, [la llave]**
fork **el tenedor**
frying pan **la sartén**
garbage can / rubbish bin **el cubo [la caneca] de la basura, el basurero**
glass **el vaso, la copa, la copita**
knife **el cuchillo**
oven **el horno**
plate **el plato**
saucepan **la cacerola, el cazo**
saucer **el platillo**
scouring pad **el estropajo**
sink **el fregadero, la pila**
sink unit **el lavadero, el fregadero**
spoon **la cuchara**
stove / gas cooker **la cocina / estufa de gas**
teapot **la tetera**
tea towel **el paño de cocina, [el trapo de cocina]**
tray **la bandeja**
washing powder **el jabón en polvo**

Dining room

candle **la vela**
candlestick **el candelero**
chair **la silla**
chandeliers **la araña, el candelero**
dresser **el aparador, la rinconera**
serviette **la servilleta**
sideboard **el aparador**
table **la mesa**
tablecloth **el mantel**
table mat **el salvaplatos, el salvamanteles**
table napkin **la servilleta**

Bedroom

alarm clock **el despertador**
bed **la cama**

bunk bed **la litera, la cama camarote**
double bed **la cama doble**
bedclothes **la ropa de cama**
bedding **la ropa de cama**
bedside table **la mesa de noche**
bedspread **el sobrecama, el cobertor, el cubrecama**
blanket **la manta, la cobija**
chest of drawers **la cómoda**
dressing table **el tocador**
duvet **el edredón, la colcha**
mattress **el colchón**
pillow **la almohada**
quilt **la colcha, el edredón**
sheet **la sábana**
wardrobe **el guardarropa, el armario (ropero)**

Bathroom

bath **el baño, la bañera**
bathmat **la estera de baño**
bidet **el bidet, el bidé**
clothes brush **el cepillo de la ropa**
faucet / tap **el grifo, [la llave]**
flannel **la manopla, el paño**
laundry basket **el cesto de la ropa sucia**
mirror **el espejo**
nailbrush **el cepillo para las uñas**
plug **el tapón**
scales **la balanza**
shampoo **el champú**
shower **la ducha**
sink **el lavabo**
soap **el jabón**
toilet **el retrete, el inodoro, el lavabo, el excusado, el wáter**
toilet paper **el papel higiénico**
toothbrush **el cepillo de dientes**
toothpaste **la pasta dentífrica**
towel **la toalla**
towel rail **el toallero**
washbasin **el lavabo, la jofaína, la palangana, [el lavamanos]**

Electrical goods

cassette player **el casete, el cassette, el tocacintas**
cassette recorder **la grabadora de cassette**
clothes dryer **la secadora**
compact disc player **el reproductor de discos compactos**
dishwasher **el lavaplatos, el lavavajillas**
electric appliance **el (aparato) electrodoméstico**
electric stove **la cocina / estufa eléctrica**
electric razor / shaver **la afeitadora (eléctrica), la rasuradora**
freezer **el (ultra)congelador, [la congeladora]**
hi-fi **el equipo de hi-fi / de alta fidelidad, [el equipo de sonido]**
iron **la plancha, el planchador**
microwave oven **el horno de microonda, el microondas**
mixer **la batidora, la mezcladora, la licuadora**
record player **el tocadiscos**
refrigerator / fridge **la nevera, el frigo, [la refrigeradora]**
sink **el lavabo, [el lavamanos]**
spin dryer **el secador centrífugo**
stereo system **el estéreo, [el equipo de sonido]**
tape player **el casete**
tape recorder **la grabadora**
trouser press **la prensa para pantalones**
TV set **el televisor**
television (TV) **la televisión**
vacuum cleaner **la aspiradora**
video recorder **la videograbadora**
walkman® **el Walkman®**
washing machine **la lavadora**

➤ TOILETRIES 9b; PLANTS 24c; VEGETABLES & FRUIT 10c; TOOLS App. 8b

8d Daily Routine

bath   el baño, [la tina]
bed   la cama
breakfast   el desayuno
clean   limpio
daily routine   la rutina diaria
dinner   la cena
dressed   vestido
evening meal   la cena
garbage / rubbish   la basura, los desperdicios *(pl)*, los desechos *(pl)*
home   la casa, el hogar
   at home   en casa
housework   los quehaceres domésticos *(pl)*
lunch   el almuerzo, la comida
maid / housekeeper   la criada
school   la escuela
shop   la tienda
shower   la ducha
sleep   el sueño
spare time   el tiempo libre, las horas libres
supper   la cena
tea   el té, la merienda
time *(commodity)*   el tiempo
   time (of day)   la hora
undressed   desnudo, desvestido
vacuum cleaner   la aspiradora
washing   el lavado, el lavar
   dirty washing   ropa sucia, ropa por lavar

washing *(hung to dry)*   el tendido, la colada
dishwashing / washing up *(act)*   el fregado, el fregar, [el lavado de platos]
   dishes *(to be washed)*   los platos para lavar
work   el trabajo

Actions

I bathe   me baño
I break   rompo
I bring   traigo
I build   construyo
I buy   compro
I carry   llevo
I change (clothes)   me cambio (de ropa)
I chat   charlo
I clean   limpio
I clear away   quito (los platos, la mesa)
I clear the table   quito la mesa
I cook   cocino
I close   cierro
I darn   zurzo
I dig   cavo, cultivo
I do   hago
I drink   bebo
I drop   dejo caer
I dry up   seco (los platos)
I dust   quito (el polvo), limpio
I eat   como

We usually get up at seven o'clock and have breakfast at eight.

Solemos levantarnos a las siete y desayunamos a las ocho.

Who is going to wash the dishes?

¿Quién va a lavar los platos?

I'll do the drying.

Voy a secar los platos.

Sweep up that mess right now!

¡Barre ese revoltijo ahora mismo!

I empty **vacío**
I fasten **abrocho**
I fill **lleno**
I get dressed **me visto**
I get undressed **me desnudo**
I get up **me levanto**
I go to bed **me acuesto**
I go to sleep **me duermo**
I go to the toilet **voy al**
   lavabo / baño / wáter
I take a bath **tomo un baño**
I have breakfast **desayuno**
I have lunch **como, almuerzo**
I have a snack / tea **meriendo**
I heat **caliento**
I hire / rent **alquilo**
I hire / rent out **alquilo**
I iron / press **plancho**
I knit **hago punto, [tejo]**
I set the table **pongo la mesa**
I let *(allow)* **dejo**
I live **vivo**
I lock **cierro con llave**
I make **hago**
I polish **limpio, saco brillo a ...**
I prepare **preparo**
I press *(button)* **aprieto, pulso**
I put on *(clothes)* **me pongo**
   I put on *(radio, TV)* **pongo,**
   conecto, enchufo, enciendo
I rest **descanso**
I call *(telephone)* **llamo por**
   teléfono
I ring *(doorbell)* **toco el timbre**
I scrub **friego**

I sew **coso**
I shine **saco brillo a, limpio**
I shop **hago las compras**
I shower **me ducho**
I sit down **me siento**
I sit **me siento, me quedo**
   sentado, estoy sentado
I sleep **duermo**
I speak **hablo**
I stand **estoy de pie**
I stand up **me levanto**
I start **empiezo, comienzo**
I stop **(me) paro**
I sweep **barro**
I take off *(clothes)* **me quito**
I take **cojo**
I throw away **tiro, echo, [boto]**
I tidy / straighten up **arreglo, pongo**
   en orden, limpio
I tie **ato, lío**
I trim **arreglo, ajusto**
I turn / switch off **apago,**
   desenchufo, desconecto
I turn / switch on **pongo, enchufo,**
   enciendo
I unblock **desatasco**
I use **utilizo, uso**
I wake up **me despierto**
I wallpaper **empapelo**
I wash the dishes **lavo los**
   platos
I wash **(me) lavo**
I watch TV **veo la televisión**
I water **riego**
I wear **llevo**

The table has not been cleared!

¡Aún no se ha quitado la mesa!

She does the dusting and cleaning for us on Fridays.

Los viernes quita el polvo y hace la limpieza en nuestra casa.

My husband cooks on Saturdays. Dinner will be at nine p.m.

Mi marido cocina los sábados. La cena será a las nueve.

▶ GARDENING 24c

Shopping

9a General Terms

article   **el artículo**
assistant   **el dependiente, la dependienta**
automatic door   **la puerta automática**
bargain   **la ganga, el artículo de ocasión**
business   **el comercio, la empresa**
cash register / desk   **la caja registradora**
cash machine   **la caja electrónica**
change *(money)*   **la moneda suelta, el suelto, el vuelto**
cheap   **barato**
checkout   **la caja**
choice   **la elección, la selección**
closed / day off   **cerrado (por vacaciones)**
coin   **la moneda**
contents   **el contenido**
costly   **costoso, caro**
credit   **el crédito**
credit card   **la tarjeta de crédito**
customer information   **el servicio de información para clientes**
customer service   **el servicio de asistencia posventa**
dear   **caro, costoso**

department   **el departamento, la sección**
discount   **la rebaja**
elevator / lift   **el ascensor**
entrance   **la entrada**
escalator   **la escalera mecánica**
exit   **la salida**
expensive   **caro, costoso**
fashion   **la moda**
fire door   **la puerta contra / de incendios**
fire exit   **la salida de incendios**
fitting room   **el probador, el vestidor**
free   **gratis**
free gift   **el regalo (gratuito)**
it is good value   **bien vale lo que pagué**
handbag   **el bolso, la bolsa, [la cartera]**
instructions for use   **el modo de empleo**
item   **el artículo**
mail order   **las ventas por correo**
manager   **el director / gerente, la directora / gerente**
market   **el mercado**
money   **el dinero**

Expressions you hear

Anything else? / Is that all?	**¿ Algo más / Es todo?**
Can I help you?	**¿ En qué puedo servirle?**
Do you want anything in particular?	**¿ Desea algo en concreto?**
What would you like?	**¿ Qué desea usted?**
Who's next?	**¿ Quién sigue?**
Whole or sliced?	**¿ Entero o en trozos?**

---

bill *(money)* **el billete**
open **abierto**
opening hours **las horas de abrir**
packet **el paquete**
pocket **el bolsillo**
pound *(weight)* **la libra**
PULL **tira, tire, hale**
purse **el monedero**
PUSH **empuja, empuje**
quality **la calidad**
real / genuine **verdadero, genuino, auténtico**
receipt **el recibo**
reduction **la reducción**
refund **el reembolso, la devolución**
sale **las rebajas, la liquidación, el saldo, [la promoción]**
salesperson / shop-assistant **el dependiente, el vendedor**
security guard / store detective **el guarda jurado**
self-service **autoservicio**
shopkeeper **el tendero / la tendera**
shoplifter **la mechera, el ratero de tiendas**
shopping **las compras**
  I go shopping **voy de compras**
shopping basket **la cesta de compras**
shopping cart **el carrito de la compra**
shopping list **la lista de compras**
shut **cerrado**
slice **el trozo, la tajada**
special offer **la oferta especial**

stairs **la escalera**
summer sale **las rebajas de(l) verano, [la promoción]**
trader **el comerciante, el traficante, el vendedor**
traveler's check / cheque **el cheque de viaje / de viajero**
wallet **la cartera, [la billetera]**
way in **la entrada**
way out **la salida**

Actions

I change **cambio**
I choose **escojo, elijo**
I decide **decido**
I exchange **cambio**
I have on / wear **llevo, [me pongo]**
I line / queue up **hago cola**
I order **pido, encargo**
I pay **pago**
I put on **me pongo**
I select **elijo, selecciono, escojo**
I sell **vendo**
I serve **sirvo**
I shop **hago las compras**
I shoplift **hurto / robo en tiendas**
I show **(de)muestro, enseño**
I spend *(money)* **gasto**
I steal **robo**
I take off **me quito**
I try on **(me) pruebo, [me mido]**
I wait **espero**
I wear **llevo, me pongo**
I weigh **peso**
I wrap up **envuelvo**

Is there a dairy around here? **¿Hay una lechería por aquí?**

Where is the nearest bakery? **¿Dónde está la panadería más cercana?**

Can I pay by check / cheque? **¿Puedo pagar por cheque?**

9b Household Goods & Toiletries

Toiletries

after-shave   **la loción para
después del afeitado**
antiperspirant   **el antiperspirante**
blusher   **el colorete**
brush   **el cepillo**
comb   **el peine, la peinilla**
condom   **el condón, el
preservativo**
cotton   **el algodón, el
hidrófilo**
deodorant   **el desodorante**
dental floss   **el hilo de higiene
dental**
eyeliner   **el lápiz de ojos**
face cream   **la crema de belleza**
glasses   **las gafas**
hairbrush   **el cepillo para el pelo**
lipstick   **la barra de labios,
el lápiz labial**
makeup   **el maquillaje, los
cosméticos**
nailfile   **la lima para las uñas**
paper handkerchief   **el pañuelo de
papel**
perfume   **el perfume**
razor   **la afeitadora, la maquinilla
de afeitar**
razor blade   **la hoja de afeitar, la
cuchilla de afeitar**
rouge   **el colorete**
sanitary napkin   **el paño higiénico,
la compresa (higiénica), [la
toalla higiénica]**
shampoo   **el champú**
soap   **el jabón**
spray   **el aerosol, el atomizador**
sunglasses   **las gafas de sol**
suntan lotion   **el bronceador**
talcum powder   **(los polvos de)
talco**
tampon   **el tampón, el tapón**
tissues   **los pañuelos de papel**

toilet water   **el agua** *(f)* **de colonia,
la colonia**
toilet paper   **el papel higiénico**
toothbrush   **el cepillo de dientes**
toothpaste   **la crema dental, la
pasta dentífrica**
tweezers   **las pinzas**

Household items

bottle   **la botella**
bowl   **la fuente, la escudilla, el
tazón**
cleanser   **el jabón en
polvo**
clothespin   **la pinza**
cup   **la taza**
dish   **el plato, la fuente**
dishwashing / washing-up liquid   **el
detergente líquido, el
lavavajillas**
foil / aluminum foil   **el aluminio
doméstico, el papel de
aluminio**
fork   **el tenedor**
glass   **el vaso**
jar   **el tarro, el pote, el frasco, la
jarra, el bote**
jug   **el jarro, la jarra**
kitchen roll   **el rollo de cocina**
knife   **el cuchillo**
matches   **los fósforos, las cerillas**
paper napkin / serviette   **la servilleta
de papel**
paper towel   **la toallita de papel**
plastic wrap   **el plástico
para envolver**
plate   **el plato**
pot   **la olla, la cacerola, la
cazuela, el cazo**
saucer   **el platillo**
scouring pad   **el estropajo**
spoon   **la cuchara**
string   **la cuerda, el cordel**

Basic foodstuffs

bacon   el tocino, el bacón
beans   las habas, las judías
beef   la carne de vaca
beer   la cerveza
biscuits   las galletas, los bizcochos
bread   el pan
butter   la mantequilla
cakes   los pasteles
carrots   las zanahorias
cereals   los cereales
chocolate spread   la pasta de chocolate
cola   la cola
coffee   el café
custard   las natillas, la crema instantánea (en polvos)
fish   el pescado
fruit   la fruta
ham   el jamón
jam   la confitura, la mermelada
juice   el zumo, el jugo
lemonade   la limonada, la gaseosa
loaf   el pan, la barra de pan
macaroni   los macarrones
margarine   la margarina
marmalade   la mermelada
mayonnaise   la mayonesa
meat   la carne
milk   la leche
mustard   la mostaza
oil   el aceite
olive oil   el aceite de oliva
pasta   las pastas alimenticias
pâté   el pâté, el pastel (de carne)
peanut butter   la mantequilla de cacahuete, [la mantequilla de maní]
peas   los guisantes, [las arvejas]
pepper   la pimienta
peppers   los pimientos
pork   el cerdo, la carne de cerdo
potatoes   las patatas, [las papas]
pudding   el púding, el pudín
salt   la sal
sardines   las sardinas
sauce   la salsa
sausage   la salchicha, el embutido
soup   la sopa
spaghetti   los espaguetis, los fideos
sugar   el azúcar
tea   el té
tea bag   la bolsita de té
tortilla   la tortilla
vegetables   las legumbres, las verduras, los vegetales
vinegar   el vinagre
wine   el vino

Expressions of quantity

a bar of . . .   una pastilla de ...
a bottle of . . .   una botella de ...
a box of . . .   una caja de ...
a hundred gram(me)s of . . .   cien gramos de ...
a kilo of . . .   un kilo de ...
a liter / litre of . . .   un litro de ...
a packet of . . .   un paquete de ...
a slice of . . .   un trozo de ..., una tajada de ...
a can / tin of . . .   una lata de ...
half a pound of . . .   media libra de ...

9c Clothing

artificial **artificial**
beautiful **hermoso**
belt **el cinturón**
big **grande**
bikini **el bikini**
blouse **la blusa**
boot **la bota**
bra **el sostén**
brand new **flamante, completamente nuevo**
cagoule **el canguro, el chubasquero**
cap **el gorro, la gorra**
cardigan **la rebeca, el cardigán**
checked **a cuadros**
clothes **la ropa, los vestidos**
clothing **la ropa, los vestidos**
coat **el abrigo, [el saco]**
colorfast / colourfast **no desteñible**
colorful / colourful **vivo, animado**
corduroy **la pana**

cravat **la corbata de fantasía, el fular, el foulard**
dress **el vestido**
elegant **elegante**
embroidered **bordado, recamado**
fashionable **de moda**
glove **el guante**
handkerchief **el pañuelo**
hat **el sombrero**
high-heeled **de tacones altos**
in the latest fashion **de última moda**
jacket **la chaqueta, la americana**
jeans **el(los) vaquero(s), el(los) tejano(s)**
jersey **el jersey, el suéter**
jewelry / jewellery **las joyas, las alhajas**
jumper **el jersey, suéter**
knitted **de punto, [tejido]**
knitwear **los géneros de punto**
ladies' wear **la ropa de señora**
lingerie **la lencería**

Expressions in clothes shops / stores

Can I try it on? **¿Puedo probarlo?**
Do you have the same in red? **¿Tiene usted uno / a parecido / a en rojo?**
I like it. **Me gusta.**
I take / wear size *(clothes)* **Llevo el ..., [Me llevo una talla ...]**
I take / wear size *(shoes)* **Calzo el ...**
I would like a ... **Quiero un / una ...**
I would like to change ... **Quisiera cambiar ...**
I would rather have ... **Preferiría ...**
I'll take it. **Me lo / la llevo.**
I'll take the big one. **Me llevo el / la grande.**

I'd like it two sizes bigger. **Lo quisiera dos números más grande.**
I'm next. **Me toca a mí.**
It suits me. **Me va bien. Me sienta bien.**
That's not quite right. **No es del todo correcto. / Eso no está del todo bien.**
They don't go together. **No armonizan., No hacen juego.**
What color / colour? **¿De qué color?**
What's it made of? **¿De qué está hecho?**
Will it shrink? **¿[Se] encogerá?**

long **largo**
long-sleeved **con mangas largas**
loose **suelto**
loud / brash **chillón, charro, cursi**
low-heeled **de tacones bajos**
man-made fiber / fibre **las fibras sintéticas**
matching **acompañado, a tono, que hace juego con**
men's wear **la ropa de caballero**
no-iron **de no planchar, que no necesita planchado**
pair **el par**
pajamas **el pijama, la pijama**
panties **las bragas, la braga, las braguitas, [los pantys]**
pants **los pantalones**
parka / anorak **el anorak / anorac, el chubasquero**
plain **sencillo, llano, sin adornos**
printed **impreso, estampado**
pure **puro**
raincoat **el impermeable, la gabardina**
sandal **la sandalia, la alpargata**
scarf **la bufanda**
shirt **la camisa**
shoe **el zapato**
shoelace **el lazo, el cordón**
short-sleeved **de mangas cortas**
size **el tamaño, la talla, el número**
skirt **la falda**
slip **las enaguas, la combinación**
small **pequeño**
smart **elegante, pulcro**
sneakers **los zapatos de lona / deportivos, las zapatillas**
sock **el calcetín, [la media]**
soft **blando**
stocking **la media**
striped **listado, rayado, a rayas**
suit **el traje**
sweater **el suéter, el jersey**
sweatshirt **la sudadera**
swimming trunks **el bañador, [el traje de baño]**

swimsuit / bathing suit **el traje de baño, el bañador**
synthetic **sintético**
tie **la corbata**
tight **estrecho, apretado, ajustado, ceñido**
tights **el panti, las medias**
too big / small **demasiado grande / pequeño**
toweling **la felpa**
training shoes **las zapatillas de deporte**
trousers **el pantalón, los pantalones**
T-shirt **la camiseta, el niki, [la playera], [la remera]**
ugly **feo**
umbrella **el paraguas**
underpants **los calzoncillos**
undershirt **la camiseta**
underwear **la ropa interior**
unfashionable **fuera de moda, pasado de moda**
velvet **el terciopelo**
vest / waistcoat **el chaleco**

Alterations & repairs

I alter **arreglo**
buckle **la hebilla**
button **el botón**
heel **el tacón**
hem **el dobladillo**
hole **el roto**
I knit **tricoto**
knitting needle **la aguja de hacer calceta**
material **el tejido**
patch **el remiendo**
pin **el alfiler**
pocket **el bolsillo, [la bolsa]**
I repair / mend **remiendo, [zurzo]**
I sew **coso**
stain **la mancha**
tailor **el sastre**
tailored **hecho por sastre**
thread **el hilo**
zipper **la cremallera**

Food & Drink

10a Drinks & Meals

Drinks

alcoholic **alcohólico**
aperitif **el aperitivo**
beer **la cerveza**
brandy **el brandy, el coñac**
champagne **el champán**
chocolate (drinking) **el chocolate (para beber)**
cider **la sidra**
cocktail **el cóctel**
coffee **el café**
cola **la cola**
draught beer **la cerveza al grifo**
drink **la bebida**
dry **seco**
juice (fruit) **el zumo / [el jugo] (de fruta)**
lemonade **la limonada**
low alcohol **de baja graduación de alcohol**
orange / lemon crush **la naranjada / la limonada**
milk **la leche**
milk shake **el batido, [la malteada]**
mineral water **el agua** *(f)* **mineral**
nonalcoholic **sin alcohol**
sherry **el vino de jerez, el jerez**

sparkling **espumoso**
spirits **los licores, las bebidas alcohólicas**
sweet **dulce**
tea **el té**
water **el agua**
noncarbonated / still water **el agua sin gas**
with ice **con hielo**
whisky **el whisky**
wine **el vino**

Drinking out

bar **el bar**
bartender **el barman**
beer hall **la cervecería**
bottle **la botella**
café **el café**
coffee shop / bar **la cafetería**
cellar **la bodega**
counter / bar **la barra**
cup **la taza, la copa**
I drink **bebo**
glass **el vaso**
refreshments **los refrescos**
sip **el sorbo**
straw **la pajita**
tavern / pub **el pub, la taberna**

---

cafeteria **la cafetería**
canteen **la cantina**
stall **el puesto**
ice cream parlor / parlour **la heladería**
pizza parlor / parlour **la pizzería**
restaurant **el restaurante**

self-service **el autoservicio**
snack bar **el bar de aperitivos, el snack-bar**
take out / take-away **para llevar**
take out / take-away restaurant **el restaurante con comida para llevar**

teaspoon **la cucharita**
wine cellar **la bodega**
wineglass **el vaso de vino**
wine tasting **el catamiento de vino**

Meals

appetizer / starter **el entremés, la entrada**
breakfast **el desayuno**
course **el plato**
dessert **el postre**
I dine **ceno**
dinner **la cena**
I eat **como**
I have a snack **tomo un aperitivo, tomo una tapa**
I have breakfast **desayuno**
I have dinner **ceno**
I have lunch **como, almuerzo**
lunch **la comida, el almuerzo**
main **principal**
meal **la comida**
snack **el aperitivo, la tapa, el refrigerio**
supper **la cena**

Eating out

I add up the bill **hago la cuenta**
bowl **el cuenco, la fuente**
charge **el precio**
cheap **barato**
check / bill **la cuenta**
I choose **elijo, escojo**

it costs **cuesta**
I decide **decido**
expensive **caro**
first course **el primer plato**
fixed price **el precio fijo**
fork **el tenedor**
inclusive **incluido, inclusive**
knife **el cuchillo**
main course **el plato principal**
menu **el menú**
menu of the day **el menú del día**
napkin **la servilleta**
I order **pido**
order **el pedido**
place setting **la colocación de la mesa**
plate **el plato**
portion **la porción**
reservation **la reserva**
I serve **sirvo**
service **el servicio**
set menu **el menú prefijado**
side dish **el plato adicional**
spoon **la cuchara**
table **la mesa**
tablecloth **el mantel**
tip / gratuity **la propina**
I tip **doy propina**
toothpick **el palillo de dientes**
tourist menu **el menú turístico**
tray **la bandeja**
waiter **el camarero**
waitress **la camarera**
wine list **la lista de vinos**

Can you tell me where the nearest café is, please? **¿Me puede decir dónde está el café más cercano, por favor?**

Where can we get a drink around here? **¿Dónde podemos tomar algo por aquí?**

I'd like a chocolate milk shake, please. **Un batido [Una malteada] de chocolate, por favor.**

➤ VEGETABLES, FRUIT, DESSERT 10c; COOKING & EATING 10d

10b Fish & Meat

Fish & seafood

anchovy **la anchoa**
clam **la almeja**
cockles **los berberechos**
cod **el bacalao**
crab **el cangrejo**
crayfish **el cangrejo de río**
eel **la anguila**
fish **el pescado**
flounder / plaice **la patija**
hake **la merluza**
herring **el arenque**
lobster **la langosta, el bogavante**
mussel **el mejillón**
octopus **el pulpo**
oyster **la ostra**

prawn **la gamba, [el camarón]**
prawns **las gambas, los langostinos**
salmon **el salmón**
sardine **la sardina**
scallop **la venera**
seafood **el marisco**
shell **el caparazón**
shellfish **el crustáceo, los mariscos**
shrimp **el camarón, el langostino**
snails **los caracoles**
sole **el lenguado**
squid **el calamar**
swordfish **el pez espada**
trout **la trucha**
tuna **el atún**
whitebait **el chanquete**

Is this fish fresh?
I'd rather have tuna than crab.

¿**Es fresco este pescado?**
Prefiero comer atún que cangrejo.

Would you prefer cod or sole?

¿**Prefiere usted bacalao o lenguado?**

"Shall we try the chicken?"
"I'd like a pork chop."

— ¿**Probamos el pollo?**
— **Me gustaría tomar una chuleta de cerdo.**

Can we both have steak, one rare and one well-done?

¿**Nos trae dos filetes de vaca, uno poco hecho y el otro muy hecho?**

I'll have a rare steak with fries / chips and salad, please.

Quisiera un biftec poco hecho con patatas [papas] fritas y una ensalada, por favor.

I want a tomato salad. Does it have garlic in it?

Quisiera una ensalada de tomate. ¿**Tiene ajo?**

Meat & meat products

bacon   **el tocino, la panceta**
beef   **la carne de vaca**
bolognese   **boloñesa**
casserole   **la cazuela, [la cacerola]**
chop   **la chuleta**
cutlet   **la chuleta**
ham   **el jamón**
hamburger / beefburger   **la hamburguesa**
hot dog   **el perrito caliente**
kid   **el cabrito**
kidney   **los riñones**
lamb   **el cordero**
liver   **el hígado**
meat   **la carne**
meatballs   **las albóndigas**
minced meat   **la carne picada**
mixed grill   **la parrillada mixta**
mutton   **la carne de cordero**
pâté   **el paté**
pork   **la carne de cerdo, el cerdo**

rabbit   **el conejo**
salami   **el salami, el salchichón**
sausage   **la salchicha**
scallop   **el escalope**
sirloin   **el solomillo**
steak   **el filete**
stew   **el guiso, el estofado**
veal   **la (carne de) ternera**

Poultry & game

capon   **el capón**
chicken   **el pollo**
   chicken breast   **la pechuga de pollo**
duck   **el pato**
goose   **el ganso**
partridge   **la perdiz**
pheasant   **el faisán**
poultry   **la carne de ave, el ave**
quail   **la codorniz**
turkey   **el pavo**
wild boar   **el jabalí**
woodcock   **la becada**

Traditional dishes

albóndigas   spiced meatballs
almejas a la marinera   clams in paprika sauce
calamares a la romana   deep-fried squid
caldo gallego   meat and vegetable broth
[chile con carne]   stew of kidney beans, chili, and minced beef
chorizo   spicy sausage made of pork, garlic, and paprika
conejo al ajillo   rabbit with garlic
empanada gallega   tenderloin of pork, onions, and chili peppers in a pie
empanadillas   savory pasties stuffed with meat or fish

gambas a la plancha   grilled prawns
menestra de pollo   casserole of chicken and vegetables
paella valenciana   saffron rice with chicken, shrimp, mussels, prawns, squid, peas, tomato, chili pepper, and garlic
riñones al jerez   kidneys braised in sherry
sopa de mariscos   seafood soup
sopa de pescado   fish soup
[taco]   cornmeal pancake stuffed with meat, chili pepper sauce, and mashed avocado

FOOD & DRINK

Vegetables

artichoke   la alcachofa
asparagus   el espárrago
avocado   el aguacate
baked beans   las judías cocidas,
   [los frijoles cocidos]
beans   las judías, las habas
beets   la remolacha
broccoli   el brécol, [el brócoli]
Brussels sprout   la col de Bruselas
cabbage   la col, [el repollo]
carrot   la zanahoria
cauliflower   la coliflor
celeriac   el apio
celery   el apio
chickpea   el garbanzo
corn / maize   el maíz
   corn on the cob   la mazorca
cucumber   el pepino, [el
   cohombro]
eggplant / aubergine   la berenjena
endive / chicory   la endivia
French bean   la judía enana, el
   frijol
garlic   el ajo
gherkin   el pepinillo
green bean   la alubia, la judía
herb   la hierba aromática
leek   el puerro
lentil   la lenteja
lettuce   la lechuga
marrow   el tuétano
mushroom   el champiñón

onion   la cebolla
parsley   el perejil
parsnip   la chirivía, la pastinaca
pea   el guisante, [la arveja]
pepper (red / green)   el pimiento
   (verde / rojo)
potato   la patata
pumpkin   la calabaza
radish   el rábano
rice   el arroz
salad   la ensalada
spinach   la espinaca
sweetcorn   el maíz dulce
tomato   el tomate
turnip   el nabo
vegetable   la verdura
   vegetable (adj)   vegetal
watercress   el berro
zucchini / courgette   el calabacín

Fruit

apple   la manzana
apricot   el albaricoque
banana   el plátano
berry   la baya, el grano
blackberry   la mora, la zarzamora
blackcurrant   la grosella
brazil nut   la nuez del Brasil
bunch of grapes   el racimo de uvas
cherry   la cereza
chestnut   la castaña
coconut   el coco
cranberry   el arándano

Traditional dishes

arroz con leche   rice pudding
bizcocho   sponge cake
crema catalana   caramel
   pudding
guacamole   mashed avocado

pastel de queso   cheesecake
[papusa]   pancake with cheese
   or bacon
tortilla de patatas   potato
   omelet

---

currant   la pasa de Corinto
date   el dátil
fig   el higo
fruit   la fruta
gooseberry   la grosella espinosa
grape   la uva
grapefuit   el pomelo
hazelnut   la avellana
kiwi fruit   el kiwi
lemon   el limón
lime   la lima
melon   el melón
nut   la nuez
olive   la aceituna
orange   la naranja
passion fruit   la fruta de la pasión,
   [el maracuyá]
peach   el melocotón
peanut   el cacahuete
pear   la pera
peel   la piel, la cáscara
I peel   pelo, quito la cáscara
peeled   pelado
piece of fruit   una fruta
pineapple   la piña
plum   la ciruela
pomegranate   la granada
prune   la ciruela seca
raisin   la pasa, [la uva pasa]
raspberry   la frambuesa
red currant   la grosella roja
rhubarb   el ruibarbo
seed   la pepita
stone   el hueso
strawberry   la fresa
sultana   la pasa

tangerine   la mandarina
walnut   la nuez

Dessert

biscuit / cookie   la galleta
cake   el pastel
caramel   el caramelo
chocolate   el chocolate
chocolates   los bombones
cream   la nata
crème caramel   el flan
custard   las natillas
dessert   el postre
flan   la tarta, [el flan]
flour   la harina
fresh fruit   la fruta fresca
fruit of the season   la fruta de
   la estación
fruit salad   la macedonia, [la
   ensalada de frutas]
ice cream   el helado
mousse   la mousse
pancake   la hojuela, [el
   panqueque]
pastry   la pastita
pie   el pastel
pudding   el puding, el dulce, el
   pudín
sweet   dulce
tart   la tarta dulce
trifle   la trufa
vanilla   la vainilla
whipped cream   la nata batida
yogurt   el yogur

I'd rather have boiled potatoes than fries / chips.

Prefiero las patatas [papas] cocidas a las patatas [papas] fritas.

Two strawberry ice creams. Have you got any apple pie?

Dos helados de fresa. ¿Tiene tarta de manzana?

FOOD & DRINK

10d Cooking & Eating

Food preparation

I bake	**cuezo al horno, horneo**
baked	**al horno**
barbecue	**la barbacoa**
I beat	**bato**
beaten	**batido**
I boil	**hiervo**
boiled	**hervido**
bone	**el hueso, la espina**
boned	**deshuesado, sin espinas**
boned *(fish)*	**sin espinas**
I bone	**deshueso, quito las espinas**
I braise	**braseo**
braised	**braseado**
in breadcrumbs	**empanado**
breast	**la pechuga**
I carve	**trincho**
I chop	**corto en trozos, pico**
I clear the table	**quito la mesa**
I cook	**cocino**
cooking / cuisine	**la cocina**
I cut	**corto**
I dice	**corto en cubitos**
dough	**la masa, la pasta**
I dry	**seco (los platos)**
egg	**el huevo**
flour	**la harina**
food preparation	**la preparación de alimentos**
fried	**frito**

I fry	**frío**
I grate	**rallo**
grated	**rallado**
gravy	**la salsa de carne**
I grill	**aso (a la parrilla)**
grilled	**asado (a la parrilla)**
ingredient	**el ingrediente**
large	**grande**
I marinate	**pongo a marinar**
marinated	**marinado**
medium	**en su punto, término medio**
milk	**la leche**
I mix	**mezclo**
mixed	**mezclado**
olive oil	**el aceite de oliva**
pastry	**la pasta**
short(crust) pastry	**la pasta quebradiza**
I peel	**pelo**
peeled	**pelado**
I pour	**sirvo**
rare	**poco hecho**
recipe	**la receta**
roast	**el asado**
I roast	**aso al horno**
in sauce	**en salsa**
I set / lay the table	**pongo la mesa**
I sift	**tamizo, cierno**
I slice	**corto en rodajas**
sliced	**en rodajas**

Chop two kilos of tomatoes and one kilo of peeled onions. Put into saucepan with 500 ml of malt vinegar. Add refined sugar and two teaspoons of salt.

Cook, stirring frequently for forty minutes until mixture thickens.

Pique dos kilos de tomates y un kilo de cebollas peladas. Póngalos en una cacerola con 500 ml de vinagre de malta. Agregue azúcar refinada y dos cucharaditas de sal.

Cocínelo durante cuarenta minutos, revolviendo continuamente hasta que espese.

I spread **extiendo**
stewed **estofado, guisado**
sunflower oil **el aceite de girasol**
I toast **tuesto**
toasted **tostado**
I wash up **friego, lavo**
I weigh **peso**
well-done **muy hecho, bien
    cocinado**
I whip **bato**
whipped **batido**
I whisk **bato (con batidora)**
whisked **batido (con batidora)**

Eating

additive **el aditivo**
I am hungry **tengo hambre**
I am thirsty **tengo sed**
appetite **el apetito**
appetizing **apetitoso**
bad **malo**
I bite **muerdo**
bitter **amargo**
calorie **la caloría**
    low calorie **bajo en calorías**
I chew **mastico**
cold **frío**
delicious **delicioso**
diet **el régimen, [la dieta]**
    I'm on a diet **sigo un régimen,
    [estoy a dieta]**
fatty / oily **graso**
fresh **fresco**

fresh(ly) *(adv)* **fresco**
healthy *(appetite)* **bueno**
    healthy *(food)* **sano**
I help myself **me sirvo**
hot **picante**
hunger **el hambre**
hungry **hambriento, con ganas
    de comer**
I like **me gusta**
mild **suave**
I offer **ofrezco**
I pass (salt) **paso**
piece **el trozo, el pedazo**
I pour **sirvo**
I provide **pongo, proporciono**
rancid *(cheese)* **rancio**
salty **salado**
I serve **sirvo**
sharp **ácido**
slice **la rebanada**
I smell **huelo**
soft **blando**
spicy **picante**
stale (bread) **duro**
still **no espumoso, sin gas**
strong **fuerte**
I swallow **trago**
tasty **sabroso**
thirst **la sed**
thirsty **sediento**
I try **pruebo**
vegan **vegetariano estricto**
vegetarian **vegetariano**

Pass the salt, please.	**Pase la sal, por favor.**
Just a small portion.	**Sólo una porción pequeña.**
Nothing more, thanks.	**Nada más, gracias.**

Health & Illness

11a Accidents & Emergencies

accident **el accidente**
ambulance **la ambulancia**
I attack **ataco**
break **la rotura, la ruptura, el rompimiento**
I break **rompo, me rompo**
I break my arm **me rompo el brazo**
breakage **la rotura, la ruptura, el rompimiento**
broken **roto**
I have broken my leg **me he roto la pierna**
bruise **la contusión, el cardenal, la magulladura, el moretón**
I bruise **contundo, magullo**
burn **la quemadura**
I burn **me quemo**
casualty **el herido, la víctima**
casualty department **la sección de accidentes**
I catch fire **me enciendo, prendo fuego**

I collide (with) **choco (con), colisiono (con)**
collision **la colisión, el choque**
I crash **choco, colisiono**
I crash (plane) **estrello (avión)**
crash **el choque, la colisión**
I crush **aplasto**
I cut (myself) **(me) corto**
I have cut my finger **me he cortado el dedo**
dead **muerto**
death **la muerte**
I die **muero**
emergency **la emergencia, urgencia**
emergency exit **la salida de emergencia / urgencia**
emergency services **las urgencias, los servicios de emergencia**
it explodes **estalla, explota, explosiona**

There has been an accident! My friend is injured.	**¡Ha habido un accidente! Mi amigo está herido.**
We need an ambulance quickly.	**Necesitamos una ambulancia, pronto!**
Call the fire brigade!	**¡Llama a los bomberos!**
I think I have broken my arm. It hurts a lot.	**Creo que tengo el brazo roto. Me duele mucho.**

explosion **la explosión, el estallido**
I extinguish **apago, extingo**
I fall **caigo**
fatal **fatal, mortal**
fine **la multa**
fire **el fuego, el incendio**
fire brigade **el cuerpo de bomberos**
fire engine **el coche de bomberos**
fire extinguisher **el extintor**
fireman **el bombero**
first aid **los primeros auxilios**
graze **el roce, la abrasión, la rozadura**
I graze **raspo**
I have an accident **sufro un accidente**
hospital **el hospital**
impact **el impacto, el choque**
incident **el incidente**
I injure **hiero, hago daño a, lastimo, lesiono**
injury **la herida**
injured **herido**
insurance **el seguro, los seguros**
I insure **aseguro**

I kill **mato**
killed **matado, muerto**
life belt **el cinturón salvavidas**
life jacket **el chaleco salvavidas**
oxygen **el oxígeno**
paramedic **el paramédico**
I recover **recupero, me recobro**
recovery **la recuperación**
I rescue **rescato, salvo**
rescue **el rescate, el salvamento**
rescue services **los servicios de rescate**
I run over **atropello**
I rush **voy de prisa, me apresuro**
safe **salvo, seguro**
safe and sound **sano y salvo**
safety belt **el cinturón de seguridad**
salvage **el salvamento, la recuperación**
I save **rescato, salvo**
seat belt **el cinturón de seguridad**
terrorist attack **el ataque de terroristas**
third party **la tercera persona**
witness **el testigo**

It was your fault, not mine. **Ha sido culpa tuya, no mía.**

Are you a doctor? **¿Es usted médico?**

Where's the nearest hospital? **¿Dónde está el hospital más cercano?**

▶ MEDICAL TREATMENT 11c; HEALTH & HYGIENE 11d

11b Illness & Disability

ache **el dolor**
alive **vivo**
I am ill / sick **estoy enfermo**
I am sick / vomit **vomito, devuelvo**
he amputates **amputa**
amputee **el amputado**
amputation **la amputación**
arthritis **la artritis**
asthma **el asma** (f)
black eye **el ojo amoratado**
I bleed **desangro, sangro**
blind **ciego**
blind man / woman **el ciego, la ciega**
blood **la sangre**
breath **el aliento, la respiración**
I breathe **respiro**
breathless **falto de aliento, desalentado, jadeante**
catarrh **el catarro**
I catch cold **cojo frío, cojo un resfriado**
cold **el resfriado, el catarro**
constipated **estreñido**
constipation **el estreñimiento**
convalescence **la convalecencia**
I am convalescing **convalezco**
cough **la tos**

I cough **toso**
cripple **el lisiado, el mutilado**
I cry **lloro**
dead **muerto**
deaf **sordo**
deafness **la sordera**
death **la muerte**
depressed **deprimido**
depression **la depresión, el abatimiento**
diarrhea **la diarrea**
I die **muero**
diet **el régimen, la dieta**
disabled **minusválido**
disease **la enfermedad, el mal**
dizziness **el mareo, el vértigo**
dizzy **mareado**
drug **la droga**
drugged **drogado**
drunk **borracho**
dumb **mudo**
earache **el dolor de oídos**
I feel dizzy **me siento mareado**
I feel ill / unwell **me siento enfermo**
I feel (well) **me siento (bien)**
fever **la fiebre**
feverish **febril**
flu **la gripe**

I feel dizzy if I stand up.	**Al levantarme me siento mareado.**
I don't usually faint!	**No suelo desmayarme.**
I have been sick / vomited several times.	**He vomitado varias veces.**
I suffer from high blood pressure.	**Padezco de hipertensión.**
My children have diarrhea. I seem to be constipated.	**Mis niños tienen la diarrea. Yo debo estar estreñido.**

I get drunk **me emborracho**
I got better **me mejoré, me repuse, me restablecí**
I had an operation **me han operado**
I have a cold **tengo un resfriado**
I have a temperature **tengo fiebre**
headache **el dolor de cabeza**
health **la salud**
healthy **bien de salud**
heart attack **el ataque cardíaco**
high blood pressure **la hipertensión**
HIV positive **VIH positivo**
hurt **el dolor**
I hurt **me duele, tengo dolor de ...**
it hurts **me duele**
ill **enfermo**
illness **la enfermedad**
jaundice **la ictericia**
I live **vivo**
I look (ill) **parezco enfermo**
mental illness **la enfermedad mental**
mentally handicapped **minusválido mental**
mentally sick **enfermo de la mente**
migraine **la jaqueca**
mute **el mudo**
  mute *(adj)* **mudo**

pain **el dolor**
painful **doloroso**
pale **pálido**
paralysis **la parálisis**
paralyzed **paralizado**
physically handicapped **mutilado, minusválido**
recovery **el restablecimiento**
rheumatism **el reumatismo**
sick **enfermo**
I sneeze **estornudo**
sore throat **el dolor de garganta**
sting **la picadura, el escozor, la picazón**
it stings **me pica, me rasca**
stomach **el estómago**
stomachache **el dolor de estómago**
stomach upset **el trastorno estomacal**
I take drugs **tomo drogas, me drogo**
temperature **la fiebre**
tonsillitis **la amigdalitis**
toothache **el dolor de muelas**
I vomit **vomito, devuelvo**
what's wrong? **¿qué (te) pasa?**
I wound **hiero**
wounded **herido**

I don't know what is wrong with her.	**No sé qué tendrá.**
She seems to have a temperature.	**Parece tener fiebre.**
I have a sore throat and I have a migraine coming on.	**Tengo dolor de la garganta y me llega [me está empezando] una jaqueca.**

11c Medical Treatment

anesthetic / anaesthetic **el anestésico**
  I am under anesthetic **estoy anestesiado**
appointment **la cita**
bandage **la venda**
blood **la sangre**
blood test **el análisis sanguíneo / de la sangre**
blood pressure **la presión sanguínea**
capsule **la cápsula**
chemotherapy **la quimioterapia**
cure **la cura**
danger to life **el peligro mortal**
dangerous **peligroso**
death **la muerte**
I diet **estoy a régimen / [dieta]**
doctor (Dr.) **el médico**
dressing **el vendaje**
drop **la gota**
drug **la droga**
I examine **examino**
examination **el examen**
I fill **(re)lleno**
glasses **las gafas**

I have **tengo**
heating **la calefacción**
hospital **el hospital**
I improve **me restablezco, me repongo**
injection **la inyección**
insurance certificate **el certificado de seguro**
I look after **cuido de**
medical **médico**
medicine **la medicina**
midwife **la comadre, la comadrona, la partera**
nurse **la enfermera**
I nurse **cuido, atiendo**
office hours **las horas de consulta**
I operate **opero**
operation **la operación, la intervención quirúrgica**
pastille **la pastilla**
patient **el paciente, el enfermo**
pharmacist / chemist **el farmacéutico**
pharmacy **la farmacia**

Call a doctor!

¡Llama a un médico!

Is he a good doctor? Can he diagnose the symptoms and prescribe a cure?

¿Es buen médico? ¿Puede diagnosticar los síntomas y recomendar una cura?

He does not like injections. He has never had an X-ray.

No le gustan las inyecciones. Nunca lo han radiografiado.

Will I need an operation? I have my medical insurance.

¿Necesitaré una operación? Tengo mi seguro de médico.

physiotherapy **la fisioterapia**
physiotherapist **el fisioterapeuta**
pill **la píldora**
plaster (of Paris) **el yeso mate**
I prescribe **receto**
prescription **la receta**
radiotherapy **la radioterapia**
receptionist **el / la recepcionista**
service **el servicio**
I set **encaso**
spa resort **el balneario, la estación balnearia, la estación termal**
specialist **el / la especialista**
stitch **el punto de sutura**
stitches **los puntos de sutura**
sticking plaster **el esparadrapo**
surgery **la cirugía**
syringe **la jeringa, la jeringuilla**
tablet **la tableta, el comprimido, la pastilla**
therapeutic **terapéutico**
therapy **la terapia, la terapéutica**
therapist **el / la terapeuta**
thermometer **el termómetro**
I treat **trato, curo, atiendo**
treatment **el tratamiento, la cura**

ward **la sala, la crujía**
wound **la herida**
X-ray **el rayo x**
I X-ray **radiografío**

Dentist & optician

abscess **el flemón**
contact lens **el lente de contacto**
dentist **el dentista**
denture **la dentadura**
I extract **saco**
eyeglass / spectacles case **el estuche para gafas**
eyesight **la vista**
farsighted / longsighted **présbite, hipermétrope**
filling **el empaste**
frame **la montura**
glasses / spectacles **las gafas**
lens **el lente**
nearsighted / shortsighted **miope**
optician **el óptico**
sunglasses **las gafas de sol**
tinted **ahumado**
I test / check **controlo**
I have a toothache **tengo dolor de muelas**

I have lost my tablets. I have to take them four times a day.

He perdido mis comprimidos [tabletas / pastillas]. Debo tomarlos [tomarlas] cuatro veces al día.

Can I have a prescription?

¿Me puede dar una receta?

He had an operation recently. He seems to be recovering.

Lo operaron recientemente. Parece que se está restableciendo.

We are so relieved — all the tests proved negative.

Estamos muy aliviados — todos los análisis salieron negativos.

▶ HOSPITAL DEPARTMENTS App. 11c

11d Health & Hygiene

Physical state

ache	**el dolor**
aching *(adj)*	**adolorido**
asleep	**dormido**
awake	**despierto**
blister	**la ampolla**
boil	**el divieso, el furúnculo**
bruise	**la contusión, el cardenal, la magulladura, el magullón, el moretón**
comfort	**la comodidad**
comfortable	**cómodo, confortable**
discomfort	**el malestar**
dizziness	**el mareo, el vértigo**
dizzy	**mareado**
drowsiness	**la somnolencia**
drowsy	**soñoliento**
I exercise	**ejercito**
exercise bike	**la bicicleta estática**
faint	**mareado**
I faint	**me desmayo, pierdo el conocimiento**
I feel	**me siento**
fit	**en buena forma, en buen estado físico, sano, bien de salud**
fitness	**la buena salud, el (buen) estado físico**
graze	**el roce, la abrasión, la raspadura**
I am hot / cold	**tengo calor / frío**
hunger	**el hambre** *(f)*
hungry	**hambriento**
I am hungry	**tengo hambre**
ill	**enfermo**

I lie down	**me acuesto**
I look	**parezco**
queasy	**mareado, bascoso**
I relax	**me relajo**
I rest	**descanso**
seasick	**mareado**
sick	**enfermo**
I sleep	**duermo**
sleepy	**soñoliento**
stamina	**la resistencia, el aguante**
strange	**extraño, curioso, raro**
thirst	**la sed**
thirsty	**sediento**
I am thirsty	**tengo sed**
tired	**cansado**
I am tired	**tengo sueño, estoy cansado**
tiredness	**el cansancio, la fatiga, el sueño**
uncomfortable	**incómodo, molesto**
under the weather	**indispuesto**
unwell	**enfermo, indispuesto, de mala salud**
I wake up	**me despierto**
well	**bien de salud**
well-being	**el bienestar**

Beauty & hygiene

bath	**el baño**
beauty	**la belleza**
beauty contest	**el concurso de belleza**
beauty salon / parlor	**el salón de belleza**

I need a shower.	**Necesito ducharme.**
I'd like a haircut, please. Don't cut it too short.	**Quiero un corte de pelo, por favor. No me lo corte demasiado.**

beauty queen **la reina de la belleza**

beauty treatment **el tratamiento de belleza**

body odor / odour **el olor a sudor**

I burp / belch **eructo**

I brush **cepillo**

brush **el cepillo**

I clean **limpio**

clean **limpio**

I clean my teeth **me limpio los dientes**

comb **el peine**

I comb my hair **me peino**

condom **el condón, el preservativo**

contraception **la contracepción, las medidas anticonceptivas**

contraceptive **el anticonceptivo**

I cut **corto, me corto ...**

dandruff **la caspa**

I defecate **defeco**

dirty **sucio**

diet *(usual food)* **la dieta**

I am on a diet **sigo un régimen**

electric razor **la afeitadora (eléctrica)**

facial **el tratamiento facial**

flannel **la manopla**

fleas **las pulgas**

hairbrush **el cepillo para el pelo**

haircut **el corte de pelo**

I get my hair cut **me hago cortar el pelo**

hairdo **el peinado**

healthy *(person)* **sano, con buena salud**

healthy *(diet, place)* **saludable**

laundry *(establishment)* **el lavadero, la lavandería**

laundry *(linen)* **la ropa sucia, la ropa por lavar**

louse / nit **el piojo**

I'm losing my hair **pierdo el pelo, me estoy quedando calvo**

manicure **la manicura, [el manicure]**

I menstruate **menstrúo**

menstruation **la menstruación**

nailbrush **el cepillo para las uñas**

period **el período, la regla**

period pains **los dolores de la regla**

razor **la afeitadora, la rasuradora, la maquinilla de afeitar**

sanitary **sanitario, higiénico**

sanitary napkin **el paño higiénico, la compresa (higiénica), [la toalla higiénica]**

scissors **las tijeras**

I shave **me afeito**

shower **la ducha**

smell *(bad)* **el olor**

I smell *(badly)* **huelo**

soap **el jabón**

I sweat **sudo**

sweat **el sudor**

I take a bath **me baño**

I take a shower **me ducho**

tampon **el tampón**

toothbrush **el cepillo de dientes**

toothpaste **la crema de dientes, la pasta dentífrica**

towel **la toalla**

I wash **me lavo**

A little more off the back and sides, please.

Un poco más por detrás y en los lados, por favor.

Please trim my mustache.

Córteme el bigote por favor.

Social Issues

12a Society

abnormal **anormal**
alternative **la alternativa**
amenity **la amenidad**
anonymous **anónimo**
attitude **la actitud**
available **disponible**
basic **básico**
basis **la base**
burden **la carga, el peso**
campaign **la campaña**
care **el cuidado**
cause **la causa**
change **el cambio**
circumstance **la circunstancia**
community **la comunidad**
compulsory **obligatorio**
contribution **la contribución**
cost **el precio, el coste, el costo**
I counsel **aconsejo, asesoro**
counseling **el asesoramiento, la asistencia**
criterion **el criterio**
debt **la deuda**
I am in debt **tengo deudas**
dependence **la dependencia**
dependent **dependiente**
depressed **deprimido, abatido**
depression **la depresión, la crisis**
deprived **privado de**
difficulty **la dificultad**

effect **el efecto**
effective **efectivo, eficiente**
fact **el hecho**
finance **las finanzas**
financial **financiero**
frustrated **frustrado**
frustration **la frustración**
guidance **la dirección, la orientación**
increase **el aumento**
inner city **el barrio céntrico de la ciudad**
institution **la institución**
loneliness **la soledad**
lonely **solitario**
long-term **a largo plazo**
measure **medida**
negative **negativo**
normal **normal, común**
policy **la política, los principios, los criterios**
positive **positivo**
power **el poder**
prestige **el prestigio**
problem **el problema, la cuestión**
protest movement **el movimiento de protesta**
I provide **proporciono, suministro**

There are immense social problems in the inner city.	**Existen enormes problemas sociales en los barrios céntricos de las ciudades.**
The unemployed often feel frustrated and lonely, as a result of unemployment.	**Los desempleados suelen sentirse frustrados y solitarios como consecuencia del paro.**

---

provision **la provisión, el suministro, la estipulación, la disposición**
psychological **psicológico**
quality of life **la calidad de vida**
question / issue **la cuestión, el asunto**
rate **la tasa**
responsibility **la responsabilidad**
responsible (ir-) **(ir)responsable**
result **el resultado**
role **el papel**
rural **rural**
scarcity **la escasez**
scheme **el esquema**
I am out of work **no encuentro trabajo**
secure (in-) **(in)seguro**
security (in-) **la (in)seguridad**
self-esteem **la autoestima**
short-term **a corto plazo**
situation **la situación**
social **social**
society **la sociedad**
stable (un-) **(in)estable**
stability (in-) **la (in)estabilidad**
statistics **las estadísticas**
status **el estatus, la posición**
stigma **el estigma, la marca**
stress **el estrés, la fatiga**
stressful **estresante**
structure **la estructura, la configuración**
superfluous **superfluo**
support **el soporte, el apoyo, el sostén, la ayuda**
urban **urbano**
value **el valor**

Some useful verbs

I adapt / conform **me ajusto, me acomodo**
it affects **afecta**
I can afford **me puedo permitir**
I alienate **enajeno, traspaso**
I break down **fracaso**
I campaign **hago campaña**
I care for **me preocupo por**
I cause **causo**
it changes **cambia**
I contribute **contribuyo**
I cope **me arreglo, me las ingenio**
I depend on **dependo de**
I deprive **privo**
I discourage **desaliento**
I dominate **domino**
I encourage **aliento, animo**
I help **ayudo**
I increase **aumento**
I lack **carezco de**
I look after **cuido de**
I need **necesito**
I neglect **descuido, abandono**
I owe **debo**
I protest **protesto**
I provide for **proporciono, suministro**
I put up with **(me) aguanto**
I rely on **confío en, cuento con**
I respect **respeto**
I share **comparto**
I solve **resuelvo**
I suffer from (disease) **tengo**
I support **mantengo**
I tackle **hago frente a**
I value **valoro**

Financial difficulties lead to loss of status and family problems. **Las dificultades económicas llevan a una pérdida de estatus y problemas familiares.**

The quality of life suffers because of it. **Como consecuencia, se compromete la calidad de la vida.**

ADDICTION & VIOLENCE 12d; PREJUDICE 12e

SOCIAL ISSUES

12b Poverty & Social Services

Social services

aid   **la ayuda**
agency   **la agencia, la oficina**
authority   **las autoridades**
benefit   **el beneficio**
I benefit   **me beneficio**
charity   **la caridad, la organización caritativa**
claim   **la solicitud**
I claim   **solicito**
claimant   **el solicitante**
disability   **la invalidez, la incapacidad**
disabled   **el inválido, el minusválido**
I am eligible for   **tengo derecho a, cumplo los requisitos para**
frail   **débil, delicado**
frailty   **la debilidad**
grant   **la concesión, la beca**
handicap   **la minusvalía, el obstáculo, la incapacidad**
handicapped   **el minusválido, el incapacitado**
homeless shelter center   **el centro de recepciones**
ill health   **la mala salud**

income support   **la pensión de subsistencia**
loan   **el préstamo**
maintenance   **el mantenimiento**
official   **oficial**
Red Cross   **la Cruz Roja**
refuge   **el refugio**
refugee   **el refugiado**
I register   **me inscribo**
registration   **la inscripción**
Salvation Army   **el Ejército de Salvación**
service   **el servicio**
social security   **la seguridad social**
social services   **los servicios sociales**
social worker   **el asistente social**
support   **la ayuda**
I support   **ayudo**
welfare   **el bienestar social**

Wealth & poverty

affluence   **la prosperidad**
I beg   **mendigo, pido**
beggar   **el mendigo**
I am broke   **no tengo un céntimo**

"What social services are available to those in need?"

"There is a homeless shelter. Many charities are active in this way. The physically handicapped can apply for help too. They are particularly vulnerable to unemployment."

— **¿Cuáles servicios sociales están a la disposición de los necesitados?**

— **Hay un centro de recepción para las personas sin hogar. Muchas sociedades benéficas son activas del mismo modo. Los minusválidos también pueden solicitar ayuda. Ellos son muy vulnerables en lo que se refiere al desempleo.**

debt **la deuda**
in debt **tengo deudas**
deprivation **la privación, la pérdida**
deprived **desventajado, desvalido**
destitute **el indigente, necesitado**
living standards **las condiciones de vida**
millionaire **el millonario**
need **la necesidad**
nutrition **la nutrición**
poor **pobre**
poverty **la pobreza, la miseria**
subsistence **la subsistencia**
tramp / vagrant **el vagabundo**
vulnerability **la vulnerabilidad**
vulnerable **vulnerable**
wealth **la riqueza**
I am well off **estoy acomodado**

Unemployment

I cut back (jobs) **recorto, reduzco**
I dismiss **despido**
dismissal **el despido**
dole **el subsidio de desempleo**
I give notice **aviso**
job **el empleo, el trabajo**
job center / employment center **la oficina de empleo**
job creation scheme **el programa de creación de empleo**
layoff / redundancy **el despido**
laid off / redundant **despedido**
long-term unemployed **el desempleado de larga duración**
I have lost my job **he perdido mi empleo**
part-time **la media jornada**
retraining **la recapacitación, el entrenamiento adicional**
I refuse a job **rechazo un empleo**
I resign **dimito, renuncio**
short-term work **la jornada reducida**
skill **la habilidad, la aptitud, la técnica, el oficio**
staffing **empleo de personal**
training program / scheme **el programa de formación**
unemployable **inútil para el trabajo**
unemployed **desempleado, parado**
unemployment **el paro, el desempleo**
unemployment benefit **el subsidio de paro / desempleo**
unemployment rate **la tasa de desempleo**
unskilled worker **trabajador no especializado**
vacancy **la vacante**

"How high is the level of unemployment?"
"In some areas it is about fifteen percent."
"Can people retrain or work part-time?"

 "Yes, sometimes, and many retire early. Not everyone gets the unemployment benefits, as many have not worked for a long time."

—¿Cuál es la tasa del desempleo?
—En algunas zonas llega al quince por ciento.
—La gente, puede recapacitarse o trabajar en horario de jornada reducida?
—Sí, a veces, y muchos se toman la jubilación anticipada. No todos reciben el subsidio del paro, pues muchos llevan mucho tiempo sin trabajar.

▶ PAY & CONDITIONS; JOB APPLICATION 14c

SOCIAL ISSUES

12c Housing & Homelessness

accommodation   **la vivienda**
apartment / flat   **el piso, el apartamento**
  apartment houses / block of flats **el bloque de pisos / apartamentos**
I build   **construyo**
building   **la construcción, el edificio**
  building land   **los terrenos edificables / urbanizables**
  building plot   **el solar para la construcción, [el lote]**
  building site   **la obra**
camp   **el campamento**
comfortable / homey   **confortable, cómodo**
commune   **la comuna**
dilapidated   **desmoronado, ruinoso**
I demolish   **demuelo**
demolition   **la demolición**
it deteriorates   **se deteriora, deteriora**

drab   **monótono, triste**
I evict   **desalojo, desahucio**
it falls down   **está en ruinas**
furnished   **amueblado**
homeless   **sin hogar**
homelessness   **la carencia de hogar**
hostel   **el hostal**
house   **la casa**
  detached house   **el chalet**
  public housing   **la casa protegida, la casa del ayuntamiento, [la vivienda estatal]**
  semidetached house   **la casa adosada**
housing   **la vivienda**
  builders' association   **la sociedad constructora**
  housing shortage   **la escasez de viviendas**
inner city   **el barrio céntrico de la ciudad**

"Why do so many houses stand empty?
The houses deteriorate fast and squatters move in.

Aren't the town planners intending to demolish those houses?"

"Yes, but at the same time so many are homeless. They sleep in the open or squat."

"Is the municipality still building public housing?"

— **¿Por qué quedan vacías tantas casas?**
Las casas se deterioran rápidamente, y luego las ocupan los squátters.

Y los urbanistas, ¿no tienen la intención de demoler estas casas?

— **Sí, pero al mismo tiempo hay tantos sin hogar. Duermen al descubierto o ocupan las casas ilegalmente.**

— **Y el ayuntamiento [la alcaldía] ¿sigue construyendo viviendas protegidas?**

landlord **el dueño, el propietario (de la casa)**

living conditions **las condiciones de vida**

I maintain **mantengo**

I modernize **modernizo**

mortgage **la hipoteca, el préstamo hipotecario**

mortgage rate **el tipo de interés hipotecario**

I move **me mudo de casa**

I occupy **ocupo**

overcrowded **lleno de gente, atestado**

overcrowding **la superpoblación, la masificación**

own **propio**

owner occupied **ocupado por el dueño**

public housing / social housing / council housing **la vivienda protegida**

I pull down **demuelo, derribo**

real estate / estate agent **el agente de propiedad / de finca raíz**

I redevelop **reorganizo, reconstruyo**

I renovate **renuevo**

I rent / let **alquilo, arriendo**

rent **la renta, el alquiler**

I repair **reparo**

repairs **las reparaciones**

shanty town **el barrio de chabolas, [el arrabal]**

shelter **el refugio**

slum **la barriada, el barrio pobre**

I sleep in the open **duermo en la calle, estoy en la calle**

slum clearance **la demolición de barrios pobres**

speculator **el especulador**

squalid **miserable, escuálido**

I squat **ocupo sin derecho, usurpo la propiedad**

squatter **el ocupante sin derecho, el intruso, el usurpador**

suburb **el suburbio**

it stands empty **está vacío**

tenant **inquilino**

town planning **el planeamiento urbano**

urban **urbano**

urban development **el desarrollo urbano**

unfurnished **desamueblado**

unfurnished rooms / digs **las habitaciones sin muebles**

wasteland **la tierra baldía**

"Yes, but not enough. Living conditions in the apartments / blocks of flats are extremely poor. They are overcrowded and the landlords no longer repair them."

Despite campaigns to help the homeless and unemployed, the situation remains serious.

It is impossible to find a furnished apartment / flat to rent. The area is fast becoming a slum.

—Sí, pero no bastan. Las condiciones de vida en los bloques de viviendas protegidas son malísimas. Están masificadas, y los propietarios ya no las reparan.

A pesar de las campañas para ayudar a los sin hogar y a los desempleados, la situación sigue siendo grave.

Es imposible encontrar un piso amueblado para alquilar. Este barrio se está convirtiendo rápidamente en un barrio bajo.

SOCIAL ISSUES

12d Addiction & Violence

abuse   **el abuso**
I abuse   **abuso**
act of violence   **el acto de violencia**
addict (adj/ n)   **adicto**
addiction   **la adicción**
addictive   **adictivo**
aggression   **la agresión**
aggressive   **agresivo**
alcohol   **el alcohol**
alcoholic   **el alcohólico**
alcoholism   **el alcoholismo**
anger   **la rabia, el enfado**
angry   **enfadado**
I attack   **ataco**
attack   **el ataque**
I beat up   **doy una paliza**
I bully   **intimido**
bully   **la intimidación**
child abuse   **el maltrato de los hijos**
consumption   **el consumo**
dangerous   **peligroso**
I drink   **bebo**
I get drunk   **me emborracho**
drunk   **borracho**
drunken driving   **la conducción bajo los efectos del alcohol**
I dry out   **me desalcoholizo**

effect   **el efecto**
fatal   **fatal, mortal**
fear   **el temor, el miedo**
I fear   **temo, tengo miedo de**
force   **la fuerza**
gang   **la banda**
harass   **hostigar, perseguir**
hoodlum   **el gamberro, el vándalo**
hostile   **hostil**
hostility   **la hostilidad**
insult   **el insulto**
I insult   **insulto**
intoxication   **la intoxicación**
legal (il-)   **(i)legal**
I legalize   **legalizo**
I mug   **asalto, aporreo**
mugger   **el asaltante**
nervous   **nervioso**
nervousness   **los nervios, el estado nervioso**
pimp   **el chulo, el proxeneta**
pornographic   **pornográfico**
pornography   **la pornografía**
prostitution   **la prostitución**
punk   **el punki**
rape   **la violación**
he rapes   **viola**
rapist   **el violador**

Violence and vandalism are common. Older people and women are sometimes afraid to go out alone.

Many young people have a drug problem. They start by sniffing solvents, or by taking soft drugs. Cannabis is the most common, and gives a feeling of intoxication. Then they go on to hard drugs.

La violencia y el vandalismo son muy frecuentes. Los ancianos y las mujeres a veces tienen miedo de salir solos.

Muchos jóvenes tienen problemas con la toxicomanía. Empiezan inhalando disolventes o tomando drogas blandas. El cánabis es el más común, y da la sensación de intoxicación. Luego pasan a las drogas duras.

rehabilitation **la rehabilitación**
I revert **revierto, reincido**
rocker **el rocker**
I seduce **seduzco, convenzo**
sexual harassment **el hostigamiento sexual**
skinhead **el cabeza rapada**
I smoke **fumo**
stimulant **el estimulante**
stimulation **la estimulación**
I terrorize **aterrorizo**
I threaten **amenazo**
thug **el gamberro, el desalmado**
vandal **el gamberro, el vándalo**
vandalism **el gamberrismo, el vandalismo**
victim **la víctima**
violent **violento**

Drugs

addicted to drugs **drogadicto**
AIDS **SIDA**
cannabis **el cánabis, la marijuana**
cocaine **la cocaína**
crack **el crack**
I deal **trafico**
drug **la droga**
drug scene **la escena de drogas, el barrio de drogas**

drug traffic **el tráfico de drogas, el narcotráfico**
I get infected **me infecto**
glue **el pegamento, el pegante**
hard drugs **las drogas duras**
hash **el hachís**
I have a fix **estoy enganchado, estoy drogado**
heroin **la heroína**
HIV positive **VIH positivo**
I inject **inyecto**
junkie **el yonqui, el drogadicto**
I kick (the habit) **me desintoxico**
LSD **LSD**
narcotic **el narcótico**
pusher **el camello, el traficante de drogas**
I sniff **esnifo, inhalo**
soft drugs **las drogas blandas**
solvent **el disolvente**
stimulant **el estimulante**
syringe **la jeringuilla**
I take drugs / a fix **tomo drogas, estoy enganchado**
tranquillizer **el tranquilizante**
withdrawal **la retirada, el desenganchamiento**

Junkies inject or smoke drugs.

Los toxicómanos se inyectan con las drogas o las fuman.

All drugs are dangerous, but injecting them brings risks of AIDS.

Todas las drogas son peligrosas, pero inyectarlas trae el peligro del SIDA.

The drug scene is troubling as so many people become dealers or turn to crime.

El mundo de las drogas es muy preocupante, pues muchas personas se hacen camellos [traficantes] o recurren a la criminalidad.

Withdrawal symptoms are very unpleasant.

El síndrome de la abstinencia es muy desagradable.

SOCIAL ISSUES

12e Prejudice

asylum seeker   **el solicitante de asilo político**
I call names   **insulto**
citizenship   **la ciudadanía**
country of origin   **el país de origen**
cultural   **cultural**
culture   **la cultura**
I discriminate   **discrimino**
discrimination   **la discriminación**
dual nationality   **la doble nacionalidad**
emigrant   **el emigrante**
emigration   **la emigración**
equal (un-)   **(des)igual**
equal opportunities   **las oportunidades iguales**
equal pay   **la paga igualitaria**
equal rights   **los derechos igualitarios**
equality (in-)   **la (des)igualdad**
ethnic   **étnico**
far right   **la extrema derecha**
fascism   **el fascismo**
fascist   **el fascista**
foreign   **el extranjero**
foreign worker   **el trabajador extranjero**

freedom   **la libertad**
 freedom of speech   **la libertad de expresión**
ghetto   **el gueto**
human rights   **los derechos humanos**
I immigrate   **inmigro**
immigrant   **el inmigrante**
immigration   **la inmigración**
I integrate   **me integro**
integration   **la integración**
intolerance   **la intolerancia**
intolerant   **intolerante**
majority   **la mayoría**
minority   **la minoría**
mother tongue   **la lengua madre**
I persecute   **persigo**
persecution   **la persecución**
politically correct   **políticamente correcto**
prejudice   **el prejuicio**
prejudiced   **lleno de prejuicios**
rabid   **fanático**
race riot   **la manifestacíon racial**
racism   **el racismo**
racist   **el racista**
 racist *(adj)*   **racista**

"Is racism a serious problem?"

"What about the ethnic minority population resident here?"
"Unfortunately they tend to get the worst jobs and to be paid less. They are more likely to be unemployed and can only afford cheap accommodation."

— ¿Es un problema serio el racismo?

— ¿Y qué pasa con la minoría étnica que vive aquí?
— Desafortunadamente suelen obtener los peores empleos, y les pagan menos. Tienen más probabilidad de quedar desempleados, y sólo llegan a tener viviendas muy malas.

refugee   el refugiado
I repatriate   repatrio
residence permit   el permiso de residencia
right   el derecho
    right to asylum   el derecho de asilo
    right to residence   el derecho de residencia
stereotypical   estereotípico
tolerance   la tolerancia
tolerant   tolerante
I tolerate   tolero
work permit   el permiso de trabajo

sexuality

female   la mujer, la hembra
feminine   femenino
feminism   el feminismo
feminist   la feminista
gay   el homosexual, el marica
gay club   el club para homosexuales
gay movement   el movimiento homosexual
heterosexual   el heterosexual
    heterosexual *(adj)* heterosexual
homosexual   el homosexual
    homosexual *(adj)* homosexual
homosexuality   la homosexualidad
lesbian   la lesbiana
    lesbian *(adj)* lesbiana
male   varón
sexual   sexual
sexuality   la sexualidad
women's lib   la liberación de la mujer
women's libber   el / la activista por la liberación de la mujer
women's rights   los derechos de la mujer

The law still discriminates against male homosexuals, although society is getting more tolerant.

La ley sigue discriminando a los homosexuales masculinos, aunque la sociedad se está haciendo más tolerante.

"Is there still antisemitism?"
"Unfortunately, although the situation has improved overall, there is still prejudice against the Jews."

—¿Existe aún el antisemitismo?
—Por desgracia, aunque la situación ha mejorado, sigue habiendo prejuicio en contra de los judíos.

The feminist movement is still demanding equal rights for

El movimiento feminista sigue exigiendo derechos iguales para las mujeres.

Religion

13a Ideas & Doctrines

agnostic **el agnóstico**
Anglican **el anglicano**
apostle **el apóstol**
atheism **el ateísmo**
atheist **el ateo**
atheistic **ateístico**
authority **la autoridad**
belief **la creencia**
I believe (in) **creo (en)**
believer **el creyente**
Bible **la Biblia**
biblical **bíblico**
blessed **bendito**
Buddha **Buda**
Buddhism **el budismo**
Buddhist **el budista**
Calvinist **el calvinista**
he canonizes **canoniza**
cantor **el cantor**
Catholic **el católico**
charismatic **carismático**
charity **la caridad**
Christ **Cristo**
Christian **el cristiano**
Christianity **la cristianidad, el cristianismo**
church **la iglesia**
commentary **el comentario**
conscience **la conciencia**
conversion **la conversión**

covenant **la alianza, el pacto**
disciple **el discípulo**
divine **lo divino**
doctrine **la doctrina**
duty **el deber, la obligación**
ecumenism **el ecumenismo**
ethical **ético**
evil **el mal**
faith **la fe**
faithful **fiel**
I forgive **perdono**
forgiveness **el perdón**
free will **la libre voluntad**
fundamentalism **el fundamentalismo**
fundamentalist **el fundamentalista**
God **Dios**
god **el dios**
goddess **la diosa**
Gospel **el evangelio**
grace **la gracia**
heaven **el cielo, el paraíso**
Hebrew **el hebreo**
hell **el infierno**
heretical **herético**
Hindu **el hindú**
Hinduism **el hinduismo**
holiness **la santidad**
holy **santo, sagrado**
Holy Spirit **el espíritu santo**

The five pillars of Islam are belief in the One True God and his Prophet, prayer, fasting, giving alms, and pilgrimage to Mecca.

Los cinco pilares de la fe musulmana son la creencia en el Unico Dios Verdadero y en su Profeta, la oración, el ayuno, la limosna y el peregrinaje a Meca.

hope **la esperanza**	prophet **el profeta**
human **humano**	Protestant **el protestante**
human being **el ser humano**	Protestantism **el protestantismo**
humanism **el humanismo**	Quaker **el cuáquero**
humanity **la humanidad**	redemption **la redención, el**
infallibility **la infalibilidad**	**perdón**
infallible **infalible**	religion **la religión**
Islam **el islam**	sacred **sagrado**
Islamic **islámico**	saint **el santo**
Jesus **Jesús**	Saint Peter **San Pedro**
Jew **el judío**	he sanctifies **santifica**
Jewish **judío**	Satan **Satanás**
Judaic **judaico**	he saves **salva**
Judaism **judaísmo**	scripture **las escrituras** *(pl)*
Koran / Q'uran **El Corán**	service **el servicio religioso, la**
Lord **El Señor**	**misa**
merciful **misericordioso**	Sikh **sij**
mercy **la misericordia**	Sikhism **sijismo**
Messiah **El Mesías**	sin **el pecado**
Mohammed **Mahoma**	sinful **pecaminoso**
moral **moral**	sinner **el pecador**
morality **la moralidad**	soul **el alma**
Muslim **musulmán**	spirit **el espíritu**
mystical **místico**	spiritual **espiritual**
mysticism **la mística, el**	spirituality **la espiritualidad**
misticismo	Talmud **el Talmud**
myth **el mito**	Taoism **el taoísmo**
New Testament **El Nuevo**	theological **teológico**
Testamento	theology **la teología**
nirvana **la nirvana**	traditional **tradicional**
Old Testament **El Viejo**	transcendental **trascendental**
Testamento	Trinity **la trinidad**
orthodox **el ortodoxo**	true **verdadero**
pagan **el pagano, el infiel**	truth **la verdad**
parish **la parroquia**	vision **la visión**
Pentateuch **el Pentateuco**	vocation **la vocación**

There is considerable disagreement about the ordination of women to the priesthood.	**Hay un desacuerdo apreciable con respecto a la ordenación de las mujeres al sacerdocio.**
John Wesley said, "The world is my parish."	**John Wesley dijo, "El mundo es mi parroquia."**

RELIGION

archbishop **el arzobispo**
baptism **el bautismo, el bautizo**
bar mitzvah **el bar-mitzah**
I bear witness to **testifico, doy testimonio**
bishop **el obispo**
bishopric / see **el obispado**
burial **el entierro**
cathedral **la catedral**
chapel **la capilla**
christening **el bautizo, el bautismo**
clergy **el clero**
clergyman **el clérigo**
communion **la comunión**
   Holy Communion **la santa comunión**
community **la comunidad**
I confess (faith) **soy**
I confess (sins) **confieso**
confession **la confesión**

confirmation **la confirmación**
congregation **la congregación**
   congregation (of cardinals) **la curia**
convent **el convento**
I convert (others) **convierto**
I convert (self) **me convierto**
Eucharist **La Eucaristía**
evangelical **evangélico**
evangelist **el evangelista**
I give alms **doy limosna**
I give thanks **doy gracias**
Imam **el Imam, el Imán**
intercession **la intercesión, la mediación**
laity **el laicado**
lay **seglar, profano**
layperson **el seglar, el laico**
the Lord's Supper **La Santa Cena**
Mass **La Misa**
I meditate **medito**

Bishops in the Church of England are not afraid to speak about social problems.

Los obispos de la Iglesia Anglicana no tienen miedo de hablar de los problemas sociales.

The sacrament of Holy Communion will be celebrated on Sunday at nine.

El Sacramento de la Sagrada Comunión se celebrará el domingo a las nueve.

The parish council meets regularly.

El Consejo Parroquial se reúne con regularidad.

Every Muslim is called to prayer five times a day.

A todos los musulmanes se les llama a rezar cinco veces al día.

During the holy month of Ramadan, Muslims fast from dawn to dusk. The month ends with the celebrations of the festival of Eid.

Durante el Mes Sagrado de Ramadán, los musulmanes ayunan desde el amanecer hasta el anochecer. El mes termina con las festividades de la fiesta de Eid.

meditation   la meditación
minister   el ministro de la iglesia
I minister to the parish   soy el párroco, administro la parroquia
ministry   el ministerio eclesiástico
mission   la misión
missionary   el misionario, el misionero
monastery   el monasterio
monk   el monje
mosque   la mezquita
mullah   mullah
nun   la monja
parish   la parroquia
parishioner   el feligrés
pastor   el pastor, el sacerdote
pastoral   pastoral
pilgrimage   el peregrinaje
Pope   el Papa
I praise   rezo, oro
I pray (for)   rezo (por), pido (por)
prayer   la oración

priest   el sacerdote, el cura
rabbi   el rabino
reformation   la reformación, la reforma
I repent   me arrepiento
repentance   el arrepentimiento
repentant   el arrepentido
I revere   venero, reverencio
reverence   la veneración, la reverencia
reverent   reverente
rite   el rito
ritual   el ritual
sacrament   el sacramento
synagogue   la sinagoga
synod   el sínodo
temple   el templo
vow   el voto
wedding   la boda
witness   el testigo
I witness   testifico
worship   la adoración
I worship   adoro

Those who are called to the ministry must demonstrate their vocation before being accepted to theological colleges.

Los que tienen vocación por el sacerdocio tienen que manifestar su vocación antes de ser aceptados en los seminarios.

The Baptist tradition is very strong in the American south.

La tradición de la iglesia Bautista es muy fuerte en el sur de los Estados Unidos.

A few Muslim schoolgirls in France have come into conflict with the authorities because they chose to wear the veil in school.

Algunas colegialas musulmanas en Francia han entrado en conflicto con las autoridades por decidir llevar el velo en el colegio.

Religious fundamentalism can lead to fanaticism and intolerance in any religion.

En cualquier religión, el fundamentalismo religioso puede llevar al fanatismo y a la intolerancia.

Business & Economics

14a The Economics of Business

I administer **administro**
I agree (to do) **acepto (hacer)**
agreement **el acuerdo**
bureaucracy **la burocracia**
business **los negocios**
  a business **un negocio, un acuerdo negocial**
capacity *(industrial)* **la capacidad**
commerce **el comercio**
commercial **comercial**
company **la empresa, la compañía, la sociedad**
deal **el trato**
I deliver **suministro, envío**
demand **la demanda**
the product is in demand **el producto está en demanda, el producto tiene demanda**
development **el desarrollo**
I earn (a living) **(me) gano (la vida)**
I employ **empleo**
employment **el empleo**
executive **el ejecutivo**
I export **exporto**
exports **las exportaciones**
fall **la caída**
goods **los bienes**
it grows **crece**
I import **importo**

I increase **incremento, aumento**
increase **el incremento, el aumento**
industrial output **la producción industrial**
industry **la industria**
I invest **invierto**
investment **la inversión**
layoffs **los despidos**
living standards **el nivel de vida**
I manage **dirijo, gestiono, administro**
management **la dirección, la gestión, la administración**
multinational **la multinacional**
I negotiate **negocio**
negotiations **las negociaciones**
  face-to-face **cara a cara**
priority **la prioridad**
I produce **produzco**
producer **el productor**
production line **la línea de producción**
productivity **la productividad**
quality **la calidad**
I raise *(prices)* **subo, incremento**
raise / rise **el aumento**
  pay raise **el aumento salarial**
reliability **la fiabilidad**
services **los servicios**

Strikers blocked the port of Bilbao and all main roads to Barajas Airport. | **Los huelguistas obstruyeron el puerto de Bilbao y todas las carreteras que llevan al Aeropuerto de Barajas.**

Unemployment is rising to twelve percent. | **El desempleo alcanza el doce por ciento.**

I set *(priorities)* **establezco**

sick leave **la baja / licencia por enfermedad**

I sign *(contracts)* **firmo**

skilled labor / labour **el trabajo especializado**

workers' unrest **el descontento laboral**

social welfare **el bienestar social**

I strengthen **refuerzo**

supplier **el proveedor**

supply **el suministro**

tax **el impuesto**

I tax **cobro un impuesto**

unemployment **el desempleo**

unemployment benefit **el subsidio de desempleo**

unskilled labor / labour **el trabajo no especializado**

work ethic **la ética laboral, la ética del trabajo**

workforce **los trabajadores**

work week **la semana laboral**

Industrial / Labor dispute

I am on strike **estoy en huelga**

I am a strike breaker / blackleg **trabajo durante una huelga, soy esquirol**

I boycott **boicoteo**

I cross the picket line **cruzo la línea de piquetes**

demonstration **la manifestación**

dispute **la disputa**

industrial / labor dispute **la disputa laboral, el conflicto laboral**

industrial relations **las relaciones industriales**

I lock out **dejo en la calle, cierro la puerta**

lockout **quedarse en la calle**

minimum wage **el salario mínimo**

I picket **hago de piquete**

picket **el piquete**

productivity bonus **el bono de productividad, la prima de productividad**

I resume work **reanudo, vuelvo al trabajo**

settlement **el ajuste**

I slow down / go slow **desciendo el ritmo de trabajo**

stoppage **la suspensión, la huelga**

strike **la huelga**

unofficial strike **la huelga no autorizada**

I strike **hago huelga**

strike ballot **la votación de la huelga**

strikebreaker **el esquirol**

striker **el huelguista**

trade union **el sindicato**

trade unionist **el sindicalista**

unfair dismissal **el despido injustificado**

I unionize **me sindico, me sindicalizo**

unionized labor / labour **los trabajadores sindicados**

unrest **el descontento**

wage demand **la demanda salarial**

work by the book / to rule **la huelga de celo, el paro técnico**

The unions called for a reduction in the average hours of the workweek.

Los sindicatos exigieron una reducción en el promedio de horas semanales de trabajo.

The President has agreed to meet union leaders for talks.

El Presidente ha consentido en entrevistarse con los líderes de los sindicatos.

14b At Work

agenda **el orden del día**
  on the agenda **en el orden del día**
I am away on business **estoy en viaje de negocios**
business trip **el viaje de negocios**
canteen **la cantina, el bar**
career **la carrera, la trayectoria profesional**
I chair a meeting **presido una reunión**
I delegate **delego**
disciplinary proceedings **el procedimiento disciplinario**
free **gratis**
grant **la beca, la ayuda**
I grant *(someone)* **beco, concedo una ayuda**
job **el trabajo, el empleo**
manager **el gerente**
management functions **las funciones directivas**
I market **comercio (al por mayor)**
meeting **la reunión**
misconduct **la mala conducta**
occupation **la ocupación, la profesión**
I'm on sick leave / off work **no trabajo, estoy de baja**
post **el puesto de trabajo**
profession **la profesión**
professional **el profesional**
publicity **la publicidad**
I qualify **satísfago los requisitos**
I report to . . . **mi superior inmediato es ...**
I am responsible for **soy responsable de**
research **la investigación**
I sell **vendo**
semiskilled **semiespecializado**
I teach **enseño**
I toil **trabajo duro**
trade **el comercio**
training **el aprendizaje, el entrenamiento**

training course **el curso de aprendizaje, el curso de entrenamiento / capacitación**
I transfer **me traslado**
vacation / holiday **las vacaciones**
vocation **la vocación**
wage earner **el asalariado**
warning *(verbal)* **la amonestación verbal**
  written warning **la amonestación por escrito**
I work **trabajo**
work **el trabajo**
worker **el trabajador**
workforce **los trabajadores, la fuerza laboral**

In the office

business lunch **la comida de negocios**
business meeting **la reunión de negocios**
computer **el ordenador, [el computador]**
conference call **la convocatoria de la conferencia**
conference room **la sala de conferencias**
correcting fluid **el líquido corrector**
desk **la mesa, el mostrador**
I dictate **dicto**
dictating machine **el dictáfono**
electronic mail **el correo electrónico**
extension **la extensión**
fax **el fax**
fax machine **la máquina de fax**
I fax **mando un fax**
file **el archivo**
I file **archivo**
filing cabinet **el archivador**
intercom **el interfono**

open plan **la oficina de plan abierto**
photocopier **la fotocopiadora**
photocopy **la fotocopia**
I photocopy **fotocopio**
pigeonhole **el casillero**
reception **la recepción**
receptionist **el / la recepcionista**
shorthand **la taquigrafía**
swivel chair **la silla giratoria**
telephone **el teléfono**
typing pool **la sala de mecanógrafos**
wastebasket **la papelera**
word processor **el procesador de textos**
workstation **el puesto de trabajo, la estación de trabajo**

In the factory & on site

automation **la automatización**
blue-collar worker **los trabajadores, los obreros**
I build **construyo**
bulldozer **la aplanadora**
car / automobile industry **la industria automotriz / del automóvil**
component **el componente, la pieza**
concrete **el hormigón**
construction industry **la industria de la construcción**

crane **la grúa**
forklift truck **la carreta elevadora**
I forge **forjo**
industry **la industria**
heavy industry **la industria pesada**
light industry **la industria ligera**
I manufacture **fabrico**
manufacturing **la fabricación**
mass production **la producción en masa**
mining **la minería**
power industry **la industria eléctrica**
precision tool **el instrumento de precisión**
prefabricated **prefabricado**
process **el proceso**
I process **proceso**
product **el producto**
on the production line **en línea de producción**
raw materials **las materias primas**
robot **el robot**
scaffolding **el andamio**
shipbuilding **la construcción naval**
steamroller **la apisonadora**
steel smelting **la fundición del acero**
textile industry **la industria textil**

Employment patterns are shifting from the traditional model of regular permanent jobs for one employer to a wide range of professional services delivered as a freelancer to various employers.

La estructura del empleo está cambiando: en lugar del modelo tradicional de puestos regulares y permanentes con un solo patrón, está cambiando a una amplia gama de servicios profesionales prestados a varios patrones por trabajadores independientes.

➤ STATIONERY App. 22b; COMPUTERS 15d

BUSINESS & ECONOMICS

14c Pay & Conditions

apprentice **el aprendiz**
bonus **la prima**
I clock in / out **ficho la entrada / salida, marco tarjeta**
commission **la comisión**
on commission **a comisión**
company car **el coche de la empresa**
contract **el contrato**
I am employed **tengo trabajo**
expenses **los gastos**
expense account **la cuenta de gastos**
flextime / flexi-time **la jornada flexible**
freelance **autónomo**
I work freelance **soy autónomo**
full-time **la jornada completa / a tiempo completo**
income **los ingresos** *(pl)*
overtime **las horas extraordinarias** *(pl)*
overworked **el recargado de trabajo**
part-time **la jornada a tiempo parcial, medio tiempo**
payday **el día de paga**
payslip **la hoja de sueldo**
pay raise / payrise **el incremento salarial, la subida de sueldo**
payroll **la nómina**
pension **la pensión**
perk **el gaje, los beneficios** *(pl)* **adicionales**
permanent **permanente, fijo**
I retire **me retiro, me jubilo**
retirement **el retiro**
salary **el salario, el sueldo**
self-employed **autónomo**
sexual harassment **el hostigamiento sexual**
shift **el turno**
day shift **el turno de día, el turno diurno**
night shift **el turno de noche, el turno nocturno**
temporary **temporal**
trial period **el período de prueba**
working hours **las horas laborales**
wages **el salario, el sueldo**

The conditions in this office are not good enough for your staff, Mr. Abril.

The place is cold, badly lit, and poorly ventilated. And you have far too many electrical appliances plugged into one socket. Unless you make considerable changes within three months, I shall be forced to close the office down. I shall come back next week to discuss your plans. Good-bye!

Las condiciones de trabajo en esta oficina no son bastante buenas para su personal, Señor Abril.

El lugar está frío, está mal iluminado, y mal ventilado. Y tienen ustedes un gran exceso de aparatos eléctricos conectados a un sólo enchufe. Si ustedes no introducen todos los cambios necesarios en un plazo de tres meses, me veré obligado a cerrar la oficina. Volveré la semana que viene para discutir con usted su plan de acción. ¡Adiós!

Job application

I advertise for a secretary **anuncio un puesto de secretaria**

advertisement **el anuncio de trabajo**

I apply for a job **solicito un trabajo**

classified ad(vertisement) **los anuncios por palabras, [los avisos clasificados]**

curriculum vitae / résumé **la hoja de vida**

discrimination **la discriminación**

racial discrimination **la discriminación racial**

sexual discrimination **la discriminación sexual**

employment agency **la agencia de trabajo**

interesting **interesante**

interview **la entrevista**

I interview **entrevisto**

job application **la solicitud de trabajo**

employment office **la oficina de empleo**

job description **la descripción del trabajo**

I find a job **encuentro un trabajo**

I have been laid off / made redundant **he sido despedido**

I look for **busco**

I promote (someone) **asciendo (a alguien)**

I am promoted **soy ascendido**

to create an opening *(vacancy)* **la creación (de un puesto)**

promotion **la promoción**

qualification **la titulación**

qualified **titulado, cualificado**

openings / situations vacant **los puestos vacantes**

I start work (for) **empiezo a trabajar (para)**

I take on *(employee)* **empleo**

vacancy **una vacante**

work experience **la experiencia laboral**

"Hello. May I speak to the personnel manager, please."

"Speaking. What can I do for you?"

"I saw your ad in the paper for a sales executive. Could you send me the job description and application forms? How many references are you asking for?"

"Two, including your present or last employer."

—Oiga. Quisiera hablar con el jefe de la administración del personal, por favor.

—Soy yo. ¿En qué puedo servirle?

—Vi su anuncio en el diario en el que se pedía un ejecutivo de ventas. ¿Podría usted mandarme la descripción del trabajo y las hojas de solicitud? ¿Cuántas referencias piden ustedes?

—Dos, incluyendo a su jefe actual o al último empleador que ha tenido.

BUSINESS & ECONOMICS

14d Finance & Industry

account   la cuenta
advance   el anticipo
  in advance   (por) adelantado
I advertise   anuncio
advertisement   el anuncio
advertising   la publicidad
advertising agency   la agencia de publicidad
audit   la auditoría
bill   la factura
board   la junta
bond   el bono
branch *(of company)*   la sucursal
budget   el presupuesto
capital   el capital
capital expenditure   los gastos de inversión
chamber of commerce   la cámara de comercio
collateral   la garantía
company   la empresa, la compañía, la sociedad
I consume *(resources)*   consumo
consumer goods   los bienes de consumo
consumer spending   los gastos de consumo
cost of living   el coste de la vida
costing   la estimación, la cotización
costs   los costes
credit   el crédito, el activo

debit   el debe, el pasivo
deflation   la deflación
economic   económico
economy   la economía
funds   los fondos
government spending   el gasto público
income   el ingreso, los ingresos
income tax   el impuesto sobre la renta
installment   el plazo
interest rate   el tipo de interés
I invest in   invierto en
investment   la inversión
invoice   la factura
labor / labour costs   los costos laborales
liability   la responsabilidad
manufacturing industry   la industria de fabricación
market   el mercado
market economy   la economía de mercado
marketing   la comercialización, el márketing
merchandise   la mercancía
national debt   la deuda nacional
I nationalize   nacionalizo
notice / advice note   el aviso
output   la producción, el rendimiento

Morales S.A. announced its takeover bid for the Dani supermarket chain.

The company informed shareholders that this year's operating profits will not match the level seen last year.

Morales S.A. anunció su oferta pública de adquisición de la cadena de supermercados Dani.

La compañía les informó a sus accionistas que los beneficios netos este año no alcanzarán el valor de los del año pasado.

pay   **el pago**
price   **el precio**
private sector   **el sector privado**
I privatize   **privatizo**
product   **el producto**
production   **la producción**
public sector   **el sector público**
quota   **la cuota**
real estate / realty   **la propiedad inmobiliaria**
retail sales   **las ventas al por menor**
retail trade   **la venta al por menor**
salaries   **los salarios**
sales tax   **el impuesto sobre las ventas**
service sector   **el sector de servicios**
share   **la acción**
shares going up / down   **la subida / bajada de las acciones**
share index   **el índice de la bolsa**
statistics   **las estadísticas**
stock exchange   **la bolsa de valores**
I subsidize   **subvenciono**
subsidy   **el subsidio**
supply and demand   **la oferta y la demanda**
supply costs   **los costos de suministro**
I tax   **cobro un impuesto**

tax   **el impuesto**
tax increase   **el incremento / la subida de los impuestos**
taxation   **la imposición**
taxation level   **el nivel de imposición**
turnover   **la facturación**
VAT / value added tax   **el IVA (impuesto sobre el valor añadido)**
viable   **viable**
wages   **el salario**

Financial personnel

accountant   **el contable**
actuary   **el actuario**
auditor   **el auditor**
banker   **el banquero**
   investment banker   **el banquero (del banco) de inversiones**
   merchant banker   **el banquero (del banco) comercial**
bank manager   **el director del banco**
broker   **el agente de negocios**
   insurance broker   **el agente de seguros**
consumer   **el consumidor**
investor   **el inversionista**
speculator   **el especulador**
stockbroker   **el agente de bolsa**
trader *(Wall St.)*   **el comerciante**

Spantax Air expressed cautious optimism and suggested that the worst recession in the history of the aviation industry is coming to an end.

La compañía aérea Spantax hizo una declaración de optimismo prudente, e indicó que está terminando la peor recesión de la historia de la industria de la aviación.

News of the budget deficit caused panic in the stock exchange today.

La Bolsa fue presa del pánico hoy al recibir las noticias del déficit presupuestario.

BUSINESS & ECONOMICS

14e Banking & the Economy

Banking & personal finance

account **la cuenta**

automatic teller / cashpoint **el cajero automático**

bank **el banco**

bank loan **el préstamo bancario**

I bank (money) **pongo dinero en el banco**

bankcard / cashcard **la tarjeta de dinero, la tarjeta para el cajero automático**

bankrupt **la bancarrota**

cash **dinero efectivo, metálico**

I cash a check / cheque **cobro un cheque, hago efectivo un cheque**

cash register / cashdesk **la caja**

I change **cambio**

check / cheque **el cheque**

credit card **la tarjeta de crédito**

currency **la moneda, la divisa**

deposit *(in a bank)* **el deposito, el ingreso**

deposit *(returnable)* **el depósito retornable**

down payment / deposit **el**

desembolso inicial, la entrada

Eurocheque **el eurocheque**

exchange rate **el tipo de cambio**

I have a credit **tengo un crédito de, tengo un saldo positivo de**

in deficit **en déficit**

installment plan / hire purchase **la venta a plazos**

in the red **descubierto, en números rojos**

I lend **presto**

loan **el préstamo**

mortgage **la hipoteca, el crédito hipotecario**

I mortgage **hipoteco, obtengo un crédito hipotecario**

I open *(account)* **abro**

overdraft **el descubierto, el sobregiro**

repayment **el reembolso**

I save **ahorro**

savings **los ahorros**

savings and loan association / building society association **la sociedad de crédito inmobiliario**

"I'd like to open an account here."
"Certainly, sir. What sort of account do you need?"
"Just a normal checking account."

—**Quisiera abrir una cuenta aquí.**
—**Con mucho gusto, señor. ¿Qué tipo de cuenta necesita usted?**
—**Una cuenta corriente, nada más.**

"Could you fill out this form with all your personal details?"

—**Haga el favor de rellenar este formulario con todos sus detalles personales.**

"Certainly. What overdraft privileges are available for students?"

—**De acuerdo. ¿Qué posibilidades de crédito al abierto tienen ustedes a disposición de los estudiantes?**

"I need to check that for you."

—**Tendré que verificarlo.**

➤ WEALTH & POVERTY 12b; CURRENCIES App. 9a

traveler's checks / travellers' cheques
los cheques de viaje
I withdraw   **retiro**

recovery   **la recuperación**
takeover   **la adquisición, la toma de control**
takeover bid   **la oferta pública de adquisición de acciones**

Growth

amalgamation   **la fusión**
appreciation   **el incremento de valor**
assets   **el activo, los bienes, el capital**
assurance   **la garantía**
auction   **la subasta**
boom   **el boom, el auge**
competition   **la competencia, la concurrencia**
economic miracle   **el milagro económico**
efficiency   **la eficacia**
material growth   **el incremento de bienes**
merger   **la fusión, el fusionamiento**
profit   **el beneficio**
profitable   **rentable, lucrativo**
progress   **el progreso**
prosperity   **la prosperidad**
prosperous   **próspero, floreciente**

Decline

bankrupt   **la bancarrota**
credit squeeze   **la restricción**
debt   **la deuda**
it is declining   **está en baja**
deficit   **el déficit**
depreciation   **la depreciación**
I dump   **hago dúmping**
inflation   **la inflación**
inflation rate   **el índice de inflación**
loss   **la pérdida**
slowdown   **la ralentización de la economía**
slump   **la recesión**
spending cuts   **los recortes presupuestarios**
stagnant   **estancado**
stagnation   **el estancamiento de la economía**
zero-growth economy   **la economía sin crecimiento**

"Did you hear about Borges & Sons?"
"No, what about them?"
"Unfortunately, they went bankrupt. They borrowed too heavily in order to introduce a new line that just didn't sell."

"And what was it?"
"A range of battery-powered toys that clearly couldn't compete with the videogames market."

— **¿Has oído las noticias acerca de Borges e Hijos?**
— **No. ¿Qué les pasa?**
— **Desafortunadamente, han quebrado. Tomaron demasiado dinero prestado para poder introducir un nuevo producto, que luego no se vendió.**
— **¿Y qué fue?**
— **Fue una gama de juguetes a pila que, está claro, no pudo hacer competencia contra el mercado de los videojuegos.**

15 Communicating with Others

15a Social Discourse

Meeting

I accept   **acepto**
appointment   **la cita**
at home   **en casa**
ball   **el baile**
banquet   **el banquete**
I bump into *(someone)*   **topo con**
I'm busy   **estoy ocupado**
I celebrate   **celebro**
celebration   **la celebración**
club   **el club**
I come and see   **vengo a ver**
dance   **el baile**
I dance   **bailo**
date *(appointment)*   **la cita, el compromiso**
diary / datebook   **la agenda**
I drop in on *(someone)*   **paso a ver**
I expect   **espero**
I'm expecting . . . for dinner   **espero a ... para cenar**
I'm free   **estoy libre**
I greet   **saludo**
guest   **el invitado, el convidado, el huésped**
handshake   **el apretón de manos**
I have fun   **me divierto**
invitation   **la invitación**
I invite   **invito**
I join   **me uno a, me reúno (con), me junto con**
   I join *(a society)*   **me hago socio de, ingreso en**
I keep *(a date)*   **cumplo**
meeting   **la reunión**
I meet   **encuentro, me reúno con**
member   **el miembro**
party   **la fiesta**
   I throw a party   **doy una fiesta**
I pick up / fetch someone   **busco a alguien**

reception   **la recepción**
I see   **veo**
I shake hands with   **estrecho manos con**
social life   **la vida social**
I socialize   **socializo**
I take part   **tomo parte**
I talk   **hablo**
visit   **la visita**
I visit   **visito**

Greetings & congratulations

bow / curtsey (to someone)   **la reverencia**
Cheers!   **¡Salud!**
Come in!   **¡Pase / Entre (usted)!**
I congratulate   **felicito**
Congratulations!   **¡Felicitaciones!, ¡Enhorabuena!, ¡Felicidades!**
Good afternoon / evening   **Buenas tardes / noches**
Good morning   **Buenos días**
Good night   **Buenas noches**
I greet   **recibo, saludo**
Happy Easter   **Feliz Pascua**
Happy New Year   **Feliz Año Nuevo**
Hello / Hallo   **Hola**
Here's to . . .   **¡Vaya por ... !, ¡Bebemos a la salud de ... ¡**
Merry / Happy Christmas   **Feliz Navidad**
toast   **el brindis**
I toast   **brindo por**
Well done!   **¡Bravo!, ¡Muy bien!**

Introduction

Bill, meet Jan.   **Bill, te presento a Jane**
Doctor . . .   **Doctor ...**
How do you do?   **¿Cómo está usted?**

I introduce **le presento a**
I introduce myself **me presento**
introduction **la presentación**
I'd like you to meet . . . **Quiero presentarle a ...**
Madam **Señora**
May I introduce . . . ? **Quiero presentarle a ...**
Miss **Señorita**
Mr. **Señor**
Mrs. **Señora**
Pleased to meet you **¡Mucho gusto!, Encantado**
Professor . . . **Profesor ...**
sir **señor**
This is . . . **Este es ...**
I welcome **doy la bienvenida, acojo, recibo**

Pleasantries

I address *(someone)* **me dirijo a**
I address as "tú" **tuteo, trato de tú**
I address as "usted" **trato de usted**
Best regards from . . . **un saludo de**
Bless you! / Gesundheit! **¡Salud / ¡Jesús!**
I'm (very) fine, thank you **Estoy (muy) bien, gracias**
health **la salud**
I hope you get well soon **(Espero) que te mejores pronto**
How are you (keeping)? **¿Cómo está usted?**
How are you feeling? **¿Cómo te sientes?**
Much better, thank you **Mucho mejor, gracias**
the same to you *(polite)* **(Y) a usted, igualmente**
so-so **regular, ni bien ni mal**
To your (very good) health! **¡Salud!**

Thanking

Many thanks **Muchas gracias**
Nice / good of you to . . . **Es usted muy amable ...**

Not at all! / It's a pleasure **¡De nada!, ¡No hay de qué!**
I thank **agradezco**
Thanks! **¡Gracias!**
Thank you so much **Muchísimas gracias**
No, thank you! **¡No, gracias!**
I'm (very) grateful to you for . . . **Le estoy (muy) agradecido por ...**

Apologizing

I apologize **me disculpo, pido perdón**
I do apologize **le ruego me disculpe**
I beg your pardon **le ruego me perdone**
I excuse **perdono**
Excuse me **Discúlpeme**
Excuse me, please **¡Perdón!, ¡Por favor!, ¡Con (su) permiso!**
Forget it! **¡Olvídelo!, ¡No se preocupe!, ¡No importa!**
I forgive **perdono, disculpo**
it doesn't matter (at all / a bit) **no importa (nada), es igual**
Oh, dear! **¡Ay!, ¡Dios mío!**
I refuse **rehuso, rechazo**
I'm (so very) sorry that . . . **Siento (muchísimo) que ...**
What a shame / pity (that . . .) **¡Qué lástima (que ...)!**

Farewells

All the best! **¡Que tenga suerte!**
Good-bye! **¡Adiós!**
Good luck! **¡Que tenga suerte!**
I say good-bye **me despido**
Have a good time! **¡Que usted se divierta!, ¡Que lo pase bien!**
Have a safe trip / journey! **¡Buen viaje!**
See you later! / Cheerio! **¡Hasta luego!**
I will see you later / tomorrow **Nos veremos más tarde / mañana**
Sweet dreams! **¡Duerma usted bien!**

COMMUNICATING WITH OTHERS

15b Comments & Interjections

Approval & disapproval

I quite agree! **¡estoy totalmente de acuerdo!**
agreement **el acuerdo**
approval **la aprobación**
I approve **apruebo**
Is this all right? **¿Vale?, ¿Está bien?**
Fine! **¡Estupendo!, ¡Magnífico!**
I'm glad / pleased (that . . .) **Me alegro (de que ...)**
Good! **¡Bueno!, ¡Muy bien!**
How nice! **¡Qué bien!**
You should(n't) have . . . **(No) debería haber ...**
Quiet! **¡Silencio!, ¡A callar!, ¡Cállate!, ¡Cállese!**
sh! **¡chitón!, ¡chist!**
tut-tut *(clicks)* **¡Vamos!, ¡Eso no!, ¡Qué horror!, ¡Pche!**
That's enough. **Basta (ya).**
That's just what I need. **Es precisamente lo que necesito.**

Permission & obligation

That's (quite) all right **(Eso) está (muy) bien**
allowed **permitido**
I allow **permito, dejo**
I am allowed to . . . **se me permite ...**
It is not allowed / permitted **No se permite**
Can I . . .? **¿Puedo ..., ¿Se puede ... ?**
I can(not) **(no) puedo**
You cannot (can't) **No puede(s)**
I have to **tengo que, debo**
May I . . . ? **¿Puedo ... ?**
I may (not) **(no) puedo**
I must (not) **(no) debo**
No **No**
Not now / here / tonight **Ahora / aquí / esta noche no**

I ought to . . . **debería ...**
you ought to . . . **deberías ...**
permission **el permiso**
permitted **permitido**
Please do! **Hágalo, por favor**
I'm (not) supposed to . . . **(no) debo ...**
Do you have time to . . .? **¿Tiene usted tiempo de ... ?**
I should **debería**
You should(n't) . . . **(No) deberías ...**

Surprise

Can that be . . . ? **¿Es posible (eso)?**
That cannot (can't) be **No puede ser**
Good grief! **¡lDios mío!**
Goodness! **¡lDios mío!**
Imagine / Fancy (that)! **¡Vaya!, ¡Fíjate!**
Is it possible that . . .? **¿Es posible que ... ?**
Just as I expected **Ya me lo figuraba.**
Oh really! **¡Eh!, ¡Ca!, ¡Qué cosas pasan!**
surprise **la sorpresa**
I surprise **sorprendo**
surprising **sorprendente**
Does that surprise you? **¿Le sorprende eso?**
So what? **¿(Pues) y qué?**
Well? **¿Y entonces?**
Wow! **¡Caramba!, ¡Caray!**

Hesitating

er . . . **pues, es decir, esto ...**
hesitation **la indecisión**
I hesitate **vacilo**
How shall I put it? **¿Cómo lo diría yo?**
Just a minute / moment! **Un minuto, momento, Un momentito**

Now let me think   **Déjame pensar, Veamos, Vamos a ver**
or rather . . .   **o bien ...**
that is to say . . .   **es decir ...**
That's not what I meant to say   **No es lo que quería decir**
thingamajig   **la cosa, el chisme**
What's his / her name?   **¿Cómo se llama (él / ella)?**

Listening & agreeing / disagreeing

I agree / don't agree (that) . . .   **(no) estoy de acuerdo que**
aha!   **¡ajá!**
Don't you agree (that)   **¿No crees que ?**
I believe so / not   **Creo que sí / no**
Certainly!   **¡Desde luego!, ¡Por supuesto!, ¡Por cierto!**
Certainly not!   **¡De ninguna manera!, ¡Ni hablar!**
correct   **correcto, exacto, justo**
I don't think so   **Creo que no**
Exactly!   **¡Exactamente!**
I find (that)   **encuentro (que)**
Indeed!   **¡Por cierto!, ¡En efecto!, ¡Claro que sí!, ¡Ya lo creo!**
Just so!   **¡Exactamente!, ¡Eso es!, ¡Perfectamente!, ¡Precisamente!**
never   **nunca, jamás**
No!   **¡No!**
Nonsense / Rubbish!   **¡Qué va! ¡Tonterías!, ¡Ni pensar!**
of course!   **¡claro!, ¡por supuesto!, ¡naturalmente!**
of course not!   **¡claro que no!**
Oh!   **¿De veras?**
Really?   **¿Verdad?, ¿De veras?**
right   **¡eso es!, ¡conforme!, ¡justo!, ¡bueno!**
That's not so   **No es así**
that's (not) right / true   **(no) es correcto, (no) es verdad**
that's right / correct   **es eso, eso es, es correcto**
I think so   **Creo que sí**

true   **verdad, verdadero**
you're wrong   **está usted equivocado**
that's wrong!   **es equivocado, es falso, no es correcto**
yes!   **¡Sí!**

Clarification & meaning

a kind / sort of . . .   **una especie de ... , algo así como ...**
Do you mean . . . ?   **¿Quiere usted decir?**
Did you say . . . ?   **¿Dijo usted que ... ?**
I explain   **explico**
How do you spell that, please?   **¿Cómo se escribe eso, por favor?**
I mean   **quiero decir**
I say   **digo**
Is that clear?   **¿Comprendido?, ¿Entendido?, ¿Está claro?**
it is spelled / you spell it . . .   **se escribe ...**
That's just what I had in mind   **Es exactamente lo que pensaba / buscaba**
That's not what I had in mind   **No es lo que yo había pensado**
What did you say?   **¿Qué dijo usted?**
What do you mean by . . . ?   **¿Qué quiere(s) decir con ... ?**
What I said was . . .   **Lo que dije fue que ...**
What is it in Spanish?   **¿Cómo es en español?**
Would you repeat that, please?   **Repite, por favor**
Would you speak more slowly, please?   **Hable (usted) más despacio, por favor**
Would you spell that, please?   **¿Quisiera usted deletrear eso, por favor?**
you know   **usted sabe**

COMMUNICATING WITH OTHERS

15c Mail / Post & Telephone

Mail / Post

abroad   **el extranjero**
addressee   **el destinatario, el consignatario**
airmail   **el correo aéreo**
airmail letter   **la carta por correo aéreo, el aerograma**
airmail paper   **el papel para avión**
answer   **la contestación, la respuesta**
collection   **la recogida**
I correspond with   **me escribo con**
correspondent   **el corresponsal**
counter   **el mostrador**
customs declaration   **la declaración aduanera**
envelope   **el sobre, la envoltura**
express delivery   **la entrega urgente**
I finish (letter)   **termino (la carta)**
first-class mail   **el correo de primera clase**
general delivery   **la lista de correos**
I get / receive   **recibo**
I hand in   **entrego**
letter   **la carta**
letter / mail rate   **la tarifa de cartas**
mail / post   **el correo**
mailbox / letter-box   **el buzón**
mailman / postman   **el cartero**

money / postal order   **el giro postal**
news   **las noticias, las nuevas**
I note down   **tomo apuntes**
notepaper   **el papel para cartas, el papel para escribir**
package   **el paquete, el bulto**
parcel   **el paquete**
parcel rate   **la tarifa de paquetes**
pen pal / pen-friend   **el amigo por correspondencia**
I post   **echo a correos, llevo a correos, echo al buzón**
post office   **correos, la oficina de correos**
postage   **los gastos de correo**
postcard   **la (tarjeta) postal**
prepaid postage / freepost   **correo libre de franqueo**
registered / recorded mail / **el correo certificado**
reply   **la contestación, la respuesta**
sealed   **sellado**
I send   **mando, envío**
I send (greetings)   **mando (un saludo / recuerdos)**
sender   **el remitente**
stamp   **el sello**
I write   **escribo**
zip code / postcode   **el código postal**

When does the mail / post arrive?   **¿A qué hora llega el cartero?**
I haven't heard from her in ages.   **Hace mucho tiempo que no tengo noticias suyas.**

Dear Sir,   **Muy señor mío:**
I am writing on behalf of my father, concerning. . . .   **Le escribo de parte de mi padre, acerca de ...**
I look forward to hearing from you,   **Quedo a la espera de sus noticias,**

Yours sincerely, . . .   **Le saluda atentamente, ...**

Telephone & telecommunications

booth **la cabina**
busy / engaged *(phone)* **está comunicando / ocupado**
button **el botón**
cell (mobile) phone **el celular, el móvil**
collect / reverse charge call **la llamada por cobro revertido**
conversation **la conversación**
dial **el disco**
electronic mail **el correo electrónico**
extension **la extensión, el supletorio, el interno**
extension number **el número de la extensión**
fax **el (tele)fax**
fax modem **el módem de fax**
local call **la llamada / conferencia local**
long-distance call **la conferencia interurbana**
operator **el / la telefonista**
out of order **no funciona**
phone booth / call-box **la cabina telefónica**
receiver **el auricular**
slot **la ranura**
subscriber **el abonado**
telecommunications links **los enlaces de telecomunicación**

telecommunications **las telecomunicaciones**
telegram **el telegrama**
telegraph **telégrafo**
telephone **el teléfono**
telephone directory **la guía telefónica**
telephone booth / kiosk **la cabina telefónica**
telephone / phone **el teléfono**
text message **el mensaje de texto**
I transmit **transmito**
unlisted / ex-directory **no figura en la guía**
word **la palabra**
wrong number **el número equivocado**
zero / nought **cero**

Telephoning

I call **llamo**
I connect with **comunico con**
I dial **marco**
I fax **mando por fax, faxeo**
I hang up **cuelgo**
I hold **estoy en espera**
I pick up **descuelgo**
I press **pulso, aprieto**
I put ... through (to) **me pongo con ..., (me) comunico con ...**
I speak to **hablo con**
I telephone / phone **llamo por / al teléfono, telefoneo**

Do you have change for the telephone?	¿Tiene usted moneda para el teléfono?
Can I dial / call direct?	¿Puedo marcar el número en directo?
Hello / Hallo! *(calling)*	¡Oíga(me), por favor!
Hello / Hallo! *(answering)*	¡Díga(me)!
Are you still there?	¿Aún está ahí?
Can you hear me?	¿Me oye usted?
Could you fax it to me?	¿Me lo puede mandar por fax, por favor?

➤ COMPUTERS 15d; USING LANGUAGE 21b

COMMUNICATING WITH OTHERS

15d Computers

Computer applications

adventure game **el videojuego de aventuras**
application **la aplicación**
artificial intelligence **la inteligencia artificial**
bar code **el código de barras**
bar code reader **el aparato lector de códigos de barras, la máquina lectora de códigos de barras**
browser **navegador**
calculator **la calculadora, la minicalculadora**
computer science / studies **la informática, las ciencias de la computación**
computerized **computerizado, informatizado**
desktop publishing / DTP **la autoedición**
electronic mail **el correo electrónico**
grammar checker **el corrector de gramática, el consultor de gramática**
information **la información**
information technology **la informática**
internet **la Internet**

optical reader **el lector óptico (de textos)**
simulation **la simulación**
simulator **el simulador**
spell check **el corrector ortográfico, el consultor de ortografía**
synthesizer **el sintetizador**
text **el texto**
thesaurus **el diccionario de sinónimos, la antología**
website **sitio Web**
word processor **el procesador de palabras, el procesador de textos**
word processing **el proceso de textos, el tratamiento de textos**

Word processing & operating

I abort **interrumpo (el programa), detengo prematuramente**
I access **entro**
I append **anexiono (al final)**
I apply boldface **pongo los caracteres en negrita**
I back up **hago una copia de apoyo**
I block (text) **agrupo**
I boot up **arranco, cebo, inicializo**
I browse **hojeo**

Is it possible to replace the central processing unit?
¿Es posible reemplazar la unidad procesadora central?
These computers are on a local area network.
Estos ordenadores están conectados a una red de área local.
I replied to your message yesterday.
Ayer mismo te contesté el mensaje.
How do you turn down the brightness?
¿Cómo se baja el brillo?
Can you repair this keyboard?
¿Puede usted reparar este teclado?

I cancel **anulo**
I click on **pulso el ratón**
I communicate **comunico**
I copy **copio**
I count **cuento**
I create **creo, abro (un archivo)**
I cut and paste **corto e inserto**
I debug **depuro, quito el duende de ...**
I delete **cancelo, borro**
I download **descargo**
I emulate **emulo**
I enter **introduzco, entro a**
I erase **borro**
I exit **salgo (del sistema)**
I export **exporto**
I file **ficho**
I format **formateo**
I forward **reenvío**
I handle (text) **trato (el texto)**
I import **importo**
I install **instalo**
I list **listo**
I log **apunto, anoto, registro**
I log off / out **salgo del sistema, finalizo la sesión, termino de operar**
I log on / in **entro al sistema, accedo, inicio la sesión**
I merge **fusiono**
I move **muevo**

I open (a file) **abro (un fichero), entro a un fichero**
I print **imprimo, grabo**
I print out **imprimo**
I (word) process **trato / manejo el texto**
I program(me) **programo**
I read **leo, estudio**
I receive **recibo**
I record **registro**
I remove **quito**
I replace **reemplazo, sustituyo**
I reply **contesto**
I retrieve **recupero, llamo**
I run **ejecuto**
I save **salvo, grabo guardo**
I search **busco**
I send a copy to **envío una copia a**
I send **envío, mando, emito**
I shift **quito**
I sort **ordeno**
I store **almaceno**
I switch off **quito, apago, desconecto**
I switch on **enciendo, pongo, conecto**
I tabulate **tabulo**
I type **tecleo**
I underline **subrayo**
I update **actualizo**

Don't show me your password!	**¡No me muestre su contraseña de acceso!**
I don't like the software package with this PC.	**No me gusta el paquete de programas que se ofrece con este ordenador personal.**
Is this spreadsheet easy to use?	**¿Esta hoja electrónica, es fácil de utilizar?**
You can always consult the pull-down menu.	**Siempre se puede consultar el menú desplegable.**
It has erased my file!	**¡Ha borrado mi fichero!**
This disk is corrupted.	**Este disco está degradado.**

Leisure & Sport

16a Leisure

activity **la actividad**	energetic **enérgico**
amateur **el amateur, el aficionado**	energy **la energía**
book **el libro**	enthusiasm **el entusiasmo**
boring **aburrido**	entrance **la entrada**
camera **la cámara**	entry fee **la tarifa de entrada**
I can **puedo**	excitement **la excitación**
card **la tarjeta**	exciting **excitante, divertido**
card game **el juego de cartas**	excursion **la excursión**
card table **la mesa de juego**	exit **la salida**
casino **el casino**	fair **la feria**
chess **el ajedrez**	fascinating **fascinante, encantador**
closed **cerrado**	
club **el club**	finished **terminado, finalizado**
I collect **colecciono**	free time **el tiempo libre**
coin **la moneda**	fun **la diversión**
collection **la colección**	I gamble **apuesto**
collectors' fair **la feria de colecciones**	I get in line / queue **hago cola**
	I go out **salgo**
connoisseur **el entendido, el conocedor**	guide **el guía**
	guided tour **el viaje con guía**
crossword puzzle **el crucigrama**	hobby / pastime **el hobby, la afición, el pasatiempo**
I decide **decido**	
discotheque **la discoteca**	interest **el interés, la afición**
do-it-yourself / DIY **hágalo usted mismo**	

"What is your favorite / favourite pastime?"
"Well, I used to go for a drive in the country every Sunday, but I have no time for hobbies nowadays. Sometimes I go fishing."

— **¿Cuál es tu pasatiempo favorito?**
— **Bueno, solía ir a conducir por el campo todos los domingos pero ahora no tengo tiempo para pasatiempos. Algunas veces voy a pescar.**

I can meet you at the swimming pool or, if you prefer, at the gym.

Puedo encontrarme contigo [Podemos vernos] en la piscina, o si prefieres, en el gimnasio.

interesting **interesante**
I join **me uno**
leisure **el ocio**
I like (dis-) **(no) me gusta**
line / queue **la cola**
I listen to **escucho, oigo**
I look **miro, veo**
market **el mercado**
  antiques market **el mercado de antigüedades**
  flea market **el mercadillo, el mercado de la pulga**
I meet **veo a, quedo con, me reúno con**
meeting place **el punto de encuentro**
member **el miembro**
membership **la calidad de socio**
movie theater / cinema **el cine**
nightclub **el club nocturno**
open **abierto**
organization **la organización**
I organize **organizo**
photograph **la fotografía**
picnic **el picnic, la comida en el campo**
place **el lugar**
I play **juego**
pleasure **la satisfacción, el placer**
politics **la política**

I prefer **prefiero**
private **privado**
public **público**
I read **leo**
season **la estación**
season ticket **el billete de abono, [el tiquete de temporada]**
secluded **aislado**
slide **la diapositiva**
spectator **el espectador**
I start (doing) **comienzo, empiezo**
I stop (doing) **termino**
I stroll **paseo**
subscription **la suscripción**
television **la televisión, el televisor**
theater / theatre **el teatro**
ticket **el billete, la entrada, [el boleto, el tiquete]**
time **el tiempo**
tour **el viaje turístico, la excursión**
vacation / holiday **las vacaciones**
I visit **visito**
visit **la visita**
I walk **ando, camino**
I watch **observo, miro**
youth club **el club juvenil**
zoo **el zoo, el (jardín / parque) zoológico**

"What do you like doing on a rainy day?"
"Perhaps playing cards but not with my brother: he cheats!"

"Shall we take the children to the zoo?"
"Good idea. If we take Eve's children and their school friends as well, we can get a group discount."

—¿Qué te gusta hacer en un día lluvioso?
—Quizás, jugar a las cartas, pero no con mi hermano: ¡hace trampas!

—¿Llevamos a los niños al zoológico?
—Buena idea. Si llevamos a los niños de Eva y a sus amigos del colegio también, nos harán un descuento de grupo.

➤ HOBBIES App. 16a; SPORTS 16c; SPORTING ACTIVITY 16b

against **contra**	fall **la caída**
I aim **apunto**	I fall **me caigo**
archer **el arquero**	field **el campo**
athlete **el atleta**	finals **la final, las finales**
athletic **atlético**	fit **en forma**
ball **la pelota, el balón**	fitness **estar en forma**
bathtowel **la toalla de baño**	I get fit **me pongo en forma**
bet **la apuesta, la postura**	game **el juego**
boat **la barca, el bote**	goal **el gol**
I bowl **juego al boliche, juego a las bolas**	gym(nasium) **el gimnasio**
boxer **el boxeador**	hit **el golpe**
captain **el capitán**	I hit **golpeo**
I catch **cojo, recojo**	ice rink **la pista de patinaje**
champion **el campeón**	I ice skate **patino sobre hielo**
championship **el campeonato**	injury **la herida, la lesión**
I climb **escalo**	instructor **el instructor**
climber **el escalador**	I jog **troto, corro**
coach **el entrenador**	jogger **el corredor**
cup (trophy) **la copa**	jump **el salto**
cycle **el ciclismo**	I jump **salto**
I cycle **hago ciclismo**	lawn **el césped**
defeat **la derrota**	league **la liga**
I dive **buceo**	I lift weights **levanto pesas**
I do (sport) **practico**	locker / changing room **el vestuario**
draw (tie) **el empate**	I lose **pierdo**
I draw (tie) **logro el empate**	marathon **el maratón**
effort **el esfuerzo**	match **el partido**
endurance **la resistencia**	medal **la medalla**
equipment **el equipo**	gold / silver / bronze **de oro / de plata / de bronce**
I exercise **hago ejercicio**	

Without sponsorship, I won't be able to train using the best facilities. I cannot then compete at the highest level.	Sin patrocinio no podré entrenar con las mejores instalaciones. Por lo mismo, no podré competir al nivel más alto.
"Did you watch the match?" "No, I had to leave before the end. Who won?" "We lost 3 to 1."	— ¿Has visto el partido? — No, me tuve que ir antes del final. ¿Quién ganó? — Perdimos 3 a 1 (tres a uno).

muscle **el músculo**
Olympics Games (winter) **los Juegos Olímpicos (de invierno)**
opponent **el adversario**
pedal **el pedal**
pentathlon **el pentatlón**
physical **físico**
I pitch **lanzo**
pitcher **el lanzador**
player **el jugador**
I play **juego**
point **el punto**
professional (adj) **profesional**
race **la carrera**
I race **participo en una carrera**
referee **el árbitro**
rest **el descanso**
result **el resultado**
I ride **monto a caballo**
riding school **la escuela ecuestre**
I row **remo**
run **la carrera**
I run **corro**
runner **el corredor**
sail **la vela**
I sail **navego**
sailing school **la escuela de náutica / navegación**
score **el tanteo, el resultado, el puntaje**
I score (a goal) **marco**
I shoot (ball, puck) **chuto, tiro**
I shoot (at a target) **tiro**
I shoot pool **juego al billar**

show **el espectáculo**
I ski **esquío**
ski lift **el remonte, la telesilla**
skier **el esquiador**
sponsor **el patrocinador**
sponsorship **el patrocinio**
sport **el deporte**
sports field **el campo de deportes**
sprint **el sprint**
stadium / ground **el estadio, el terreno**
stamina **el vigor, la resistencia**
strength **la fuerza**
supporter **el seguidor, el hincha**
I swim **nado**
team **el equipo**
team sport **el deporte de equipos**
touchdown **el tocado en tierra**
I throw **lanzo**
tournament **el torneo**
track **la pista**
I train **me entreno**
trainer **el entrenador**
training **el entrenamiento**
triumph **el triunfo**
trophy **el trofeo**
I am unfit **no estoy en forma**
victory **la victoria**
I win **gano**
workout **el entrenamiento, la preparación**
world championship **el campeonato del mundo**
world cup **la copa del mundo**

I still cannot understand how such a capable team could lose so disastrously after a brilliant season.
All sports commentators agree that they were particularly unlucky when the referee insisted on the penalty kick.

**Todavía no puedo entender cómo un equipo tan bueno pudo perder tan desastrosamente tras una magnífica temporada.
Todos los comentaristas deportivos están de acuerdo en que tuvieron muy mala suerte cuando el árbitro insistió en la sanción.**

➤ PHYSICAL STATE 11d

LEISURE & SPORT

16c Sports & Equipment

Sports

aerobics **los ejercicios aeróbicos**
archery **el tiro con arco**
athletics **el atletismo**
badminton **el bádminton**
baseball **el béisbol**
basketball **el baloncesto**
bowling **la bolera, los bolos**
  tenpins / ten-pin bowling **el boliche**
boxing **el boxeo**
climbing **el montañismo, el alpinismo**
  free climbing **la escalada libre**
  rock climbing **la escalada en rocas**
crew **el equipo**
cricket **el cricket, el críquet**
cycling **el ciclismo**
decathlon **el decatlón**
diving **el buceo**
  deep water diving **el buceo en aguas profundas**
football **el fútbol norteamericano**
handball **el balonmano**
hockey **el hockey**
horse racing **las carreras de caballos**
horseback riding **montar a caballo**
ice hockey **el hockey sobre hielo**
ice skating **el patinaje sobre hielo**
jogging **el footing**

motor racing **el automovilismo, las carreras de coches**
paragliding **el planeador**
polo **el polo**
pool **el billar**
racing **las carreras**
riding **montar a caballo**
roller skating **el patinaje sobre ruedas**
rugby **el rugbi, el rugby**
sailing **la navegación**
skiing **el esquí**
  water skiing **el esquí acuático**
  cross-country skiing **el esquí nórdico**
  downhill skiing **el esquí alpino**
snooker **el snooker**
soccer **el fútbol**
swimming **la natación**
table tennis **el tenis de mesa, el pinpón, el ping-pong**
volleyball **el vóleibol**
water polo **el polo acuático**
weight training **el entrenamiento con pesas**
windsurfing **el windsurf**

Leisure wear & sport clothes

anorak **el anorak**
bathing suit **el traje de baño**
boots **las botas**
cycling shorts **los pantalones de ciclista**
dancing shoes **los zapatos de baile**

The most popular sports in North America are baseball, (American) football, basketball and (ice) hockey. In South America, soccer is the major passion.

Los deportes más populares en Norteamérica son el béisbol, el fútbol norteamericano, el baloncesto y el hockey sobre hielo. En Sudamérica la pasión es el fútbol.

➤ CLOTHING 9c; TOOLS App. 8b

gardening gloves **los guantes de jardinería**
leotard **el leotardo**
parka **la parka**
ski outfit / salopette **el mono de esquiar**
swimsuit **el bañador [el traje de baño] de mujer**
swimming trunks **el bañador [el traje de baño] de hombre**
rugby shirt **la camiseta de rugbi**
track suit **el chandal**
trainers **las zapatillas de deporte**
walking boots **las botas para andar**
waterproof jacket **el chaleco impermeable**
Wellington boots **las botas de agua**
wet suit **el traje de buceo**

Leisure & sport equipment

arrow **la flecha**
ball **la pelota, el balón**
bat **el bate, la maza, la paleta**
binoculars **los anteojos, los prismáticos**
bow **el arco**
boxing gloves **los guantes de boxeo**
camera **la cámara**
crash helmet **el casco**
equipment **el equipo, el material**
exercise bike **la bicicleta de ejercicio, la bicicleta estática**
fishing rod **la caña de pescar**

headphone **el auricular**
hi-fi **hi-fi, (de) alta fidelidad**
knapsack / rucksack **la mochila**
knitting needles **las agujas de hacer punto**
javelin **la javalina**
mountain bike **la bicicleta de montaña**
net **la red**
outrigger **el portarremos, el bote con portarremos exterior**
pruning shears / secateurs **las tijeras de podar, la podadora**
puck **el disco, el puck**
racket **la raqueta**
rifle **el rifle**
roller skates **los patines de ruedas**
rowing machine **el aparato de remo**
rowing boat **el bote de remo**
sailboat **el barco de vela**
sewing kit **el costurero**
skate **el patín**
skis **los esquís**
ski boots **las botas de esquí**
ski poles / sticks **los bastones de esquí**
spinning wheel **la rueca**
sports bag **la bolsa de deporte**
stick *(hockey)* **el palo**
surfboard **la tabla de surf**
weights **las pesas**
yacht **el yate**
zoom lens **el zoom**

In the final minutes, the goalkeeper made a spectacular save with his stick to flick the puck off the line and out of the goal.

En los últimos minutos, el portero impidió un gol de una manera espectacular con el palo quitando el puck de la línea y echándolo lejos de la portería.

127

The Arts

17a Appreciation & Criticism

abstract **abstracto**
abstruse **abstruso**
action **la acción**
aesthete **el esteta**
aesthetics **la estética**
I appreciate **aprecio**
appreciation **la apreciación**
art **el arte**
artist **el artista**
artistic **artístico**
atmosphere **la atmósfera**
atmospheric **atmosférico**
author **el autor**
award **el premio**
I analyze **analizo**
avant-garde *(adj)* **en vanguardia**
believable **creíble**
character **el personaje**
characterization **la caracterización**
characteristic **característico**
climax **el clímax, el punto culminante**
it closes **cierra**
comic **cómico**
commentary **el comentario**
conflict **el conflicto**
contemporary **contemporáneo**
contrast **el contraste**
it creates **crea**
creativity **la creatividad**
credible **creíble, verosímil**
critic **el crítico**
criticism **la crítica**
cultivated **cultivado**
culture **la cultura**
it deals with **trata de**
it describes **describe**
it develops **desarrolla**
development **el desarrollo**

device **la estratagema, el mecanismo**
dialogue **el diálogo**
disturbing **inquietante**
empathy **la empatía**
ending **el final, el fin**
it ends **finaliza, termina**
entertaining **divertido, entretenido**
entertainment **el divertimiento, el entretenimiento**
epic *(n)* **la épica**
event **el acontecimiento, el suceso, el evento**
eventful **memorable**
example **el ejemplo**
exciting **emocionante**
I explain **explico**
explanation **la explicación**
it explores **explora**
it expresses **expresa**
fake **falso**
fantastic **fantástico**
fantasy **la fantasía**
figure **la figura**
funny **gracioso, divertido**
image **la imagen**
imaginary **imaginario**
imagination **la imaginación**
inspiration **la inspiración**
inspired by **inspirado por**
intense **intenso**
intensity **la intensidad**
invention **la invención**
inventive **inventivo, imaginativo**
ironic **irónico**
irony **la ironía**
issue **la cuestión, el problema**
life **la vida**
long-winded **prolijo, extenso**

lyrical **lírico**
modern **moderno**
mood **el humor, la atmósfera**
moral **moral**
morality **la moralidad**
moving **conmovedor**
mystery **el misterio**
mysterious **misterioso**
mystical **místico**
nature **la naturaleza**
obscene **obsceno**
obscenity **la obscenidad**
obscure **oscuro, obstruso**
opinion **la opinión**
optimism **el optimismo**
optimistic **optimista**
parody **la parodia**
passion **la pasión**
passionate **apasionado**
pessimism **el pesimismo**
pessimistic **pesimístico**
it portrays **representa, describe**
portrayal **la representación, el retrato**
precious **valioso, precioso**
protagonist **el protagonista**
I read **leo**
reader **el lector**

realistic **realista**
reference **la referencia**
I reflect **reflejo**
reflection **la reflexión, el pensamiento**
relationship **la relación, la conexión**
review **la revisión, el análisis**
sad **triste**
satire **la sátira**
it satirizes **satiriza**
satirical **satírico**
style **el estilo**
   in the style of **al estilo de**
stylish **con estilo, elegante**
subject **el tema, el contenido**
technique **la técnica**
tension **la tensión**
theme **el tema**
tone **el tono**
tragedy **la tragedia**
tragic **trágico**
true **verdadero, auténtico**
vivid **vívido**
viewpoint **el punto de vista**
witty **ingenioso**
work of art **la obra de arte**

Artistic styles & periods

Art Nouveau **el art nouveau**
Aztec **azteca**
baroque **barroco**
classical period **el período clásico**
Enlightenment **el Siglo de las luces**
existentialist **existencialista**
expressionist **expresionista**
futuristic **futurístico**
Georgian **georgiano**
Gothic **gótico**
Greek **griego**
medieval **medieval**
naturalistic **naturalístico**

Norman **normando**
Persian **persa**
poetic **poético**
postmodernist **pos-modernista**
realism **el realismo**
Renaissance **el Renacimiento**
rococo **rococó**
Romanesque **románico**
romantic **romántico**
structuralist **estructuralista**
surrealist **surrealista**
symbolist **simbolista**
twentieth century **el siglo veinte**
Victorian period **el período victoriano**

THE ARTS

antique   **antiguo**
antiquity   **la antigüedad**
architect   **el arquitecto**
art   **el arte**
artifact   **el artefacto**
artist   **el artista**
art student   **el estudiante de arte**
auction sale   **la subasta**
auctioneer   **el subastador**
balance   **el equilibrio**
baroque   **barroco**
beam   **la viga**
bronze   **el bronce**
brush   **el pincel**
I build   **construyo**
building   **la construcción, el edificio**
bust   **el busto**
caricature   **la caricatura**
I carve   **esculpo, tallo**
I cast   **fundo**
ceramics   **la cerámica**
charcoal   **el carbón, el carboncillo**
chisel   **el cincel**
chiseled   **cincelado**
classical   **clásico**
clay   **la arcilla**
collage   **el collage**
decorated   **decorado**
decoration   **la decoración**
decorative arts   **las artes decorativas**
I design   **diseño**
design   **el diseño**

dimension   **las medidas, la dimensión**
I draw   **dibujo**
drawing   **el dibujo**
easel   **el caballete**
elevation   **la elevación**
enamel   **el esmalte**
I engrave   **grabo**
engraving   **el grabado**
I etch   **grabo al aguafuerte**
etching   **el aguafuerte**
exhibition   **la exposición**
figure   **la figura**
figurine   **la figurilla**
filigree   **la filigrana**
fine arts   **las bellas artes**
flamboyant   **rimbombante, llamativo**
form   **la forma**
freehand   **hecho a pulso**
fresco   **el fresco**
frieze   **el friso**
genre   **el género**
graphic arts   **las artes gráficas**
gravity   **la gravedad**
holograph   **el ológrafo, el olograma**
interior   **interior, interno**
intricate   **intrincado**
ironwork   **el herraje**
landscape   **el paisaje**
landscape gardener   **el arquitecto de jardines**

We have a very good view of the cupola from this terrace. Look, in the foreground you can see the monastery, which dates back from 1679 and which is such a good example of religious architecture, and in the background the medieval towers are still visible.

La vista de la cúpula desde esta terraza es muy buena. Mira, al fondo puedes ver el monasterio que fue construido en 1679 y es un buen ejemplo de la arquitectura religiosa, y detrás pueden verse todavía las torres medievales.

landscape painter **el paisajista**
large-scale works **las obras a gran escala**
later works **las últimas obras**
light **la luz**
    light *(adj)* **luminoso**
lithography **la litografía**
luminosity **la luminosidad**
luminous **luminoso**
masterpiece **la obra maestra**
metal **el metal**
miniature **la miniatura**
model **el modelo**
monochrome **monocromo, de un solo color**
moorish **árabe**
mosaic **el mosaico**
museum **el museo**
oil painting **la pintura al óleo**
ornate **ornado, florido**
I paint **pinto, dibujo**
paint **la pintura**
painting **el cuadro, la pintura**
pastel **el pastel**
portrait **el retrato**
potter **el ceramista**
pottery **la cerámica**
it represents **representa**
representation **la representación**
reproduction **la reproducción**
restoration **la restauración**
I restore **restauro**
restored **restaurado**
restorer **el restaurador**

school **la escuela**
I sculpt **esculpo**
sculptor **el escultor**
sculpture **la escultura**
seascape **el paisaje marino, la marina**
shadow **la sombra**
shape **la forma**
I shape **doy forma, moldeo**
sketch / roughcast **el boceto, el esbozo**
I sketch **hago un boceto**
sketching **el dibujo, el boceto**
stained glass **la vidriera**
statuary **el estatuario**
statue **la estatua**
still life **el bodegón, la naturaleza muerta**
I stipple **punteo**
studio **el estudio**
style **el estilo**
surrealism **el surrealismo**
tapestry **el tapiz**
tempera **la témpera, la pintura al temple**
town planning **el urbanismo**
traditional **tradicional**
translucent **translúcido**
transparent **transparente**
visual arts **las artes visuales**
watercolor / -colour **la acuarela**
wood **la madera**
wood carving **la talla de madera**
woodcut **la incisión**

I have just been to the exhibition at the Royal Academy, which has already attracted thousands of visitors. There is the most wonderful collection of drawings and sculptures of the Italian artist. Two of the paintings have been very skillfully restored.

Acabo de visitar una exposición en la Real Academia que ya ha atraído a miles de visitantes. Tiene la mejor colección de dibujos y esculturas del artista italiano. Dos de los dibujos han sido muy bien restaurados.

THE ARTS

17c Literature

autograph **el autógrafo**	literal(ly) **literal(mente)**
book **el libro**	map **el mapa**
bookstore / shop **la librería**	myth **el mito**
bookseller **el librero**	mythology **la mitología**
character **el personaje**	it narrates **narra**
main character **el personaje**	narrative **la narrativa**
principal, el protagonista	narrator **el narrador**
secondary character **el**	note **la nota**
personaje secundario	page **la página**
comic **cómico**	paperback **la cubierta rústica**
dialogue / dialog **el diálogo**	paragraph **el párrafo**
fictional **ficticio**	poem **el poema**
hardback **la cubierta dura**	poetic **poético**
I imagine **imagino**	poetry **la poesía**
imagination **la imaginación**	punctuation **la puntuación**
inspiration **la inspiración**	quote **la cita**
inspired by **inspirado por**	I quote **cito**
it introduces **introduce**	I read **leo**
introduction **la introducción**	I recount **cuento, refiero**
I leaf through **hojeo**	rhyme **la rima**
librarian **el bibliotecario**	it is set in **está situado en**
library **la biblioteca**	table **la tabla**
public library **la biblioteca**	text **el texto**
pública	title **el título**
reference library **la biblioteca**	verse **el verso**
de consulta	

"What are you reading at the moment?"	— ¿Qué lees ahora?
"A spine-chilling story with a tragic conclusion.	— Una historia escalofriante con un final trágico.
It is set in contemporary Buenos Aires."	Está situado [Tiene lugar] en el Buenos Aires actual.
It is a vivid account of life in the thirties. The writer explores the theme of lost innocence.	Es un retrato vivo de la vida de los años treinta. El escritor explora el tema de la inocencia perdida.

Types of books

adventure story   **la historia de aventuras**

atlas   **el átlas**

autobiography   **la autobiografía**

biography   **la biografía**

children's literature   **la literatura infantil**

comic novel   **la novela cómica**

cookbook   **el libro de cocina**

detective story   **la novela policíaca**

diary   **el diario**

dictionary   **el diccionario**

   bilingual   **el diccionario bilingüe**

   monolingual   **el diccionario monolingüe**

encyclopedia   **la enciclopedia**

epic poem   **el poema épico**

essay   **el ensayo**

fable   **la fábula**

fairy tale   **el cuento de hadas**

feminist novel   **la novela feminista**

fiction   **la ficción, la narrativa**

Greek tragedy   **la tragedia griega**

horror story   **la historia / el cuento de terror**

letters   **las cartas**

manual   **el manual**

memoirs   **las memorias**

modern play   **la obra teatral moderna**

mystery play   **la obra teatral de misterio**

nonfiction   **la literatura no novelesca**

novel   **la novela**

picaresque novel   **la novela picaresca**

poetry   **la poesía**

reference book   **el libro de consulta**

restoration comedy   **la comedia de la restauración**

satirical poem   **el poema satírico**

science fiction story   **la historia de ciencia ficción**

short story   **el cuento, la historia corta**

spy story   **la historia de espionaje**

teenage fiction   **la literatura juvenil**

travel book   **el libro de viajes**

war novel   **la novela de guerra**

A collection of modern foreign fiction.

Una colección de narrativa extranjera actual.

My novel deals with changes in nineteenth century Spanish rural society.

Mi novela trata de los cambios de la vida rural española en el siglo diecinueve.

It opens with a lyrical description of the valley. It ends with the last entry in the hero's diary.

Comienza con una descripción lírica del valle. Termina con lo último que el héroe escribió en su diario.

THE ARTS

acoustics   la acústica
agent   el agente
album   el álbum
amplifier   el amplificador
audience   el público, la audiencia
audition   la audición
auditorium   el auditorio
ballet   el balet
bandleader   el director de la banda
baton   la batuta
brass band   la banda, la charanga
cassette tape   la cinta de casete
cassette deck   el casete
chamber music   la música de
  cámara
choir   el coro
choral   la coral
chorale   coral
choreography   la coreografía
chorister   el corista
chorus   el coro, el estribillo
compact disc / disk   el compact
  disc, el disco compacto
competition   el concurso
compilation   la recopilación
I compose   compongo
composer   el compositor
composition   la composición
concert   el concierto
concert hall   la sala de conciertos
I conduct   dirijo
conductor   el director de orquesta
dance   la danza

I dance   danzo
dancer   el danzarín
dance music   la música de danza
discotheque   la discoteca
disc jockey   el disc jockey
drummer   el batería
ensemble   el conjunto, la
  agrupación
euphony   la eufonía
folk music   la música folk, la
  música popular
gig   la actuación
group   el grupo
harmony   la armonía
harmonic   la armónica
hit (song)   la canción de éxito
hit / chart parade   la lista de éxitos
I hum   canturreo
instrument   el instrumento
instrumental music   la música
  instrumental
instrumentalist   el instrumentalista
I interpret   interpreto
interpretation   la interpretación
jazz   el jazz
judge / adjudicator   el juez del
  concurso
jukebox   la máquina de música
key   la clave
lesson   la lección
I listen to   escucho, oigo
listening   la audición
microphone   el micrófono

"There is a concert at the students' union."
"What is the name of the band?"
"I don't know. Their lyrics are quite good but the music is dreadful."

Rehearsals will be held in the cathedral on Friday evening

— Hay un concierto en el Sindicato de Estudiantes.
— ¿Cómo se llama el grupo?
— No lo sé. La letra es bastante buena pero la música es malísima.

Los ensayos se harán el viernes por la tarde en la catedral.

music **la música**
musically **musicalmente**
musician **el músico**
musicologist **el musicólogo**
note **la nota**
orchestra **la orquesta**
orchestration **la orquestación**
it is performed **es tocado, es representado**
performance **la representación**
performed by **representado por, ejecutado por**
performer **el ejecutor**
pianist **el pianista**
piano **el piano**
piece **la pieza musical**
I play **toco**
player **el músico**
portable **portátil**
I practice / practise **practico**
promotional video **el vídeo promocional**
I put on a record **pongo un disco**
recital **el recital**
record **el disco, la grabación**
I record **grabo**
recording **la grabación**
recording studio **el estudio de grabación**
refrain **el estribillo**
I rehearse **ensayo**
rehearsal **el ensayo**
repertoire **el repertorio**
rhythm **el ritmo**

rhythmic **rítmico**
rock **el rock**
show **el espectáculo**
I sing **canto**
singer **el cantante**
solo **el solo**
soloist **el solista**
song **la canción**
songwriter **el autor de canciones**
string **la cuerda**
string orchestra **la orquesta de instrumentos de cuerda**
symphony **la sinfonía**
tape **la cinta**
tour **la gira**
  on tour **de gira**
tune **el tono**
  in tune **entonado, [afinado]**
  out of tune **desentonado, [desafinado]**
I tune **entono**
tuner (of instruments) **afinador de instrumentos**
tuning fork **el diapasón**
violin maker **el fabricante de violines**
vocal music **la música vocal**
voice **la voz**
I whistle **silbo**
whistling **el silbido**
wind band **la orquesta de instrumentos de viento**
wind instruments **los instrumentos de viento**

"Do you play an instrument?"
"I play the viola."
"I never learned to play an instrument but I have just bought an electric guitar."

The conductor was greeted by a standing ovation.

— ¿Tocas algún instrumento?
— Toco la viola.
— Nunca he aprendido a tocar un instrumento pero acabo de comprar una guitarra eléctrica.

El público aplaudió en pie al director.

THE ARTS

act   **la actuación**
I act   **actúo**
acting school   **la escuela de teatro**
actor   **el actor**
actress   **la actriz**
I applaud   **aplaudo**
applause   **el aplauso**
audience   **el público**
auditorium   **el auditorio**
I book   **reservo**
box   **el palco**
box office   **la taquilla**
cabaret   **el cabaret, el espectáculo de variedades**
camera   **la cámara**
camera crew   **los operadores de cámara**
cameraman   **el cámara, el camarógrafo**
cartoons   **los dibujos animados**
choreographer   **el coreógrafo**
circle   **la galería**
circus   **el circo**
I clap   **aplaudo**
clapping   **el aplauso**
coatroom / cloakroom   **el guardarropa**
comedian   **el comediante, el actor cómico**
comedienne   **la comediante, la actriz cómica**
curtain   **el telón**
I design   **diseño**
designer   **el diseñador**
I direct   **dirijo**
director   **el director**
drama   **el drama**
dress rehearsal   **el ensayo general**
dubbed   **doblado**
dubbing   **el doblaje**
effect   **el efecto**
expectation   **la expectación**
farce   **la farsa**
farcical   **farsesco, absurdo**
first night   **el estreno**
floor show   **el espectáculo de variedades / de cabaret**
flop   **el fracaso**
gaffer   **el Iluminista**
intermission   **el intervalo, el descanso**
interval   **el descanso**
lights   **las luces, los focos**
in the limelight   **en candelero**
lobby   **el pasillo, el vestíbulo**
location work   **los exteriores, el rodaje fuera del estudio**
I make a movie / film   **hago una película**
masterpiece   **la obra maestra**

It does not transfer well to the screen.

No se transfiere bien a la pantalla.

Foreign films are usually dubbed, but some film clubs show them in the original language.

Las películas extranjeras generalmente se doblan, pero algunos clubs de cine las dan en el idioma original.

Stuntpersons have been used for the most dangerous scenes.

Se han usado dobles para las escenas más peligrosas.

matinée **la función de tarde**
melodrama **el melodrama**
mime **el mimo**
movie/film **la película**
movie/cinema buff **el cinéfilo**
movie/film maker **el cineasta**
movie/film producer **el productor de cine**
movie/film star **la estrella de cine**
movies/cinema **el cine**
music hall **la sala de fiestas**
offstage **entre bastidores**
opening night **el estreno**
ovation **la ovación**
pantomime **la pantomima**
performance **la actuación, la ejecución**
photography **la fotografía**
play **la obra de teatro**
I play **actúo**
playwright **el dramaturgo**
premiere **el estreno**
I produce **produzco**
producer **el productor**
production **la producción**
public **el público**
retrospective **la retrospectiva**
role **el papel**
row **la fila**
scene **la escena**
scenery **el escenario**
screen **la pantalla**
screen test **la prueba de proyección, la toma**

screening **la proyección**
script **el guión**
scriptwriter **el guionista**
seat **la butaca**
sequel **la continuación, el desenlace**
sequence **la secuencia**
it is shot **está filmado**
I show *(a movie/film)* **muestro**
sold-out **vendido**
sound track **la banda sonora**
special effects **los efectos especiales**
stage *(theater/theatre)* **el escenario, la escena**
  stage *(movies/cinema)* **el escenario, el decorado**
stage directions **la acotación**
stage effects **los efectos escenográficos, los efectos teatrales**
stage fright **el miedo al público**
stalls **las butacas**
stuntperson **el doble que realiza las escenas peligrosas**
trailer **el tráiler, el avance**
understudy *(theater/theatre)* **el suplente**
understudy *(movies/cinema)* **el doble**
usherette **la acomodadora**
walk-on part **el papel de figurante**
I zoom **capto, doy un golpe de zoom**

Sci-fi films were popular in the sixties.

Las películas de ciencia-ficción eran populares en los años sesenta.

I want to see the latest production of her three-act play. All the critics will be there.

Quiero ver la última producción de su obra de teatro en tres actos. Toda la crítica acudirá.

He is playing one of the most demanding roles of his career.

Está jugando uno de los papeles más difíciles de su carrera.

➤ APPRECIATION & CRITICISM App. 17a

The Media

18a General Terms

admission **la admisión**
I admit **admito**
I analyze **analizo**
analysis **el análisis**
I appeal to **apelo a, recurro a**
I argue **discuto**
argument **el argumento**
attitude **la actitud**
biased **parcial**
campaign **la campaña**
censorship **la censura**
cogent **lógico, convincente, fuerte**
comment **el comentario**
conspiracy **la conspiración**
criticism **la crítica**
critique **la crítica**
cultural **cultural**
culture **la cultura**
cultured **culto**
current events **los sucesos de actualidad**
declaration **la declaración**
it declares **declara**

detailed **detallado**
it discriminates **discrimina**
disaster **el desastre**
disinformation **la desinformación**
educational **educativo**
I entertain **divierto, entretengo**
ethical **ético**
event **el suceso, el acontecimiento**
example **el ejemplo**
expectations **las expectativas**
I exploit **exploto**
fallacious **engañoso, falaz**
fallacy **la falacia, el engaño**
freedom **la libertad**
full / detailed **detallado, extenso**
gullible **crédulo, simplón**
hidden **escondido, oculto**
homophobic **homofóbico**
ignorance **la ignorancia**
I ignore **ignoro, desconozco**
influential **influyente, prestigioso**
information **la información**
informative **informativo**

| During the recent elections it was difficult to find an example of unbiased reporting. | **Durante las elecciones recientes fue difícil encontrar un ejemplo de información objetiva en los medios de comunicación.** |

interview **la entrevista**
it intrudes **se entromete, obstruye**
intrusion **la intrusión, la intromisión**
intrusive **intruso**
issue *(problem)* **el problema, el asunto, la cuestión**
I keep up with *(news)* **estoy al día con**
libel **la difamación, la calumnia**
libellous **difamante, calumnioso**
likely **probable**
it is likely **es probable**
local interest news **las noticias de interés local**
(mass) media **los medios (masa) de comunicación**
material **el material**
meddling **entrometido**
news **las noticias**
news item **la noticia, el asunto**
partisan **partidario**
persuasive **persuasivo**
prejudice **el prejuicio**
political **político**
politics **la política**
press **la prensa**
privacy **la intimidad, la privacidad**
privacy law **la legislación para la protección de la intimidad**

problem **el problema**
review **el análisis de las noticias**
I review **analizo**
scoop **la exclusiva, la primicia informativa**
sensational **sensacional**
sensationalism **el sensacionalismo**
sexism **el sexismo**
sexist **sexista**
silence **el silencio**
silent **silencioso**
social **social**
society **la sociedad**
specious **especioso**
summary **el sumario**
summary *(adj)* **sumario**
it takes place **tiene lugar**
trust **la confianza**
I trust **confío**
trustworthy **fiable**
truth **la verdad**
truthful **verdadero**
unbiased **objetivo**
untrustworthy **no fiable**
up-to-date **actualizado**
violent **violento, agresivo**
violence **la violencia**
weekly **semanal**

I am a freelance journalist specializing in investigative journalism.

Soy periodista independiente, especializado en periodismo investigativo.

In recent years many war correspondents have lost their lives while reporting from the front or have been taken as hostages.

En años recientes, muchos corresponsales de guerra han perdido la vida informando desde el frente o han sido hecho [tomados como] rehenes.

▶ ADVERTISING 18d

THE MEDIA

advice column / problem page **el consultorio**

advice for the lovelorn / agony aunt **el columnista del consultorio sentimental**

article **el artículo**

back page **la última página**

barons **los magnates de la prensa**

broadsheet **el periódico sábana / de gran formato**

cartoon **el tebeo, la caricatura**

chief editor **el jefe de edición**

circulation **la circulación**

color / colour supplement **el suplemento en color**

column **la columna**

comic **el cómic, el tebeo**

correction **la corrección**

correspondent **el corresponsal**

foreign correspondent **el corresponsal extranjero**

crossword puzzle **el crucigrama**

daily newspaper **el diario**

I edit **edito, redacto**

edition **la edición, la tirada**

editor **el editor, el redactor, el director**

editorial **editorial**

forgotten **olvidado**

front page **la primera página, la portada**

glossy magazine **la revista de lujo**

gutter press **la prensa basura, la prensa amarilla, la prensa sensacionalista**

headline **el titular**

heading **el título, el encabezamiento**

illustration **la ilustración**

it is published **está publicado**

journalist **el periodista**

layout **la distribución, la diagramación**

leader **el editorial, el artículo de fondo**

local paper **el periódico local**

magazine **la revista**

monthly **la revista mensual**

national newspaper **el periódico nacional**

newsagent **la tienda de prensa**

newspaper **el periódico**

newsstand **el kiosco de prensa, el quiosco de prensa**

page **la página**

pamphlet **el panfleto**

periodical **la revista / la publicación periódica**

power **el poder**

powerful **poderoso**

press agency **la agencia de prensa**

press conference **la conferencia de prensa**

European current affairs are not always reported in the American press, though all quality papers have foreign correspondents in all the European capitals.

Las noticias de actualidad europea no siempre aparecen en la prensa americana, a pesar de que todos los periódicos de calidad tienen corresponsales en todas las capitales europeas.

The gutter press has a surprisingly high readership.

La prensa sensacionalista tiene una sorpendente cantidad de lectores.

I print **imprimo**
print **la impresión**
print room **la sala de impresión**
I publish **publico**
publisher **el dueño de la casa editorial**
publishing company **la casa editora, la editorial**
quality press **la prensa de calidad**
reader **el lector**
I report **informo**
report **el reportaje**
reporter **el reportero**

short news item **las noticias breves, las breves**
small ad **los anuncios por palabras**
special correspondent **el corresponsal especial**
special issue **la edición especial**
sports page **la página de deportes**
I subscribe to **me suscribo a**
subscription **la suscripción**
tabloid **la prensa sensacionalista**
type(face) **el tipo de letra, el formato de la letra**
weekly **el semanario**

Newspaper sections

Advice column / Problem page **consultorio**
Announcements **anuncios**
Arts **arte**
Economy **economía**
Editorial **artículo de fondo**
Entertainment **ocio**
Finance **finanzas**
Food and Drink **gastronomía**
Games **pasatiempos**
Gossip column **la columna rosa**
Horoscope **horóscopo**

International news **noticias internacionales**
Letters to the editor **cartas al director**
National / Home news **noticias nacionales**
Obituary **necrológicas, obituario**
Property **propiedad, inmobiliaria**
Sport **deportes**
Travel **viajes**
Women **mujer**

Media barons have dominated the press in many western countries.

Los magnates de la prensa han dominado la prensa en muchos paises occidentales.

When is the color / colour supplement published?

¿Cuándo se publica el suplemento en color?

What a scoop! I guess the circulation of the paper has increased significantly in the last two weeks.

¡Qué primicia! Supongo que la circulación del periódico ha subido mucho en las dos últimas semanas.

▶ PUBLISHING App. 17c

THE MEDIA

aerial **la antena**
anchorman **el presentador**
anchorwoman **la presentadora**
announcer **el presentador, el locutor**
audience **el público, la audiencia**
boob tube / goggle box **la caja boba, la caja tonta**
I broadcast **emito**
broadcasting station **la emisora**
cable TV **la televisión por cable**
cameraman **el cámara, el camarógrafo**
channel **el canal**
commercial **el anuncio de televisión**
couch potato **el haragán del sofá**
dubbed **doblado**
earphones **los auriculares, [los audífonos]**
episode **el episodio**
high frequency **la alta frecuencia**
interactive **interactivo**
listener **el oyente**
live broadcast **la emisión en directo**

live coverage / commentary **el reportaje en directo**
loudspeaker **el altavoz**
low frequency **la baja frecuencia**
microphone **el micrófono**
newsreader **el locutor**
personal stereo **el walkman®**
production studio **el estudio de producción**
program(me) **el programa**
radio **la radio**
on radio **en la radio**
I record **grabo**
recording **la grabación**
remote control **el mando a distancia, el control remoto**
I repeat **repito**
repeat **repetir**
satellite dish **la antena parabólica**
satellite TV **la televisión por satélite**
screen **la pantalla**
I show **presento, muestro**
signal **la señal**

"What! Still glued to the set? You have been watching the box all evening! You have become a real couch potato!"

— ¡Que! ¿Todavía pegado a la televisión? Has estado viendo la caja boba toda la tarde. Te has convertido en un verdadero haragán de la televisión.

"I'm just going to record this movie / film then I'll join you. Have you got any blank videocassettes?"

— Voy a grabar esta película y entonces voy contigo. ¿Tienes alguna cinta de video en blanco?

Until recently most television commercials portrayed women in exclusively traditional roles.

Hasta hace muy poco tiempo, en los anuncios de televisión las mujeres aparecían exclusivamente en papeles tradicionales.

station **la estación**
subtitles **los subtítulos**
I switch off **apago**
I switch on **enciendo**
teletext **el teletexto**
television **la televisión**
 on television **en televisión**
I transmit **retransmito**
TV / telly **la tele**
TV set **el aparato de televisión**

TV studio **el estudio de televisión**
video clip **el videoclip**
videogame **el videojuego**
video library **la videoteca**
video recorder **el aparato de vídeo**
viewer **el teleespectador, el televidente**
I watch **veo**

TV & radio program(me)s

cartoons **los dibujos animados**
children's program(me) **el programa infantil**
comedy **la comedia**
current affairs **la actualidad**
drama **el drama**
documentary **el documental**
education programs **los programas educativos**
feature movie / film **el largometraje**
light entertainment **el programa de variedades**

news **las noticias**
quiz program(me)s **los programas concurso**
regional news **las noticias regionales**
soap **la telenovela**
school broadcasting **la emisión escolar**
science program(me) **el programa científico**
sports program(me) **el programa deportivo**
weather forecast **el pronóstico del tiempo**

Was the Pink Floyd concert broadcast live from Venice?

There should be a program / programme on student grants on this channel, but perhaps the children would prefer watching the cartoons. Where is the TV guide?

During the summer the traffic bulletin is broadcast every hour in four languages for the benefit of foreign visitors.

¿El concierto de Pink Floyd se emitió en directo desde Venecia?

Debería haber un programa sobre becas para estudiantes en este canal, pero quizás los niños preferirían ver los dibujos animados. ¿Dónde está el programa [la programación] de la televisión?

Durante el verano el boletín de información del tráfico se emite cada hora en cuatro idiomas como servicio a los visitantes extranjeros.

▶ MOVIE / FILM GENRES App. 17e

THE MEDIA

18d Advertising

I advertise **anuncio**
advertisment **el anuncio**
advertising **la publicidad**
advertising industry **la industria de la publicidad**
appeal **el atractivo**
it appeals to **atrae, tiene atractivo para**
billboard **la cartelera, la valla publicitaria**
brand **la marca**
brochure **el folleto**
campaign **la campaña publicitaria**
catalog(ue) **el catálogo**
it catches the eye **se mete por los ojos**
commercial **el anuncio comercial**
competition *(rival)* **la competencia**
competition *(game)* **el concurso**
consumer **el consumidor**
consumer society **la sociedad de consumo**
copywriter **el escritor de material publicitario**
I covet **codicio, deseo**

it creates a need **crea una necesidad**
demand **la demanda**
disposable income **la renta disponible**
distributor **el distribuidor, el concesionario**
ethical **ético**
goods **los bienes**
hidden persuasion **la persuasión oculta**
image **la imagen**
junk mail **la propaganda de buzón**
I launch **lanzo**
lifestyle **el estilo de vida**
market **el mercado**
  down-market **inferior, la sección popular del mercado**
  up-market **superior, la sección superior del mercado**
market research **el análisis de mercados**
materialism **el materialismo**
model **el modelo**

"Do you think that TV ads are more effective than ads in newspapers?"

"National television reaches many more potential consumers but is extremely expensive."

This image will reach about a million potential consumers.

This has been his least successful campaign: next time we will use another agency or perhaps a freelance copywriter.

— ¿Piensas que los anuncios de la televisión sean más eficaces que los anuncios de los periódicos?
— La televisión nacional llega a muchos más consumidores potenciales, pero es muy cara.

Esta imagen llegará a un millón de consumidores potenciales.

Esta ha sido su campaña de menos éxito; la próxima vez usaremos otra agencia, o quizás un periodista independiente.

I motivate **motivo**
need **la necesidad**
persuasion **la persuasión**
poster **el póster, el afiche**
product **el producto**
I promote **promociono**
promotion **la promoción**
publicity **la publicidad**
I publicize **doy publicidad a,
    anuncio**
public relations **las relaciones
    públicas**
purchasing power **el poder
    adquisitivo**
radio advertisements **los
    anuncios de la radio**
it sells **vende**
slogan **el eslogan, el lema**
status symbol **el símbolo del
    estatus**
stunt **el truco publicitario**
I target **mi objetivo es, me dirijo a**
target group **el grupo objeto**
I tempt **tiento**
trend **la tendencia**
trendy **muy al día**
truthful **verdadero**
TV advertisements **los anuncios
    de televisión**
unethical **no ético**

Small ads

accommodation **el alojamiento**
appointments **citas**
births **natalicios, nacimientos**
courses and conferences
    cursos y conferencias
deaths **necrológicas, obituario**
engagements **compromisos**
exchange **divisa**
exhibitions **exposiciones**

for sale **se vende**
health **salud**
lonely hearts **encuentros**
marriages **bodas**
personal services **servicios
    personales**
property **propiedad inmobiliaria**
travel **viajes**
vacations / holidays **vacaciones**
wanted **se quiere, se requiere**

The buildings are covered in ugly publicity billboards.

Los edificios están cubiertos con vallas publicitarias feas.

This publicity can be offensive to some ethnic groups.

Esta publicidad puede ser ofensiva para algunos grupos étnicos.

SPECIAL OFFER! For one week only! Buy two and get one free! Plus twenty percent discount on your next purchase!

¡OFERTA ESPECIAL! ¡Durante una semana nada más! ¡Compre dos y le regalamos uno! ¡Más veinte por ciento de descuento en su próxima compra!

▶ THE PRESS 18b; TELEVISION & RADIO 18c

Travel

19a General Terms

I accelerate / speed up **acelero**
accident **el accidente**
adult **el adulto**
announcement **el anuncio**
arrival **la llegada**
I arrive (at) **llego (a)**
assistance **la ayuda, la asistencia**
I ask for assistance **pido ayuda**
bag **la bolsa**
baggage **el equipaje**
baggage checkroom / left-luggage
    office **la consigna**
I book **reservo**
booking office **la oficina de
    reservas**
briefcase **el maletín**
business trip **el viaje de negocios**
I buy a ticket **compro un billete**
I call at **paso (por), hago escala
    en**
I cancel **cancelo**
I carry **llevo**
I catch **cojo**
I check (tickets) **confirmo**
child **el niño, la niña**
class **la clase**
I confirm **confirmo**
connection **el transbordo**
I cross **cruzo**
delay **el retraso**
I am delayed **tengo retraso, voy
    con retraso, [estoy retrasado]**
I depart **salgo**
departure **la salida**
destination **el destino**
direct **directo**
direction **la dirección**
disabled **el inválido**

distance **la distancia**
documents **los documentos**
driver (car) **el conductor**
early **temprano, pronto**
emergency **la emergencia, la
    urgencia**
emergency call **la llamada de
    emergencia / urgencia**
emergency stop **la parada de
    emergencia**
en route **en ruta**
entrance **la entrada**
exit **la salida**
extra charge **el recargo, el
    suplemento**
fare **la tarifa**
    fare reduction **la reducción de
    tarifa**
    reduced fare **la tarifa reducida**
fast **rápido, veloz**
I fill out a form **relleno un
    formulario**
free **gratis**
from **de**
information **la información**
information office **la oficina de
    información**
I inquire **pregunto, pido
    información**
inquiry **la pregunta, la consulta**
insurance **el seguro**
help **la ayuda, el socorro**
helpful **útil**
late **tarde**
I leave (place) **salgo**
I leave (person / object) **dejo**
I leave at **salgo a**
lost **perdido**

lost and found / lost property office
la oficina de objetos perdidos
loudspeaker **el altavoz, el altoparlante**
luggage / baggage **el equipaje**
message **el mensaje, el recado, la nota**
I miss **pierdo**
money **el dinero**
nonsmoker **no-fumador**
notice **el aviso**
nuisance **la molestia**
occupied **ocupado**
on board **a bordo**
on time **a tiempo**
one-way / single ticket **el billete de ida**
I pack **hago la maleta**
passenger **el pasajero**
porter **el mozo**
porter *(hotel)* **el portero, el conserje**
perfect timing **el horario perfecto**
reduction **el descuento, la rebaja**
rescue **el rescate**
reservation **la reserva**
I reserve **reservo**
restroom / toilet **el servicio**
I return **vuelvo**
return **la vuelta**
round-trip / return ticket **el billete de ida y vuelta**
safe **seguro**
safety **la seguridad**
seat **el asiento**
seatbelt **el cinturón de seguridad**
I set off **salgo**
signal **la señal**
slow **lento**
I slow down **reduzco la velocidad**
smoking **fumar**
speed **la velocidad**
staff **el personal**
I start from **salgo de**

stop **la parada**
I stop **paro**
on strike **de huelga**
I take *(bus, train)* **cojo**
ticket **el billete**
ticket desk **la ventanilla de billetes, el despacho de billetes, la taquilla**
ticket office **la oficina de billetes, la taquilla**
timetable **el horario**
I travel **viajo**
travel **el viaje**
travel agent **el agente de viajes**
travel agency **la agencia de viajes**
travel documents **los documentos**
travel information **la información de viajes**
travel pass **el pase de viaje, el pasaporte**
travel sickness *(car)* **el mareo**
traveler **el viajero, el pasajero**
tunnel **el túnel**
turn **el giro, la vuelta**
I turn **giro**
I unpack **deshago la maleta**
useless **inútil**
valid **válido**
via / through **a través, pasa por**
visitor **el visitante**
warning **el aviso**
way in **la entrada**
way out **la salida**
weekdays **los días de la semana**
weekend **el fin de semana**
Welcome! **¡Bienvenido!**
welcoming **acogedor**
window **la ventana**
window seat **el asiento al lado de la ventana**

19b Going Abroad & Travel by Boat

Going abroad

I cross (the English Channel) **atravieso / cruzo (el canal de la Mancha)**

currency **la moneda**

currency exchange office **la oficina de cambio de moneda**

customs **la aduana**

customs control **el control de aduanas**

customs officer **el oficial de aduana**

customs regulations **la legislación / el reglamento de aduanas**

declaration **la declaración**

I declare **declaro**

duty **el derecho, el impuesto**

duty-free goods **los productos libres de impuestos**

duty-free shop **la tienda de productos libres de impuestos**

English Channel **la Mancha** Channel Tunnel **el túnel de la Mancha**

exchange rate **la tasa de cambio**

expired **caducado, vencido**

foreign currency **la moneda extranjera**

frontier **la frontera**

I go through customs **paso la aduana**

I go through passport control **paso el control de pasaportes**

immigration office **la oficina de inmigración**

immigration rule **el reglamento de inmigración**

passport **el pasaporte**

I pay duty on **pago el impuesto de**

smuggler **el contrabandista**

smuggling **el contrabando**

visa **la visa**

Travel by boat

boat **el barco**

bridge **el puente**

cabin **el camarote**

calm sea **el mar calmado, el mar en calma**

"Here are my documents. My final destination is Santiago."
"Thank you. Have a nice trip!"

— **Aquí están mis documentos. Mi destino final es Santiago.**
— **Gracias. Buen viaje.**

"I have nothing to declare. This is for my personal use."

— **No tengo nada que declarar. Esto es para mi uso personal.**

"What! All forty bottles of whisky and one hundred cartons of cigarettes?"

— **¡Qué! ¿Cuarenta botellas de whisky y cien cajas de cigarillos?**

For your comfort and safety, please fasten your seatbelts.

Por su comodidad y seguridad, por favor, abróchense los cinturones de seguridad.

captain **el capitán, el comandante**

coast **la costa**

crew **la tripulación**

crossing **la travesía**

cruise **el crucero**

deck **la cubierta**

  lower deck **la cubierta inferior**

  upper deck **la cubierta superior**

deck chair **la butaca de cubierta**

I disembark **desembarco**

disembarkation **el desembarco**

dock **el muelle**

I embark **embarco**

embarkation card **la tarjeta de embarque**

ferry **el ferry**

I go on board **entro a bordo**

harbor / harbour **el puerto**

lifeboat **el bote de salvamento**

lifejacket **el chaleco salvavidas**

lounge **la sala**

ocean **el océano**

offshore **el mar abierto, la alta mar**

on board **a bordo**

overboard **por la borda**

port **(a) babor**

port (of call) **el puerto (de escala)**

quay **el muelle**

reclining seat **el asiento reclinable**

sea **el mar**

  calm sea **el mar en calma**

  choppy sea **el mar picado / agitado**

  heavy sea **el mar grueso**

  stormy sea **el mar borrascoso**

seaman **el marino, el marinero**

seasickness **el mareo**

ship **el buque**

shipping forecast **el pronóstico del mar**

shipyard **el astillero**

smooth **en calma**

starboard **(a) estribor**

storm **la tormenta**

tide **la marea**

waves **las olas**

wind **el viento**

windy **ventoso**

yachting **la navegación en yate, el deporte de la vela**

From which quay does the ship leave?

¿De qué muelle sale el barco?

"Do you have any remedy against seasickness?

—¿Tiene algo para el mareo?

"Yes, I have some pills in my cabin. Meet me on C deck in ten minutes."

—Sí, tengo pastillas en mi camarote. Lo veo en la cubierta C dentro de diez minutos.

"Thanks, but I don't think I'll survive that long."

—Gracias, pero no creo que sobreviva tanto tiempo.

Is passport control carried out on board?

¿Se controlan los pasaportes a bordo?
[¿El control de pasaportes se lleva a cabo a bordo?]

19c Travel by Road

access   **el acceso**
I allow   **permito**
automatic   **automático**
I back up / reverse   **doy marcha atrás**
bicycle / bike   **la bicicleta**
black ice   **el hielo invisible en la carretera**
bottleneck   **el embotellamiento**
breathalyzer   **el respirador para la prueba de alcoholemia, el alcoholímetro**
breathalyzing test   **la prueba de alcoholemia**
breakdown   **la avería**
breakdown service   **el servicio de avería**
I breakdown   **tengo avería**
broken   **roto**
bus   **el autobús, [la guagua]**
bus fare   **la tarifa del autobús**
bus stop   **la parada del autobús**
car   **el coche, [el carro]**
car parts   **las piezas del coche**
car rental / hire   **el alquiler de coches**
car wash   **el lavado de coches, el autolavado**
caution   **la prudencia**
caution (legal)   **la amonestación**
I change gear   **cambio de marcha**
chauffeur   **el chófer**
check   **el control**
I collide   **me estrello, choco**
collision   **la colisión, el choque**
company car   **el coche / [el carro] de la empresa**
competent   **competente**
conductor (bus)   **el cobrador**
I cross   **cruzo, atravieso**
dangerous   **peligroso**
detour / diversion   **la desviación**
diesel   **el diesel**

I do thirty miles per hour   **voy a treinta millas por hora**
I drive   **conduzco**
drive / driving   **la conducción**
driver   **el conductor**
driver's license / driving licence   **el carné / carnet de conducir**
driving instructor   **el profesor de conducir**
driving lesson   **la lección de conducir**
driving school   **la autoescuela, [la escuela de conducción]**
driving test   **el examen de conducir**
drunken driving   **la conducción bajo los efectos del alcohol**
engine trouble   **el problema del motor**
I fasten (seatbelt)   **me ajusto**
I fill up   **lleno**
filling station   **la gasolinera, la estación de servicio / de gas, [la bomba]**
fine   **la multa**
I fix / repair   **arreglo**
flat / puncture   **el pinchazo**
forbidden   **prohibido**
for rent / hire   **en / para alquiler**
garage   **el garaje**
gear   **la marcha**
  in gear   **en marcha**
  in first gear   **en primera (marcha)**
  in neutral   **en punto muerto, [en neutro]**
  in reverse   **en marcha atrás, en reversa**
I get in the car   **me monto en el coche, subo al coche**
I get in lane   **me meto en el carril**
I get out   **salgo**

highway **la carretera**
highway police **la policía de carreteras**
I hitchhike **hago autoestop**
hitchhiker **el autoestopista**
hitchhiking **el autoestop**
I honk / sound the horn **toco la bocina, [pito]**
I am insured **estoy asegurado**
insurance **el seguro**
insurance policy **la póliza del seguro**
jack **el gato**
it is jammed **está bloqueado**
I keep my distance **guardo mi distancia**
key ring **el llavero**
keys **las llaves**
kilometer **el kilómetro**
line of cars **la fila de coches**
logbook **los documentos del coche**
make of car **la marca de coches**
mechanics **la mecánica**
mechanical **mecánico**
motel **el motel**
motor caravan **la caravana**
auto show **la exposición de coches / de automóviles**
one-way only **la dirección única, [una sola vía]**
I overtake / pass **adelanto, doblo**
overtaking / passing **el adelantamiento, el paso**
I park **aparco, estaciono, [parqueo]**
parking **el aparcamiento**
parking ban **la prohibición de aparcar**
parking lot / car park **el aparcamiento de coches, el estacionamiento, el párking, [el parqueadero]**
multistoried / multistorey **de muchos pisos**

parking meter **el contador de aparcamiento / [parqueadero]**
parking ticket **el ticket / la multa de aparcamiento / estacionamiento**
I pass **paso**
passenger **el pasajero**
pedestrian **el peatón**
gasoline / petrol **la gasolina**
leaded **con plomo**
regular / two-star **normal**
super / four star **súper**
unleaded / lead-free **sin plomo**
picnic area **la zona de picnic**
police **la policía**
policeman **el policía**
policewoman **la mujer policía**
police station **la comisaría / [estación] de policía**
position **la posición**
private car **el coche particular**
public transportation **el transporte público**
ramp **la rampa**
registration papers **los papeles de inscripción**
I rent / hire **alquilo**
rental / hired car **el coche alquilado**
rental charge **el precio de alquiler**
repair **la reparación**
I repair **reparo**
I reverse **doy marcha atrás, doy reversa**
(in) reverse **(en) marcha atrás, (en) reversa**
right of way **la preferencia**
road **la carretera**
road accident **el accidente de carretera**
road block **el bloqueamiento de la carretera**
road hog **el loco del volante**
road map **el mapa de carreteras**
road sign **la señal de tráfico**
road works **las obras de la carretera**

route **la ruta**
I run over **atropello**
rush hour **la hora de punta, [la hora pico]**
safety / traffic-free zone **la zona libre de tráfico, la zona peatonal**
seatbelt **el cinturón de seguridad**
self-service **el autoservicio**
service **el servicio**
service area **el área de servicio**
I set off **salgo**
signal **la señal**
signpost **el poste de señales, el poste indicador**
slippery **resbaladizo**
slow **lento**
I slow down **reduzco la velocidad**
speed **la velocidad**
I speed up **acelero**
speed limit **el límite de velocidad**
I start *(engine)* **enciendo**
student / learner driver **el conductor novato**
I switch off / on **apago / enciendo**
taxi / cab **el taxi**
taxi / cab driver **el taxista**
taxi stand / rank **la parada de taxis**
I test **compruebo**
toll **el peaje**

I tow away **quito remolcando, retiro a remolque**
city plan **el plano de la ciudad**
city traffic **el tráfico urbano**
traffic **el tráfico, la circulación**
traffic code **el código de la circulación**
traffic jam **el atasco de tráfico, [el trancón]**
traffic light **el semáforo**
traffic news **el informe del tráfico**
traffic police **la policía de tráfico**
traffic violation / offence **el incumplimiento de las normas de tráfico**
trailer / caravan **la caravana**
trailer truck / lorry **el camión articulado / a remolque**
trip **el viaje**
truck / lorry **el camión [el carro]**
truck / lorry driver **el conductor de camiones, el camionero**
I turn left **giro a la izquierda**
I turn right **giro a la derecha**
I turn off at **giro a**
I turn off *(engine)* **apago**
underground **subterráneo**
used / second-hand car **el coche de segunda mano**
U-turn **el giro en U**

I have a flat / punctured tire, and the lights are not working. Could you also have a look at the clutch?

Tengo una rueda pinchada y las luces no funcionan. ¿Puede echarle un vistazo al embrague también?

Fill it up with unleaded, please.

Lleno. Gasolina sin plomo, por favor.

I had to stop on the road shoulder. Thankfully, emergency phones are found on all highways / expressways.

Tuve que parar en el arcén de la autopista. Afortunadamente, hay teléfonos de emergencia en todas las autopistas.

This new model has very low gas / petrol consumption. It also has excellent handling around corners.

Este nuevo modelo consume muy poca gasolina. También se maneja muy bien en las curvas.

vehicle **el vehículo**
vehicle inspection / MOT **la ITV**
(**Inspección Técnica de Vehículos**)
I wait **espero**
warning **el aviso**
witness **el testigo**
I yield / give way **doy paso**

Roads

access / slip road **el carril de acceso**
alley **el callejón**
avenue **la avenida**
beltway / ring road **la carretera de circunvalación**
bridge **el puente**
built–up area **la zona edificada, la zona urbanizada**
bump **el badén, el bache**
bypass **la carretera de circunvalación**
closed (*road*) **cerrada**
corner **la esquina**
crossing **el cruce**
crossroad **el cruce de carreteras**
cul-de-sac **la calle sin salida**
curve / bend **la curva**
highway / expressway **la autopista**
entry **la entrada, el acceso**

exit **la salida**
junction **el cruce**
inside lane **el carril interior**
intersection **el cruce, la intersección**
junction **el cruce**
lane **el carril**
level crossing **el paso a nivel**
main street **la calle principal**
median divider / central reservation **la mediana**
one-way street **la calle de dirección única**
outside lane **el carril exterior**
pedestrian crossing **el cruce de peatones**
pedestrian island **la isleta de peatones**
road **la carretera**
road / hard shoulder **el arcén**
roundabout **la rotonda**
side road / lay-by **el apartadero**
side street **la calle lateral**
sidewalk / pavement **el pavimento**
square **la plaza**
street **la calle**
underground passage **el pasaje subterráneo**
white / yellow line **la raya blanca / amarilla**

Because of black ice on the roads, there is a risk of collision: so keep your distance.

There has been a serious accident on highway / expressway A1 between junction 7 and 8. A truck traveling towards Madrid has crashed against the divider. Three vehicles are involved, and one of the drivers is seriously injured. I have put on the hazard lights. Send an ambulance immediately.

Debido al hielo invisible en la carretera, hay riesgo de choque: así que guarda la distancia.

Ha habido un accidente grave en la autopista A1 entre los cruces 7 (siete) y 8 (ocho). Un camión viajando a Madrid ha chocado contra la barrera central. Tres vehículos han sufrido y uno de los conductores está gravemente herido. He encendido la luz de emergencia. Mande una ambulancia inmediatamente.

TRAVEL

aircraft **la nave aérea**
airplane / aeroplane **el avión**
airline **la aerolínea**
airline counter **la ventana de la línea aérea**
air travel **el viaje de avión**
airport **el aeropuerto**
I am airsick **estoy mareado**
baggage **el equipaje**
body search **el registro personal, la requisa**
I board a plane **subo a bordo de un avión**
boarding card **la tarjeta de embarque**
business class **la clase de ejecutivo**
by air **por avión**
cabin **la cabina**
canceled flight **el vuelo cancelado**
carousel **la cinta de equipaje**
charter flight **el vuelo chárter**
I check in **facturo**
check-in operations **las operaciones de facturación**

control tower **la torre de control**
copilot **el copiloto**
crew **la tripulación**
desk **la ventana**
direct flight **el vuelo directo**
domestic flight **el vuelo interior / interno**
during landing **durante el aterrizaje**
during takeoff **durante el despegue**
during the flight **durante el vuelo**
duty-free goods **los productos libres de impuestos**
economy class **la clase económica**
emergency exit **la salida de emergencia**
emergency landing **el aterrizaje de emergencia**
excess baggage **el exceso de equipaje**
I fasten **ajusto**
flight **el vuelo**

Can I make a connection to Zaragoza? Do I have to change flights?

¿Puedo hacer un transbordo para Zaragoza? ¿Tengo que cambiar el vuelo?

"I have some excess luggage."
"Have you packed your luggage yourself?"

—Tengo exceso de equipaje.
—¿Ha hecho su equipaje usted mismo?

There is some turbulence in the Andes.
The expected landing time is now 11:40, local time.

Hay algunas turbulencias en los Andes.
La hora de aterrizaje está prevista para las 11.40, hora local.

flight attendant **el asistente de vuelo**
I fly **vuelo**
I fly at a height of **vuelo a una altura de**
flying **la aviación**
fuselage **el fuselaje**
gate **la puerta**
instructions **las instrucciones**
hand luggage **el equipaje de mano**
headphones **los auriculares**
highjacker **el secuestrador (aéreo)**
immigrant **el inmigrante**
immigration **la inmigración**
immigration rules **las normas de inmigración**
I land **aterrizo**
landing **el aterrizaje**
landing lights **las luces de aterrizaje**
lifejacket **el chaleco de salvavidas**
no-smoking sign **la señal de no fumar**
nonstop **sin parada**

on board **a bordo**
parachute **el paracaídas**
passenger **el pasajero**
passengers' lounge **la sala de pasajeros**
passport control **el control de pasaportes**
pilot **el piloto**
plane **el avión**
refreshments **los refrescos**
runway **la pista de aterrizaje**
security measures **las medidas de seguridad**
security staff **el personal de seguridad**
steward **el auxiliar de vuelo**
stewardess / air hostess **la azafata**
I take off **despego**
take-off **el despegue**
terminal **el terminal**
tray **la bandeja**
turbulence **la turbulencia**
view **la vista, el panorama**
window **la ventana, la ventanilla**
window seat **el asiento junto a la ventana**

"Will Mr. / Ms. Bosé traveling on flight IB 131 to Alicante please contact the information desk immediately."
"Where do I check in for flight IB 131?"

This is the last call for passengers traveling on flght IB 881 to Buenos Aires.

How long is the delay?

My luggage has not yet been unloaded.

What is the flight number?

—**El señor / la señora Bosé viajando en el vuelo IB 131 para Alicante, por favor preséntense en el mostrador de información.**
—**¿Dónde facturo para el vuelo IB 131?**

Última llamada para los pasajeros del vuelo IB 881 para Buenos Aires.

¿Cuánto dura el retraso?

Mi equipaje no ha sido descargado todavía.

¿Cuál es el número del vuelo?

TRAVEL

announcement   **el anuncio**
barrier   **la barrera**
buffet   **el menú**
club / buffet car   **el vagón-cafetería, el coche-comedor**
coach   **el vagón**
compartment   **el compartimiento**
connection   **la conexión, el transbordo**
dining car   **el vagón restaurante**
exemption   **la exención**
fare   **la tarifa**
inspector   **el inspector, el revisor**
I lean out   **me asomo**
level crossing   **el paso a nivel**
luggage rack   **la reja de equipaje, la baca**
menu / buffet   **el menú**
I miss   **pierdo**
nonrefundable   **sin devolución**

(non)smoking car   **el compartimiento de (no) fumadores**
occupied   **ocupado**
on time   **a tiempo**
platform   **el andén, [la plataforma]**
porter   **el portero**
I punch (ticket)   **perforo**
railroad / railway   **la red ferroviaria**
elevated railway   **el ferrocarril elevado**
ramp   **la rampa**
reduction   **el descuento**
reservation   **la reserva**
reserved   **reservado**
sleeper   **el coche cama**
smokers   **fumadores**
speed   **la velocidad**
stairs   **las escaleras**
stationmaster   **el jefe de estación**
stop   **la parada**

A special announcement:
On Sundays and holidays
the service to Valencia does not
operate, and on weekdays after nine
in the morning fares are subject to
supplementary charges.
In addition, reservations are
required for seats in the
nonsmoking cars on the
Gijón service. We apologize for
any inconvenience.

Un anuncio especial:
Los domingos y festivos no sale
el servicio para Valencia y en
los días laborales después de
las nueve de la mañana las
tarifas están sujetas a cargos
suplementarios. Además, se
necesitan reservas para los
compartimientos para
no fumadores en el servicio para
Gijón. Pedimos disculpas por
los inconvenientes.

The 11:45 to Lima is now leaving
from platform 10.

El tren de las 11.45 (las doce
menos cuarto) para Lima
sale del andén 10.

The subway / underground is closed
until seven in the morning.

El metro está cerrado hasta las
siete de la mañana.

subway / underground   **el metro**
supplement   **el suplemento**
taxi stand / rank   **la parada de taxis**
ticket   **el billete, [el tiquete, el boleto]**
   first class   **de primera clase**
   group   **de grupo**
   one-way / single   **de ida**
   round-trip / return   **de ida y vuelta**
   second class   **de segunda clase**
ticket collector   **el revisor de billetes, [el controlador de boletos]**
ticket office   **la oficina / el despacho de billetes, la taquilla**
timetable   **el horario**
   summer timetable   **el horario de verano**
   winter timetable   **el horario de invierno**

timetable changes   **los cambios de horario**
track   **la vía**
traveler   **el viajero**
train   **el tren**
   direct train   **el tren directo**
   express train   **el tren expreso, el rápido**
   Intercity train   **el tren interurbano / de largo recorrido**
   local train   **el tren local**
   night train   **el tren nocturno**
train / rail station   **la estación de tren**
train / rail tracks   **el raíl, la vía, la carrilera**
trolley   **el tranvía**
user   **el usuario**
I wait   **espero**
waiting room   **la sala de espera**
warning   **el aviso**
window   **la ventana**

Where do I have to change?

¿Dónde tengo que cambiar?

When is the first train?

¿Cuándo es el primer tren?

Excuse me, this a nonsmoking compartment.

—Perdone, éste es un compartimiento para no fumadores.

Is this the Intercity to Barcelona?

¿Es este el servicio de largo recorrido para Barcelona?

There are no facilities for disabled travelers on this train.

No hay servicios para pasajeros inválidos en este tren.

This is a public announcement for all passengers travelling to Seville. We are sorry to announce that this service is subject to delays. There will also be a platform change.

Anuncio para los pasajeros viajando a Sevilla. Sentimos anunciar que este servicio tiene retraso. También se hará un cambio de andén [plataforma].

Vacation / Holidays

20a General Terms

abroad **el extranjero**
accommodation **la vivienda, la estancia, el alojamiento**
alone **solo**
area **el área, la zona**
arrival **la llegada**
available **disponible**
beach **la playa**
camera **la cámara**
city map / town plan **el mapa de la ciudad**
clean **limpio**
climate **el clima**
closed **cerrado**
clothes **la ropa**
cold **frío**
comfort **el confort, la comodidad**
comfortable **confortable, cómodo**
congested **congestionado, lleno**
cost **el costo, el precio**
country **el país**
countryside **el campo**
dirty **sucio**
disadvantage **la desventaja**
disorganized **desorganizado**
exchange **el cambio**
fire **el fuego**
folding chair **la silla plegable**
folding table **la mesa plegable**
food **la comida**
free **gratis**
full / full-up **lleno, completo**
I go **voy**
group **el grupo**
group travel **el viaje en grupo**
guide **el guía**
guidebook **la guía**
guided tour **el viaje con guía**
guided walk **la visita con guía**
land **el país, la tierra**

landscape **el paisaje**
journey **el viaje**
knapsack / rucksack **la mochila**
mild *(climate)* **templado**
money **el dinero**
open **abierto**
organization **la organización**
I organize **organizo**
organized **organizado**
plan *(town)* **el plano**
I plan **planeo**
portable **portátil**
I return *(to a place)* **vuelvo**
sea **el mar**
seascape **el paisaje marino**
seaside resort **punto de veraneo en la playa, el lugar de veraneo**
show **el espectáculo**
I show **muestro, demuestro, exhibo**
sight **la vista**
I spend time **paso tiempo**
stay **la estancia**
I stay **estoy en**
sun **el sol**
sunny **soleado**
I sunbathe **tomo el sol**
I tan / get brown **me bronceo**
tour **la gira, el viaje, la excursión**
tourism **el turismo**
tourist **el turista**
tourist menu **el menú turístico**
tourist office **la oficina de turismo**
town **la ciudad, el pueblo**
travel **el viaje**
I travel **viajo**
travel adaptor **el adaptador de viaje**
trip **el viaje**
I understand **entiendo**

I unpack **deshago la maleta**
vacation / holiday **las vacaciones**
visit **la visita**
I visit **visito**
visiting hours **las horas de visita**
visitors **los visitantes**
welcome **la bienvenida**
worth seeing **visita recomendada**

Holiday activities

beach vacation / holiday
vacaciones en la playa
boating vacation / holiday **las vacaciones en barco**
bus trip **las vacaciones en autobús**
camping **el camping**
canoeing **el viaje en canoa**
car trip / motoring holiday **las vacaciones en coche / [carro]**
cruise **el crucero**
cycling **el ciclismo**

fishing **la pesca**
fruit picking **la recolección de fruta**
home exchange **el intercambio de casas**
hunting **la caza**
mountain climbing **el montañismo, la escalada de una montaña**
rock climbing **la escalada en rocas**
sailing **la navegación**
shopping **las compras**
sightseeing **el excursionismo**
skiing **el esquí**
study vacation / holiday **las vacaciones de estudio**
sunbathing **el baño de sol**
volunteer work **el trabajo voluntario**
walking **caminar, andar**
wine tasting **la cata de vinos**

Dear all at work,

Having a wonderful vacation. The weather is hot (I have a great tan), the campsite is clean, and the local food is excellent.

The kids are having a great time too, enjoying the water sports, building sandcastles, and making lots of friends.

I'm not looking forward to coming home!
Best wishes, María.

Mis queridos colegas

Me estoy divirtiendo en estas vacaciones. Hace calor (estoy muy bronceada), el camping está limpio, y la comida regional es excelente.

Los chicos están pasándolo bien también, disfrutando de las actividades acuáticas, haciendo castillos de arena, y haciendo muchos amigos.

¡ No tengo ganas de volver!

Un afectuoso saludo de María.

➤ TRAVEL 19; HOBBIES 16a; ON THE BEACH App. 20a; WEATHER 24d

20b Accommodations & Hotel

Accommodations

apartment   **el apartamento**
bed and breakfast   **la pensión**
campsite   **el camping, la zona de camping**
efficiency unit / self-catering   **el piso con cocina propia**
farm   **la granja**
full board   **la pensión completa**
half board   **la media pensión**
home exchange   **el intercambio de casas**
hotel   **el hotel**
mobile home   **la caravana**
inn   **la posada, la fonda, el mesón**
trailer / caravan   **la caravana**
villa   **la villa**
youth hostel   **el albergue juvenil**

Booking & payment

affordable   **asequible, razonable**
all-included   **todo incluido**
bill   **la cuenta**
I book / reserve   **reservo**
brochure   **el folleto**
I cash   **hago efectivo, cobro**
cheap   **barato**
check / cheque   **el cheque**
cost   **el costo, el coste**
credit   **el crédito**
credit card   **la tarjeta de crédito**
economical   **económico**
Eurocheque   **el eurocheque**
excluding   **excluido**
exclusive   **exclusivo**

expensive   **caro**
extra charge   **el suplemento, el recargo**
evening meal   **la cena**
fee   **el precio**
I fill in   **relleno, lleno**
form   **el impreso, el formulario**
free   **gratis**
inclusive   **completo, que incluye**
I pay   **pago**
payment   **el pago**
pricelist   **la lista de precios**
receipt   **el recibo**
reduction   **el descuento, la rebaja**
refund   **la devolución, el reembolso**
reservation   **la reserva**
I reserve   **reservo**
sales tax / VAT   **el IVA**
I sign   **firmo**
signature   **la firma**
traveler's check / traveller's cheque   **el cheque de viaje / viajero**

Hotel

adjoining / en-suite bathroom   **el baño adjunto**
air-conditioning   **el aire acondicionado**
amenities   **los servicios**
balcony   **el balcón**
bath   **el baño**
bed   **la cama**
bedding / bed linen   **la ropa de cama**
bedspread   **el cubrecama, el cobertor, la colcha**

I'd like to reserve a double room with a double bed and a bath for three days from March 5th.

Quisiera reservar una habitación doble con baño por tres días desde el cinco de marzo.

We are checking out now. I shall collect the luggage at ten thirty.

Ahora pagamos. Recogeré el equipaje a las diez y media.

Do not disturb.

No molestar.

bed and breakfast **la pensión (desayuno incluido)**
billiard room / pool hall **la sala de billar**
board **la pensión**
 full board **pensión completa**
 half board **media pensión**
breakfast **el desayuno**
broken **roto, estropeado**
business meeting **la reunión de negocios**
call **la llamada**
I check in / out **facturo / me retiro**
coathanger **la percha, el perchero**
comfortable **cómodo, confortable**
I complain **me quejo, reclamo**
complaint **la queja, el reclamo**
conference **la conferencia**
conference facilities **el salón de conferencias**
damage **el daño, el perjuicio**
dining room **el comedor**
early morning call **la llamada por la mañana temprano**
elevator / lift **el ascensor**
facilities **los servicios**
fire exit **la salida de incendios**
fire extinguisher **el extintor de fuego, el extinguidor**
guest **el huésped**
hairdresser **el peluquero**
hairdryer **el secador de pelo**
heating **la calefacción**
hotel **el hotel**
key **la llave**

laundry **la lavandería**
laundry service **el servicio de lavandería**
meal **la comida**
night porter **el portero de noche**
noisy **ruidoso**
nuisance **la molestia**
overnight / weekend bag **el maletín de fin de semana**
pants / trouser press **la prensa de pantalón**
parking space **el espacio para aparcar**
plug **el enchufe**
porter **el portero**
privacy **privacidad, intimidad**
private toilet **el wáter particular, el baño privado**
reception **la recepción**
receptionist **el recepcionista**
room **la habitación**
 double room **la habitación doble**
 family room **la habitación familiar**
 twin-bedded room **la habitación con camas gemelas**
room service **el servicio a la habitación**
shower **la ducha**
showercap **el gorro de ducha**
stay **la estancia**
I stay **estoy en, me alojo en**
view **la vista**
water **el agua**

I'd like to complain. The hot water tap does not work, and the elevator is out of order. There is only one coathanger in the wardrobe, and I asked for a room with a view.

Quiero hacer un reclamo. Ni el grifo de agua caliente ni el ascensor funcionan. Sólo hay una percha en el armario, y había pedido una habitación con vista.

Press the button.

Apriete el botón.

➤ ROOMS 8a; FURNITURE & FURNISHINGS 8c; EATING OUT 10a

VACATION / HOLIDAYS

20c Camping & Self-Service / -Catering

air bed **el colchón inflable**
antihistamine cream **la crema antihistamínica**
ants **las hormigas**
barbecue **la barbacoa**
battery **la pila**
I camp **acampo**
camp bed **la cama de camping**
camper **el campista**
camping **el camping**
camping equipment / gear **el equipo de camping**
camping gas **el camping gas**
campsite **el camping**
can / tin opener **el abrelatas**
connected **conectado**
cooking facilities **la posibilidad de cocinar**
disconnected **desconectado**
drinking water **el agua potable**
extension cord **la extensión**
flashlight / torch **la interna, la antorcha**
forbidden **prohibido**
fun **la diversión**

gas cylinder **la bombona de gas**
gas stove / cooker **la cocina de gas**
ground-sheet **la tela impermeable**
guy rope **el viento de la tienda**
laundromat / launderette **la lavandería**
I make friends **hago amigos**
medicine kit **el botiquín**
mosquito bite **la picadura de mosquito**
mosquito net **la red contra los mosquitos, el mosquitero**
mosquitos **los mosquitos**
pan **la sartén, el cazo, la cacerola, la cazuela**
peg **la estaca**
I pitch / put up my tent **pongo mi tienda de campaña**
registration **la inscripción**
services **los servicios**
sheet **la sábana**
showers / washing facilities **las duchas**
site **el emplazamiento, el sitio**
sleeping bag **el saco de dormir**

"Where shall we put up the tent?" —¿Dónde ponemos la tienda de campaña?

"Away from the main block." —Lejos del bloque principal.
"I'll pitch it in the shade." —La montaré a la sombra.
"No, it is a bit damp there. This is better here, and there are no mosquitos." —No, está un poco húmedo allí. Está mejor aquí, y no hay mosquitos.

"Where's the flashlight / torch? It's not in the tent." —¿Dónde está la linterna? No está en la tienda de campaña.
"It was in the knapsack / rucksack just now." —Justo ahora estaba en la mochila.
"Keep your voice down, please, we are trying to sleep!" —Baja la voz por favor, estamos tratando de dormir.

Do you have a few spare pegs? ¿Tienes algunas estacas que me podrías dejar?

space **el espacio**
I take down (tent) **quito (la tienda de campaña)**
tent **la tienda de campaña**
toilet **el servicio, el baño**
trailer / caravan **la caravana**
trashcan / dustbin **el bote / la caneca de la basura**
uncomfortable **incómodo, poco confortable**
vehicles **los vehículos**
water filter **el filtro de agua**

Self-service / -catering

agency **la agencia**
agreement **el acuerdo**
amenities **las facilidades**
apartment **el apartamento**
I clean **limpio**
I cook **cocino**
damaged **dañado, estropeado**
damages **los daños, los perjuicios**
dangerous **peligroso**

electricity **la electricidad**
equipment **el equipo**
farm **la granja**
maid **la criada**
meter **el contador**
owner **el dueño, el propietario**
rent **el alquiler, la renta**
I rent **alquilo, arriendo**
I rent out **doy en alquiler**
repair **la reparación**
I repair **reparo**
I return (*give back*) **devuelvo**
ruined **en ruinas, estropeado, dañado**
self-service **el autoservicio**
set of keys **el juego de llaves**
I share **comparto**
shutters **las contraventanas**
smelly **oloroso, que huele**
spare keys **las llaves de repuesto**
water supply **el suministro de agua**
well **el pozo**
well-kept **bien guardado**

I'm making a packed lunch. | **Estoy preparando un almuerzo empaquetado.**

The apartment is close to the town center / centre, just a few kilometers / kilometres from the nearest stores / shops and convenient for the swimming pool. | **El apartamento está cerca del centro de la ciudad, a sólo unos kilómetros de las tiendas más cercanas, y cerca de la piscina.**

You will find the electric meter under the stairs. | **El contador de electricidad está debajo de las escaleras.**

There are no blankets, the stove / cooker doesn't work, and there is a frog in the bathroom. | **No hay mantas, no funciona el horno, y hay una rana en el baño.**

Is there no more water? | **¿No queda agua?**
Beware of the dog! | **¡Perro peligroso!**

➤ FURNISHINGS 8b, 8c; COOKING UTENSILS App. 10d

Language

21a General Terms

accuracy   **la exactitud**
accurate   **exacto**
I adapt   **adapto**
I adopt   **adopto**
advanced   **avanzado**
aptitude   **la aptitud**
artificial language   **el lenguaje artificial**
based on   **basado en**
bilingual   **bilingüe**
bilingualism   **el bilingüismo**
borrowing   **el préstamo**
branch   **la rama**
classical languages   **las lenguas clásicas**
it derives from   **se deriva de, viene de**
development   **el desarrollo**
difficult   **la dificultad**
easy   **fácil**
error   **el error**
foreign language   **el idioma extranjero**
I forget   **olvido, me olvido de**
grammar   **la gramática**
grammatical   **gramático**

I improve   **mejoro**
influence   **la influencia**
known   **conocido**
language   **el idioma, la lengua**
language course   **el curso de idiomas**
language family   **la familia de idiomas**
language school   **la escuela de idiomas**
language skills   **las habilidades para los idiomas**
Latin   **el latín**
I learn   **aprendo**
learning   **el aprendizaje**
level   **el nivel**
linguistics   **la lingüística**
link   **el nexo**
living   **vivo**
major languages   **los idiomas principales**
it means   **significa, quiere decir**
I mime   **represento con gestos**
minor languages   **los idiomas secundarios**
mistake   **el error**

Minor languages may disappear; however, thanks to the oral tradition in some communities, some have been preserved.

Los idiomas secundarios podrían desaparecer, sin embargo gracias a la tradición oral en algunas comunidades, algunos se han preservado.

modern languages **las lenguas modernas**
monolingual **monolingüe**
mother tongue **la lengua madre, la lengua materna**
mutation **la mutación, el cambio**
name **el nombre**
nation **la nación**
national **nacional**
native **el nativo**
natural **natural**
official **oficial**
offshoot **el ramal**
origin **el origen**
phenomenon **el fenómeno**
I practice / practise **practico**
preserved **preservado**
question **la pregunta**
register **el registro**
self-assessment **la autoevaluación**
separate **separarado, independiente**
sign language **el lenguaje de señas**
survival **la supervivencia**
it survives **sobrevive**
I teach **enseño**
teacher **el profesor**
teaching **la enseñanza**
test **la prueba, el examen**

I test **evalúo, corrijo un examen, ensayo**
I translate **traduzco**
translation **la traducción**
I understand **entiendo, comprendo**
unknown **desconocido**
widely **ampliamente**
witticism **la agudeza**

Words & vocabulary

antonym **el antónimo**
colloquial **familiar**
consonant **la consonante**
dictionary **el diccionario**
expression **la expresión**
idiom **la expresión idiomática**
idiomatic **idiomático**
jargon **la jerga**
lexicographer **el lexicógrafo**
lexicon **el léxico**
phrase **la frase, la oración**
phrase book **el libro de frases**
sentence **la frase, la oración**
slang **el argot**
syllable **la sílaba**
synonym **el sinónimo**
vocabulary **el vocabulario**
vowel **la vocal**
word **la palabra**
wordplay **el juego de palabras**

I am not very good at languages, but my sister is a gifted linguist.

No soy muy bueno para los idiomas, pero mi hermana es dotada para las lenguas.

She learned French and Italian in school, then she traveled extensively and picked up Bulgarian and Urdu while working as a volunteer.

Aprendió francés e italiano en el colegio, y ha viajado mucho y aprendió un poco de búlgaro y de urdú mientras trabajaba como voluntaria.

➤ MAIN LANGUAGE FAMILIES, LANGUAGES App. 21a

LANGUAGE

Speaking & listening

accent   **el acento**
   regional accent   **el acento regional**
articulate   **elocuente**
I articulate   **articulo**
clear   **claro**
I communicate   **comunico**
conversation   **la conversación**
I converse   **converso, hablo**
dialect   **el dialecto**
diction   **la dicción**
I express myself   **me expreso**
fluent   **la fluidez, la soltura, la facilidad**
fluently   **con fluidez, con soltura, con facilidad**
I interpret   **interpreto**
interpreter   **el intéprete**
intonation   **la entonación**
lisp   **el ceceo**
I lisp   **ceceo**
I listen   **escucho, oigo**
listener   **el oyente**
listening   **la audición**
listening skills   **las habilidades para audición**

I mispronounce   **pronuncio mal**
mispronunciation   **el error de pronunciación**
oral(ly)   **oral(mente), verbal(mente)**
I pronounce   **pronuncio**
pronunciation   **la pronunciación**
rhythm   **el ritmo**
sound   **el sonido**
I sound   **sueno**
I speak   **hablo**
speaker   **el hablante**
speaking   **el habla**
speaking skills   **las habilidades para hablar, las habilidades verbales**
speech   **el discurso**
speed   **la velocidad**
spoken   **hablado**
spoken language   **el lenguaje hablado**
stress   **la entonación**
stressed (un-)   **(in)acentuado**
I stutter / stammer   **tartamudeo, balbuceo**
unpronounceable   **impronunciable**
verbally   **verbalmente**

"I have no difficulty in reading Spanish, but I don't understand it when people speak very fast or with a strong regional accent."

—No tengo dificultad para leer el español, pero no lo entiendo cuando la gente habla muy rápido o con un acento regional fuerte.

"Do you practice Spanish with a native speaker?"
"No, I prefer to attend a class."

—¿Practicas español con un nativo?
—No, prefiero ir a clase.

Don't worry about spelling mistakes for the moment.

No te preocupes por los errores de ortografía de momento.

Writing & reading

accent **el acento**
   acute accent **el acento agudo**
   tilde **la tilde**
alphabet **el alfabeto**
alphabetically **alfabéticamente**
in bold **en negrita, en negrilla**
Braille **el Braille**
character **el carácter**
code **el código**
I correspond (with) **estoy en correspondencia (con)**
correspondence **la correspondencia**
I decipher **descifro**
graphic **gráfico**
handwriting **la escritura a mano, la letra**
ideogram(me) / ideograph **el ideograma**
illiterate **analfabeto**
italic **en bastardilla**
I italicize **pongo en bastardilla**
letter *(alphabet)* **la letra**
literate **alfabetizado, que sabe leer y escribir**
literature **la literatura**
note **la nota**

paragraph **el párrafo**
philology **la filología**
philologist **el filólogo**
pictograph **el pictograma**
I print **imprimo**
I read **leo**
reading **la lectura**
reading skills **las habilidades para la lectura**
I rewrite **escribo de nuevo**
scribble **los garabatos**
I scribble **garrapateo, hago garabatos**
sign **el signo**
I sign **firmo**
signature **la firma**
I spell **deletreo**
spelling **la ortografía**
text **el texto**
I transcribe **transcribo**
transcription **la transcripción**
I underline **subrayo**
I write **escribo**
writing **la escritura**
writing skills **las habilidades para la escritura**
written language **el lenguaje escrito**

Which languages have a Slavic alphabet? — **¿Qué idiomas tienen un alfabeto eslavo?**

Portuguese spoken here. — **Aquí se habla portugués.**

Do you have any previous knowledge of Russian? — **¿Tienes algún conocimiento previo de ruso?**

"Which is the easiest language to learn for an English speaker?" — **—¿Cuál es el idioma más fácil de aprender para un hablante de inglés?**

"Spanish, of course!" — **—¡El español, por supuesto!**

Education

22a General Terms

achievement **el éxito, el logro**
admission **la admisión**
   I am admitted to school **estoy admitido en el colegio**
absent **ausente**
age group **el grupo etario, [el grupo de la misma edad]**
I am away **estoy ausente**
aptitude **la aptitud, la facilidad**
I analyze **analizo, estudio**
answer **la respuesta**
I answer (someone) **respondo, contesto (a alguien)**
   I answer (a question) **respondo (a una pregunta)**
I ask **pregunto**
I attend (a school) **voy (al colegio)**
board of education **la delegación, el consejo local de educación**
boring **aburrido**
career **la carrera, la profesión**
career counseling **el asesoramiento sobre la profesión**
caretaker **el cuidador, el bedel, el vigilante, el conserje**
I catch up **me pongo al día**
chapter **el capítulo**
cheat **el tramposo, el petardista**
class **la clase**
class council **la reunión de delegados de clase**
class representative **el delegado de la clase**
class teacher **el profesor**
class trip **el viaje escolar, el viaje con la clase**
club **el club, el grupo**
I complete **completo**
comprehension **la comprensión**

compulsory schooling **el colegio obligatorio**
computer **el ordenador, [el computador]**
concept **el concepto**
I copy(out) **copio**
copy **la copia**
course **el curso**
deputy head **el subdirector**
detention **la detención**
   I am in detention **estoy castigado**
difficult **difícil**
discuss **la discusión**
easy **fácil**
education **la educación**
educational system **el sistema educativo**
I encourage **aliento, doy ánimo**
essay **la redacción, el ensayo**
example **el ejemplo**
excellent **excelente**
extracurricular / out of school activity **la actividad fuera del colegio**
favorite / favourite **el favorito**
favorite / favourite subject **la asignatura favorita**
I forget **olvido**
governing body **la junta directiva**
holidays **las vacaciones**
homework **la tarea, los deberes**
instruction **la instrucción, la enseñanza**
interesting **interesante**
I learn **aprendo**
I leave **salgo, dejo**
lesson **la lección, la clase**
   lesson *(chapter)* **la lección**
   lessons **las lecciones**

I listen **escucho, oigo**

I look at **miro, considero**

I misunderstand **entiendo mal, no entiendo bien, malinterpreto**

mixed ability group **el grupo de alumnos con capacidades diversas**

modular **modular**

module **el módulo**

occupational career education **la guía vocacional / profesional**

occupational education teacher **el profesor encargado del asesoramiento profesional de los alumnos**

oral **oral**

outdoor **exterior**

parents' evening **la tarde de reunión de los padres**

pastoral care **la tutoría**

I play truant **hago rabona, hago novillos, me ausento**

I praise **alabo**

principal **principal**

principal / headteacher **el director**

project **el proyecto**

punctual **puntual**

I punctuate **escribo los signos de puntuación**

I punish **castigo**

punishment **el castigo**

pupil **el alumno**

qualification **el título, los requisitos**

I qualify **saco un título, lleno los requisitos**

question **la pregunta**

I question **pregunto**

question mark **el signo de interrogación**

I read **leo**

reading **la lectura**

I repeat a year **repito un curso**

report **las notas, el certificado escolar**

research **la investigación**

I research **investigo**

resource center / centre **el centro de servicios escolares / de recursos**

scheme of work **el esquema de trabajo, el plan de trabajo**

school administration **la administración**

school book **el libro escolar**

school council **el consejo escolar**

schoolfriend / pal **el amigo del colegio**

set **el grupo**

school sets **los grupos, las clases**

skill **la habilidad**

specialist teacher **el profesor especializado**

spelling **la ortografía**

staff **el personal**

I stay in **me quedo en casa**

I stay down (year) **repito curso**

strict **estricto**

I study **estudio**

sum **la suma**

I summarize **resumo, sumarizo**

I cram / swot **empollo**

task **el deber, la tarea**

I teach **enseño**

teacher **el profesor, el maestro**

teaching **la enseñanza**

term / semester **el semestre**

I train **preparo, entreno**

training **la preparación**

I translate **traduzco**

translation **la traducción**

tutor **el tutor**

I understand **entiendo, comprendo**

understanding **el entendimiento, la comprensión**

unit (of work) **la unidad de trabajo**

I work **trabajo, estudio**

I work hard **estudio mucho**

work experience **la experiencia laboral**

I write **escribo**

written (work) **escrito**

EDUCATION

athletic field   **el campo de deportes**
blackboard   **la pizarra**
blackout   **el bloqueo**
book   **el libro**
break   **el recreo**
briefcase   **la maleta del colegio, el maletín**
canteen   **el bar del colegio, la cantina del colegio**
cassette (audio / video)   **la cinta**
cassette recorder   **la grabadora**
classroom   **la clase**
computer   **el ordenador, [la computadora]**
desk   **el pupitre**
dormitory   **el dormitorio**
gym(nasium)   **el gimnasio**
headphone   **el auricular, [el audífono]**
interactive TV   **la televisión interactiva**
laboratory   **el laboratorio**
(language) laboratory   **el laboratorio (de idiomas)**
library   **la biblioteca**
lunchtime   **el descanso para comer, la hora de almuerzo**
note   **la nota**
office   **la oficina**
playground   **el patio de juego**
radio   **la radio**
ruler   **la regla**

slide   **la diapositiva**
satellite TV   **la television por satélite**
schoolhall   **la sala**
schoolbag / bookbag / satchel   **la maleta del colegio**
sports center   **el polideportivo**
staffroom   **el cuarto de profesores**
studio   **el estudio**
timetable   **el horario**
video   **el vídeo**
   video (adj)   **de vídeo**
video camera   **la cámara de vídeo**
video cassette   **la cinta de vídeo**
video recorder   **el aparato de vídeo**
workshop   **el taller**

Type of school

boarding school   **el internado**
boarder   **el interno**
comprehensive school   **el colegio de enseñanza secundaria**
day school   **el colegio (que no es internado)**
further education   **la formación profesional, la educación media**
grammar school   **la escuela pública elemental**
high school   **el colegio de segunda enseñanza, el instituto**

"At what age do children start school?"
"They have to go to school when they are six years old."

Our son already goes to kindergarten and is looking forward to school.

— ¿ **A qué edad empiezan los niños la escuela?**
— **Tienen que ir a la escuela a la edad de seis años.**

Nuestro hijo ya va al jardín de infancia, y tiene ganas de ir a la escuela.

---

nursery school **el colegio infantil, la guardería**
playgroup **el grupo de juego**
primary **primario**
primary / elementary school **el colegio de enseñanza primaria**
school **el colegio, la escuela**
school type **el tipo de colegio**
of school age **en edad escolar**
secondary **secundario**
secondary school / junior high school **el colegio de enseñanza secundaria**
secondary school / senior high school **el colegio de enseñanza secundaria**
senior year / sixth form **el último curso de la enseñanza secundaria**
special school **el colegio especial**
technical school **el colegio técnico**

Classroom commands

Answer the question! **¡Contesta la pregunta!**
Be careful! **¡Ten cuidado!**
Be quiet! **¡Cállate!**
Be quick! **¡Sé rápido!**
Bring me your workbook! **¡Tráeme tu cuaderno!**
Clean the blackboard! **¡Limpia la pizarra!**
Close the door! **¡Cierra la puerta!**
Come here! **¡Ven aquí!**

Come in! **¡Entra!**
Copy these sentences! **¡Copia estas frases!**
Do your homework! **¡Haz la tarea!**
Don't talk / chatter! **¡No charles!**
Fill in the boxes! **¡Rellena los cuadrados!**
Go out! **¡Salte fuera!, ¡Fuera!**
Learn by heart! **¡Aprende de memoria!**
Listen carefully! **¡Escucha con atención!, ¡Escucha atentamente!**
Make less noise! **¡No hagas tanto ruido!**
Open the window! **¡Abre la ventana!**
Pay attention! **¡Atiende!**
Read the text! **¡Lee el texto!**
Show me your book! **¡Enséñame tu libro!**
Sit down! **¡Siéntate!**
Stand up! **¡Levántate!**
Take notes! **¡Toma apuntes!, ¡Coge apuntes!**
Work in pairs! **¡Trabajad en parejas!**
Work in groups! **¡Trabajad en grupos!**
Write it down! **¡Escribe esto!**
Write out in rough / draft! **¡Escribe en sucio!, ¡Escribe en borrador!**
Write out neatly / in neat! **¡Escribe con buena letra!, ¡Escribe claramente!**

Our daughter goes to elementary / primary school. She reads to her teacher every day and can read well now. | **Nuestra hija va a la escuela primaria. Lee a su maestra todos los días y ya sabe leer bien.**

"Do you move up a class every year?"
"No, last year I had to repeat the year." | **—¿Subes una clase todos los años [un grado cada año]?**
—No, el año pasado tuve que repetir el curso.

EDUCATION

22c School Subjects & Examinations

Subjects

arithmetic   la aritmética
art   el arte
biology   la biología
business studies   los estudios empresariales / de negocios
chemistry   la química
commerce   el comercio
compulsory subject   la asignatura obligatoria
computer studies   la informática
design technology   la tecnología de diseño
economics   la economía
English   el inglés
foreign language   el idioma extranjero
geography   la geografía
gymnastics   la gimnasia
history   la historia
home economics   la economía doméstica
information technology   la informática
Italian   el italiano
Latin   el latín
law   el derecho

main subject   la asignatura principal
mathematics   las matemáticas
metalwork   el trabajo con metal
minor / subsidiary subject   la asignatura secundaria
music   la música
occupational / careers education   la formación profesional
option(al subject)   la asignatura optativa
philosophy   la filosofía
physical education   la educación física
physics   la física
religious education   la educación religiosa
science   la ciencia, las ciencias
sex education   la educación sexual
social studies   los estudios sociales
sociology   la sociología
Spanish   el español
sport   el deporte
   type of sport   el tipo de deporte
subject   la asignatura

"Which school do you go to?"	— ¿A qué escuela vas?
"I go to the high school. I enjoy it a lot. There are lots of clubs and activities."	— Voy al instituto. Me gusta mucho. Hay muchos clubs y actividades.
"Which is your favorite subject?"	— ¿Qué asignatura prefieres?
"I like math / maths, but prefer physics."	— Me gustan las matemáticas, pero prefiero la física.
My favorite / favourite subject is physical education.	Mi asignatura preferida es la educación física.
I don't like history, it is so boring.	No me gusta la historia, es tan aburrida.
I'm good at English, since I did an exchange.	Estoy fuerte en inglés, desde que hice un intercambio.
I work very hard at it.	Trabajo mucho en inglés.

technical drawing   **el dibujo técnico**
technology   **la tecnología**
textiles   **los estudios textiles**
woodwork   **el trabajo con madera**

Examinations

I assess   **evalúo, corrijo**
assessment   **la evaluación**
certificate   **el certificado**
degree   **el grado**
diploma   **el diploma, el título**
dissertation   **el proyecto de fin de carrera, [la tesis]**
distinction   **la matrícula de honor**
doctorate   **el doctorado**
examination   **el examen**
  external   **externo, exterior**
  final   **final**
grade / mark   **la nota**
I grade   **califico, doy nota a**
grading / mark system   **el sistema de notas**
graduate (in engineering)   **el licenciado (en ingeniería)**
listening comprehension   **la comprensión de escucha**
mark   **la nota**

masters degree   **el título de máster**
merit   **el mérito**
oral   **oral**
point   **el punto**
post-graduate course   **el curso de post-licenciado, [el curso de posgrado]**
reading comprehension   **la comprensión de textos**
I pass (an exam)   **apruebo**
I sit for / take an exam   **me presento a un examen**
I test   **examino**
test   **el examen, el test, la prueba**
thesis   **la tesis**
trainee   **el aprendiz, el estudiante**
written test   **el examen escrito**

Grades / Marks

very good   **sobresaliente**
good   **notable**
satisfactory   **bien, satisfactorio**
pass   **aprobado**
poor   **insuficiente**
very poor   **muy deficiente**

Here are your grades!
Well done! Isabel, you have done excellent work.
Teodoro, you will need to work harder. Your spelling is very poor.

Anna, this is very satisfactory, but please improve your handwriting. Your work is so sloppy.

Next month we are having another test. It will count towards your final grade.

¡Aquí tenéis vuestras notas!
¡Bravo! Isabel, tu trabajo es sobresaliente.
Teodoro, tendrás que trabajar más. Tu ortografía es muy deficiente.

Ana, esto es muy satisfactorio, pero haz lo que puedas para mejorar tu escritura. Tu trabajo es tan descuidado.

El mes que viene haremos otra prueba / evaluación. Se incluirá en vuestra nota final.

EDUCATION

adult **de adultos**
adult education **la educación de adultos**
alumnus **el graduado**
apprentice **el aprendiz**
apprenticeship **el aprendizaje**
chair *(university)* **la cátedra**
college **el colegio universitario**
  college of further education **el colegio de formación profesional**
course of study **el curso**
diploma **el diploma, el título**
faculty **el profesorado**
further education **la formación profesional**
graduate **licenciado**
in-service training **el cursillo de formación de profesorado**
lecture **la clase, la conferencia**
lecture hall **el aula, el salón de conferencias**

lecturer **el profesor universitario**
masters degree **el título de máster**
part-time education **la educación a tiempo parcial / de medio tiempo**
polytechnic **el politécnico**
practical **la clase práctica**
principal **el director**
professor **el profesor universitario, el catedrático**
quota *(for university entry)* **el cupo**
research **la investigación**
residence hall / hall of residence **la residencia de estudiantes**
retraining **la reeducación, la recapacitación**
I retrain **hago un curso de reeducación**
scholarship *(grant)* **la beca, la ayuda escolar**
seminar **el seminario**
student **el / la estudiante**

We have increased the number of universities and are aiming for a broader provision.	**Hemos aumentado el número de universidades, y aspiramos a conseguir una provisión más amplia.**
The technical colleges now belong to the university sector and we now speak of a comprehensive university.	**Los colegios técnicos ya pertenecen al sector universitario, y ahora nos referimos a una universidad abierta.**
The length of course is four years (eight semesters).	**La duración del curso es de cuatro años (ocho semestres).**
Financial support is of the greatest importance. Many students get a state grant.	**El apoyo económico es muy importante. Muchos estudiantes reciben una beca del estado.**
Many students apply for places, but they cannot all be admitted.	**Muchos estudiantes solicitan puestos, pero no se les puede admitir a todos.**

student council **la junta de delegados de clase**
student grant **la beca de estudios**
student union **el sindicato de estudiantes, la asociación de estudiantes**
teacher-training college **la escuela de magisterio**
technical college **el colegio técnico**
university / college **la universidad**
university admission qualification **el certificado de selectividad, [el exámen de clasificación]**

Faculties & departments

accounting / accountancy **la contabilidad**
architecture **la arquitectura**
business management **la organización de negocios**
catering **la hostelería**
classics **los clásicos**
civil engineering **la ingeniería civil**
commerce **el comercio**
construction **la construcción**
education **la educación**

electronics **la electrónica**
electrical engineering **la ingeniería eléctrica**
economics **las ciencias económicas**
engineering **la ingeniería**
environmental sciences **las ciencias del medioambiente**
history of art **la historia del arte**
hotel management **la dirección hotelera**
languages **los idiomas**
law **el derecho**
literature **la literatura**
mechanical engineering **la ingeniería mecánica**
medicine **la medicina**
pharmacy **la farmacia**
nuclear science **la ciencia nuclear**
office skills **el secretariado**
philosophy **la filosofía**
psychology **la psicología**
sociology **la sociología**
theology **la teología**
tourism **el turismo**

There is now an entrance restriction.	**Ahora la entrada tiene restricciones.**
College admission depends on SAT scores.	**El derecho a un puesto universitario depende de las notas obtenidas en los exámenes de SAT.**
They require particularly high grades / marks for medicine.	**Se exigen notas especialmente altas para poder estudiar medicina.**
Our results are always outstanding.	**Nuestros resultados siempre son sobresalientes.**
Many students want job / vocational qualifications.	**Muchos estudiantes quieren sacar títulos profesionales.**
They can easily transfer between courses.	**Pueden cambiar fácilmente los cursos.**

▶ LANGUAGES App. 21b; SCIENTIFIC DISCIPLINES App. 23a

23 Science: The Changing World

23a Scientific Study & Life Sciences

Scientific study

academic paper **el artículo académico, [la ponencia]**
I analyze **analizo**
analysis **el análisis**
authentic **auténtico**
Bunsen burner **el mechero Bunsen**
I challenge **desafío**
I check **compruebo, reviso**
classification **la clasificación**
I classify **clasifico**
control **el control**
I discover **descubro**
discovery **el descubrimiento**
(electron) microscope **el microscopio (electrónico)**
experiment **el experimento**
I experiment **experimento**
flask **el frasco, el matraz**
hypothesis **la hipótesis**
I identify **identifico**
I investigate **investigo**
I invent **invento**

invention **el invento**
laboratory **el laboratorio**
material **el material**
I measure **mido**
measurement **la medición**
I observe **observo**
origin **el origen**
pipette **la pipeta**
process **el proceso**
research **la investigación**
I research **investigo**
result **el resultado**
I solve *(problem)* **resuelvo**
test **la prueba**
I test **compruebo**
test tube **el tubo de ensayo**
theory **la teoría**
I transfer **transfiero**

Biology

bacteria **la bacteria**
botanical **botánico**
I breathe **respiro**
cell **la célula**

The researcher took a sample, mounted it on a slide, and put it under the microscope for examination.

La investigadora tomó una muestra, la fijó en una platina y la puso debajo del microscopio para examinarla.

All the results from the experiments support her hypothesis.

Todos los resultados de los experimentos apoyan su hipótesis.

chlorophyll   **la clorofila**
it circulates   **circula**
decay   **la decadencia**
decline   **el descenso, la disminución**
it declines   **desciende**
it excretes   **excreta**
excretion   **la excreción**
it feeds   **alimenta**
food chain   **el ciclo alimenticio, la cadena alimenticia**
gene   **el gen, el gene**
genetic   **genético**
genetic disorder   **la alteración genética**
it grows   **crece**
growth   **el crecimiento**
habitat   **el hábitat**
it inherits   **hereda**
membrane   **la membrana**
it mutates   **se transforma, cambia**
nucleus   **el núcleo**
organic   **orgánico**
organism   **el organismo**
photosynthesis   **la fotosíntesis**
population   **la población**
it reproduces   **se reproduce**
respiration   **la respiración**
sensitivity   **la sensibilidad**
survival   **la sobrevivencia**
it survives   **sobrevive**
virus   **el virus**

Medical science & research

DNA   **el ADN**
donor   **el donante**
embryo   **el embrión**
embryo research   **la investigación embrionaria**
ethical consideration   **la consideración ética**
experiments on animals   **los experimentos con animales**
hereditary illness   **la enfermedad hereditaria**
IVF (in vitro fertilization)   **FIV (la fertilización / fecundación in vitro)**
I justify   **justifico**
microorganism   **el microorganismo**
organ transplant   **el transplante de órgano**
pacemaker   **el marcapasos**
I permit   **permito**
plastic / cosmetic surgery   **la cirugía plástica**
recipient   **el recipiente**
I reject *(organ)*   **rechazo**
risk   **el riesgo**
I risk   **me arriesgo**
survival rate   **la tasa de sobrevivencia**
test-tube baby   **el niño probeta**
transplant   **el transplante**
X ray   **el rayo X**

A girl of seventeen was today given a new heart in a transplant operation that lasted ten hours.

A una chica de diecisiete le dieron hoy un nuevo corazón, en una operación de transplante que duró diez horas.

Research on human embryo tissue is likely to remain highly controversial.

Los trabajos de investigación sobre los tejidos de embrión humano probablemente serán siempre una cuestión muy controvertida.

➤ EARTH & SPACE 23c; THE ENVIRONMENT 24; MEDICAL TREATMENT 11c

SCIENCE: THE CHANGING WORLD

23b Physical Sciences

Chemistry

acid **el ácido**
air **el aire**
alkali **el álcali**
alkaline **alcalino**
I analyze **analizo**
I calculate **calculo**
chemical **químico**
compound **el componente**
composition **la composición**
it dissolves (in water) **se disuelve (en agua)**
element **el elemento**
emulsion **la emulsión**
equation **la ecuación**
gas **el gas**
inorganic **inorgánico**
insoluble **insoluble**
liquid **el líquido**
    liquid *(adj)* **líquido**
litmus paper **el papel de tornasol**
matter **la materia**
metal **el metal**
natural gas **el gas natural**
opaque **opaco**
it oxidizes **oxida**
periodic table **la tabla periódica**
physical **físico**
pure **puro**
it reacts **reacciona**
reaction **la reacción**
salt **la sal**
solid **el sólido**
    solid *(adj)* **sólido**
soluble **soluble**
solution **la solución**
stable **estable**
substance **la sustancia**
transparent **transparente**

Physics & mechanics

it accelerates **acelera**
acceleration **la aceleración**
acoustics **la acústica**
artificial **artificial**
automatic **automático**
ball bearing **de bolas**
boiling point **el punto de ebullición**
circuit **el circuito**
cog **el diente, la rueda dentada**
conservation **la conservación, la preservación**
density **la densidad**
dial **la esfera, el dial**
distance **la distancia**
energy **la energía**
it expands **se expande**
fiber / fibre **la fibra**
force **la fuerza**
it freezes **se congela**
formula **la fórmula**
freezing point **el punto de congelación**
friction **la fricción, el rozamiento**
gauge *(measuring)* **el calibrador, el indicador**
gear **el engranaje**
gravity **la gravedad**
I heat **caliento**
heat **el calor**
heat loss **la pérdida de calor**
laser **el láser**
laser beam **el rayo láser**
lever **la palanca**
light **la luz**
light beam **el rayo de luz, el haz de luz**
lubricant **el lubricante**

Water has a boiling point of
one hundred degrees centigrade.

**El agua tiene un punto de
ebullición de cien grados
centígrados.**

machinery **la maquinaria, el mecanismo**
magnetism **el magnetismo**
magneto **la magneto**
mass **la masa, el peso**
mechanics **la mecánica**
mechanical **mecánico**
mechanism **el mecanismo**
metallurgy **la metalurgia**
microwave **la microonda**
mineral **el mineral**
missile **el misil**
model **el modelo**
motion **el movimiento**
observation **la observación**
I operate *(machinery)* **manejo**
operational **operacional**
optics **la óptica**
pressure **la presión**
property **la propiedad**
proportional **proporcional**
ray **el rayo**
reflection **la reflexión**
refraction **la refracción**
relativity **la relatividad**
resistance **la resistencia**
resistant **resistente**
robot **el robot, el autómata**
I sort **clasifico**
sound **el sonido**
speed **la velocidad**
structure **la estructura**
synthetic **sintético**
temperature **la temperatura**
theory **la teoría**
time **el tiempo**
transmission **la transmisión**
turbine **la turbina**
vapor / vapour **el vapor**
it vibrates **vibra**
vibration **la vibración**

wave **la onda**
long waves **las ondas largas**
medium / short waves **las ondas medías / cortas**
wavelength **la longitud de onda**
it works **funciona**

Electricity

battery *(large)* **la batería**
battery *(small)* **la pila**
charge **la carga**
I charge the battery **cargo la batería**
current **la corriente**
electrical **eléctrico**
electricity **la electricidad**
electrode **el electrodo**
electron **el electrón**
electronic **electrónico**
electronics **la electrónica**
positive **positivo**
negative **negativo**
voltage **el voltaje**

Nuclear physics

atom **el átomo**
atomic **atómico**
it emits **emite**
fission **la fisión, la escisión**
fusion **la fusión**
molecular **molecular**
molecule **la molécula**
neutron **el neutrón**
nuclear **nuclear**
nuclear energy **la energía nuclear**
nucleus **el núcleo**
particle **la partícula**
proton **el protón**
quantum theory **la teoría cuántica**
radiation **la radiación**
reactor **el reactor**

What's the voltage of this equipment?

¿Cuál es el voltaje de este aparato?

SCIENCE: THE CHANGING WORLD

23c The Earth & Space

Geology & minerals

bauxite **la bauxita**
carbon dating **la prueba del carbono**
chalk **la creta**
chalky **cretoso**
clay **la arcilla**
diamond **el diamante**
I excavate **excavo**
exploration **la exploración**
geologist **el geólogo**
geology **la geología**
gemstone **la gema**
granite **el granito**
graphite **el grafito**
layer **la capa**
lime **la cal**
limestone **la piedra caliza**
loam **la marga**
marble **el mármol**
mine **la mina**
I mine **trabajo en la mina**
ore **la mena, el mineral**
quartz **el cuarzo**
quarry **la cantera**
raw materials **las materias primas**
sand **la arena**
sandstone **la piedra arenisca**
sediment **el sedimento**
silica **la sílice**
slate **la pizarra**
soil **la tierra, el suelo**
stalactite **la estalactita**
stalagmite **la estalagmita**

Energy & fuels

atomic energy **la energía atómica**
coal **el carbón**
concentration **la concentración**
coolant **el refrigerante**
energy **la energía**
energy conservation **la conservación de energía**
energy consumption **el consumo de energía**
energy needs **las necesidades energéticas**
energy saving **el ahorro de energía**
energy source **la fuente de energía**
fossil fuels **el combustible fósil**
fuel **el carburante, el combustible**
fuel consumption **el consumo de combustible**
it generates **genera, produce**
geothermal energy **la energía geotérmica**
hydroelectric dam **la presa hidroeléctrica**
hydroelectric power **la fuerza hidroeléctrica**
natural gas **el gas natural**
nuclear energy **la energía nuclear**
nuclear power station **la central nuclear**
nuclear reactor **el reactor nuclear**
oil **el petróleo**
oil production **la producción de petróleo**
oil-producing countries **los países productores de petróleo**
ozone layer **la capa de ozono**
petroleum **el petróleo**
solar cell **la célula solar**
solar energy **la energía solar**
I strike oil **descubro un yacimiento de petróleo**
thermal energy **la energía térmica**
wave power **la energía de las ondas**
tidal power station **la planta colectora de energía de las mareas**
wind energy / power **la energía eólica**

Space

asteroid   **el asteroide**
big bang theory   **la teoría del big-bang**
black hole   **el agujero negro**
eclipse   **el eclipse**
it eclipses   **eclipsa**
galactic   **galáctico**
galaxy   **la galaxia**
gravitational pull   **la fuerza de atracción planetaria, la fuerza de gravedad**
the heavens   **los cielos**
light-year   **el año luz**
meteorite   **el meteorito**
moon   **la luna**
   full moon   **la luna llena**
   new moon   **la luna nueva**
nova   **la nova**
orbit   **la órbita**
planet   **el planeta**
shooting star   **la estrella fugaz**
solar system   **el sistema solar**
solstice   **el solsticio**
space   **el espacio**
star   **la estrella**
sun   **el sol**
sunspot   **la mancha solar**
universe   **el universo**

Space research & travel

antenna   **la antena**
astrologer   **el astrólogo**
astronomer   **el astrónomo**
astronaut   **el astronauta**
cosmonaut   **el cosmonauta**
dish antenna   **la antena parabólica**

I launch   **lanzo**
launch pad   **la plataforma de lanzamiento**
lunar module   **el módulo lunar**
moonbuggy   **el vehículo lunar**
moonwalk   **el paseo sobre la superficie lunar**
observatory   **el observatorio**
orbit   **la órbita**
planetarium   **el planetario**
it reenters   **vuelve a entrar, reentra**
relativity   **la relatividad**
rocket   **el cohete**
rocket fuel   **el combustible del cohete**
satellite   **el satélite**
   communications   **de comunicaciones**
   spy   **espía**
   weather   **meteorológico**
sky lab   **el laboratorio espacial**
space flight   **el vuelo espacial**
space probe   **la prueba espacial**
space shuttle   **el transbordador espacial**
space walk   **el paseo espacial**
spacecraft   **la nave espacial**
spacesuit   **el traje de astronauta**
stratosphere   **la estratosfera**
telescope   **el telescopio**
time warp   **el salto en el tiempo**
touchdown on land   **el aterrizaje**
   on sea   **el amerizaje**
   on moon   **el alunizaje**
zodiac   **el zodíaco**

By studying the light received from stars many millions of light years away, scientists hope to discover the origins of the universe.

Los científicos esperan descubrir el orígen del universo por medio de sus estudios de la luz que nos llega de estrellas que están a muchos millones de años luz.

24 The Environment: The Natural World

24a Geography

archipelago **el archipiélago**
area **el área, la zona**
bank (river) **la ribera (del río)**
bay **la bahía**
beach **la playa**
bog **el pantano, la ciénaga**
bottom **el fondo**
canyon **el cañón**
clean **limpio**
cliff **el acantilado, el precipicio**
coast **la costa**
coastline **el litoral**
continent **el continente**
copse / coppice **el soto, el bosquecillo**
country **el país**
   in the country **en el campo**
countryside **el campo**
creek **la cala, el riachuelo, la ensenada**
dangerous **peligroso**
deep **profundo**
delta **el delta**
desert **el desierto**
dirty **sucio**
dune **la duna**
earth tremor **el temblor de tierra**
earthquake **el terremoto**
equator **el ecuador**
equatorial **ecuatorial**
eruption **la erupción**
it erupts **erupciona**
escarpment **la escarpa**
estuary **el estuario**
field **el campo**
fjord **el fiordo**
flat **plano, llano**
it flows **fluye, discurre**
foothills **las estribaciones**
forest **el bosque**

friendly **no perjudicial**
geographical **geográfico**
geography **la geografía**
geyser **el géiser**
globe **el globo terráqueo, la esfera terrestre**
gradient **la pendiente, la inclinación**
hemisphere **el hemisferio**
high **alto**
hill **la colina**
incline / slope **la inclinación, la pendiente**
it is situated **está situado**
island **la isla**
jungle **la jungla**
lake **el lago**
land **la tierra**
it is located **está situado, se localiza en**
location **la situación, la localización**
map **el mapa**
marsh **el pantano, la ciénaga, la marisma**
meridian **el meridiano**
mountain **la montaña**
mountain range **la cordillera**
national **nacional**
national park **el parque nacional**
nature **la naturaleza**
nice / pleasant **agradable**
ocean **el océano**
ocean floor **el fondo del mar**
peaceful **tranquilo, silencioso**
peak **el pico, la cumbre**
peninsula **la península**
plateau **la meseta, el altiplano**
pole **el polo**
province **la provincia**

reef **el arrecife**
region **la región**
regional **regional**
ridge **la cresta, la sierra**
river **el río**
riverbed **el lecho del río**
rockpool **la charca entre rocas**
sand **la arena**
scenery **el escenario, la vista**
sea **el mar**
seaside **el borde del mar**
shore **la orilla del mar**
spring **la fuente, el manantial**
steep **escarpado, empinado**
steppe **la estepa**
stream **el arroyo, la corriente**
summit **la cima, la cumbre**
tall **alto, elevado**
territory **el territorio**
top **la cima, la cumbre**
tropics **los trópicos**
tundra **la tundra**
unfriendly **perjudicial**
valley **el valle**
volcano **el volcán**
water **el agua** *(f)*
  freshwater **el agua dulce /**
  limpia
   saltwater **el agua salada**
   seawater **el agua de mar**
waterfall **la catarata, el salto**
wood **la madera, el bosque**

woodland **el bosque, la región**
  boscosa
zenith **el zénit**
zone **la zona**

Man-made features
_____

aqueduct **el acueducto**
bridge **el puente**
canal **el canal**
capital (city) **la capital**
city **la ciudad**
country road **la carretera**
  secundaria, el camino
dam **la presa, la represa, el**
  dique
embankment **el terraplén**
factory **la fábrica**
farm **la granja**
farmland **las tierras de labranza**
hamlet **la aldea, el caserío**
harbor / harbour **el puerto**
industry **la industria**
marina **el puerto deportivo**
oasis **el oasis**
reclaimed land **la tierra ganada al**
  mar
reservoir **el pantano, el embalse**
town **la ciudad, el pueblo**
track **el camino, la pista**
village **la aldea, el pueblo**
well **el pozo, el manantial**

The area was marshy and
unsuitable for development.

**La zona no era apta para el
desarrollo por ser pantanosa.**

The village is situated in a valley
about five kilometers / kilometres
north of a small provincial Chilean
town.

**El pueblo está situado en un
valle a unos cinco kilómetros al
norte de una pequeña ciudad
provincial chilena.**

The inhabitants of the small towns
at the foot of Everest were among
the poorest people in the world
before 1950.

**Los habitantes de los pequeños
pueblos al pie del Everest
figuraban entre la gente más
pobre del mundo antes de 1950.**

THE ENVIRONMENT: THE NATURAL WORLD

24b The Animal World

Animals

animal   **el animal**
it barks   **ladra**
it bites   **muerde**
it bounds   **salta hacia delante**
it breeds   **cría**
burrow   **la madriguera**
cage   **la jaula**
carnivore   **el carnívoro**
cat   **el gato**
it crawls   **anda a gatas**
den   **la guarida, la madriguera**
dog   **el perro**
I feed   **doy de comer, alimento**
it feeds   **alimenta**
food   **la comida, el alimento**
gerbil   **el gerbo**
goldfish   **el pez de colores**
guinea pig   **el conejo de Indias, el curí**
habitat   **el hábitat**
hamster   **el hámster**
herbivore   **el herbívoro**
it hibernates   **hiberna**
it howls   **aúlla**
hutch / hut   **la conejera**
I keep a cat   **tengo un gato**
kitten   **el gatito**
lair   **el cubil, la guarida**
it leaps   **salta**
litter   **la camada**

mammal   **el mamífero**
it meows   **hace miau**
mouse   **el ratón**
omnivore   **el omnívoro**
pack   **la manada, la jauría**
parakeet / budgerigar   **el periquito**
predator   **el depredador**
prey   **la presa**
pet   **el animal doméstico**
puppy   **el perrito**
rabbit   **el conejo**
rabies   **la rabia**
reptile   **el reptil**
it roars   **ruge**
safari park   **el parque de safari**
it squeaks   **chilla**
I stroke   **acaricio**
tortoise   **la tortuga**
I walk *(the dog)*   **paseo**
wildlife park   **la reserva natural**
zoo   **el (jardín / parque) zoológico**

Birds

bird   **el pájaro**
it flies   **vuela**
flock   **la bandada**
it hovers   **permanece inmóvil en el aire**
it migrates   **migra, emigra**
nest   **el nido**
it nests   **anida**
it pecks at   **pica**
it sings   **canta**

| Guinea pigs and hamsters are popular pets in Britain. | **Los conejillos de Indias y los hámsteres figuran entre los animales domésticos más populares en Gran Bretaña.** |
| The campaign to save the whale is increasing in popularity. | **La campaña para salvar la ballena está ganando popularidad.** |

Sealife / Waterlife

alligator   **el caimán**
anemone   **la anémona**
angling   **la pesca con caña**
coral   **el coral**
crab   **el cangrejo**
crocodile   **el cocodrilo**
dolphin   **el delfín**
fish   **el pez**
I fish   **pesco**
harpoon   **el arpón**
hook   **el anzuelo**
marine   **marino, marítimo**
mollusk   **el molusco**
net   **la red**
octopus   **el pulpo**
plankton   **el plancton**
rod   **la caña de pescar**
seal   **la foca**
shark   **el tiburón**
shoal   **el banco**
starfish   **la estrella de mar**
it swims   **nada**
turtle   **la tortuga marina**
whale   **la ballena**
whaling   **la pesca de ballenas**

Insects

ant   **la hormiga**
bee   **la abeja**
   queen bee   **la abeja reina**
   worker bee   **la abeja obrera**
bedbug   **el chinche**
beetle   **el escarabajo**

bug   **el insecto,**
   el bicho
butterfly   **la mariposa**
it buzzes   **zumba**
caterpillar   **la oruga**
cocoon   **el capullo**
cockroach   **la cucaracha**
cricket   **el grillo**
dragonfly   **la libélula**
flea   **la pulga**
fly   **la mosca**
grasshopper   **el saltamontes,**
   [el chapulín]
hive   **la colmena**
insect   **el insecto**
invertebrate   **el invertebrado**
ladybug / ladybird   **la mariquita**
larva   **la larva**
locust   **la langosta**
it metamorphoses   **metamorfosea**
mosquito   **el mosquito**
moth   **la polilla**
scorpion   **el escorpión**
silkworm   **el gusano de seda**
slug   **la babosa**
snail   **el caracol**
spider   **la araña**
it spins (a web)   **teje (una tela)**
it stings   **pica**
termite   **la termita**
tick   **la garrapata**
web   **la red**
wasp   **la avispa**
worm   **el gusano**

The panda is in danger of extinction in the wild, because the bamboo, which it eats, inexplicably dies away every fifty years.

El panda corre riesgo de extinción en la selva, pues el bambú que come desaparece por completo cada cincuenta años sin que nadie sepa por qué.

Don't forget to walk the dog, feed the cat, and talk to the goldfish!

¡No olvides de llevar al perro de paseo, de darle de comer al gato y de hablarle al pez de colores!

➤ FISH & SEAFOOD 10b; PARTS OF THE ANIMAL BODY App. 24b

24c Farming & Gardening

Farm animals

bull   **el toro**
cattle   **el ganado**
chicken   **el pollo**
cow   **la vaca**
it crows   **canta, cacarea**
dairy *(adj)*   **lácteo**
duck   **el pato**
it eats   **come**
feed   **el alimento**
it feeds   **se alimenta**
colt   **el potro**
fodder   **el pienso, el forraje**
food *(for animals)*   **el alimento de los animales**
it gallops   **galopa**
goat   **la cabra**
goose   **el ganso**
it grazes   **pace, pasta**
it grunts   **gruñe**
horse   **el caballo**
horseshoe   **la herradura**
it kicks   **da patadas**
kid   **la cría**
I milk   **ordeño**
it moos   **muge**
it neighs   **relincha**
ox   **el buey**
it pecks   **picotea**
pig   **el cerdo**
pony   **el poni, el caballito**
poultry   **las aves**
produce   **los productos agrícolas**
it quacks   **hace cua-cua**
I ride *(a horse)*   **monto**
rooster / cock   **el gallo**

I shear   **esquilo**
sheep   **la oveja**
sheepdog   **el perro pastor de ovejas**
I slaughter   **mato, sacrifico**
stallion   **el semental**
it trots   **trota**

On the farm

agricultural   **agrario**
arable   **arable, cultivable**
barn   **la granja**
combine harvester   **la cosechadora, la segadora**
crop   **el cultivo**
dairy   **la quesería**
farm   **la granja**
farmhouse   **la casa de la granja**
farm laborer / labourer   **el granjero**
farmyard   **el patio de la granja**
fence   **la valla, el seto, la cerca**
I groom   **cepillo al caballo**
harvest   **la cosecha**
I harvest   **cosecho**
hay   **el heno**
bale of hay   **la bala de heno**
I irrigate   **riego**
milk churn   **la lechera**
milking machine   **la ordeñadora**
pasture   **el pasto**
pen   **el corral**
pigsty   **la porqueriza, la pocilga**
silage   **el silo**
slaughterhouse   **el matadero**
stable   **el establo**
stud farm   **la caballeriza**

In the developing countries, arable land is often owned by rich landlords.

En los países en desarrollo, la tierra cultivable a menudo es de propietarios ricos.

Agriculture & gardening

acorn   **la bellota**
agriculture   **la agricultura**
barley   **la cebada**
it blooms   **florece**
bloom   **la flor**
bouquet   **el ramo, el bouquet**
branch   **el ramo**
bud   **el capullo**
bulb   **el bulbo**
bush   **el arbusto**
cactus   **el cactus**
compost   **el abono**
corn / maize   **el maíz**
I cultivate   **cultivo**
cutting   **el esqueje**
I dig   **cavo**
ear   **la espiga**
I fertilize   **abono**
fertilizer   **el fertilizante,
   el abono**
fir   **el abeto**
flower   **la flor**
it flowers   **florece**
flowerpot   **el tiesto, la maceta, [la
   malera]**
foliage   **el follaje**
garden / yard   **el jardín**
I gather   **recojo**
grain   **el grano**
grass   **la hierba**
I grow   **planto, cultivo**
it grows   **crece**
hedge   **el seto**
horticulture   **la horticultura**
lawn   **el césped**
leaf   **la hoja**

I mow   **corto la hierba**
oats   **la avena**
orchard   **la huerta**
petal   **el pétalo**
I pick   **cojo, recojo**
pine   **el pino**
pine forest   **el bosque de pinos**
I plant   **planto**
plant   **la planta**
pollen   **el polen**
I reap   **cosecho, recojo**
ripe   **maduro**
it ripens   **madura**
root   **la raíz**
rotten   **podrido**
rye   **el centeno**
sap   **la savia**
seed   **la semilla**
sorghum   **el sorgo**
species   **la especie**
stalk   **el tallo, la caña**
stamen   **el estambre**
stem   **el tallo**
thorn   **la espina**
I transplant   **transplanto**
tree   **el árbol**
trunk   **el tronco**
undergrowth   **la maleza, el monte
   bajo**
vegetables   **las verduras**
vegetation   **la vegetación**
I water   **riego**
weeds   **las malas hierbas**
I weed   **mato las malas hierbas**
wheat   **el trigo**
wildflower   **la flor salvaje, la flor
   silvestre**
it wilts   **se marchita**

Let's go for a walk in the country and stop at the old farmhouse. We'll probably see some newborn lambs in the fields.

Vámonos a dar un paseo en el campo hasta el cortijo viejo. Probablemente veremos unos corderos recién nacidos en los campos.

THE ENVIRONMENT: THE NATURAL WORLD

24d Weather

anticyclone **el anticiclón**
avalanche **la avalancha**
average temperature **la temperatura media**
bad weather **el mal tiempo**
bright **despejado, claro**
bright period **el período despejado**
centigrade **centígrado**
changeable **variable**
climate **el clima**
climatic **climático**
cloud **la nube**
clouded over **cubierto**
cloudless **despejado, sin nubes**
cloudy **nuboso, nublado**
cold **frío**
it is cold **hace frío**
cold front **el frente frío**
it is cool **hace fresco**
cyclone **el ciclón**
damp **húmedo**
degree **el grado**
   above zero **sobre cero**
   below zero **bajo cero**
depression **la depresión**

drizzle **el chirimiri, [la llovizna]**
it drizzles **llovizna**
drought **la sequía**
dry **seco**
dull weather **el tiempo gris**
it's fine **hace buen tiempo**
flash **el relámpago**
fog **la niebla**
it is foggy **está nuboso / nublado**
it's freezing **está helando**
frost **la helada, la escarcha**
frosty **helado**
gale **el vendaval, el ventarrón**
gale warning **el aviso de tormenta**
it's hailing **está granizando**
hail **el granizo**
heat **el calor**
heatwave **la ola de calor**
high pressure **la presión alta**
highest temperature **la temperatura máxima**
it's hot **hace calor**
ice **el hielo**
Indian summer **el verano de San Martín**
lightning **el relámpago, el rayo**

It will be cold over the whole country tomorrow, maximum temperatures four to six Celsius (thirty-nine to forty-three Fahrenheit).

Mañana hará frío en todo el país, con una temperatura máxima de entre cuatro y seis grados Celsius (treinta y nueve a cuarenta y tres Fahrenheit).

Freezing fog patches in the Ebro valley should clear by midday.

Las zonas de niebla helada que se encuentran en la Cuenca del Ebro desaparecerán con toda probabilidad antes de mediodía.

Outlook for the weekend — very warm and sunny.

El pronóstico para el fin de semana — sol y mucho calor.

The whole country will be affected by rain, turning to sleet in the mountains.

El país entero será afectado por la lluvia, que caerá como aguanieve en las zonas montañosas.

low pressure **la presión baja**
lowest temperature **la temperatura mínima**
mild **suave**
mist **la bruma**
misty **brumoso**
monsoon **el monzón**
moon **la luna**
occluded front **el frente ocluso**
rain **la lluvia**
it's raining **está lloviendo**
rainy **lluvioso**
shade **la sombra**
it shines **brilla**
shower **el chaparrón**
snow **la nieve**
snowball **la bola de nieve**
snowdrift **la ventisca de nieve**
snowfall **la nevada**
snowflake **el copo de nieve**
snowman **el muñeco de nieve**
snow report *(for skiing)* **el pronóstico de la nieve**
it's snowing **está nevando**
snowstorm **la tormenta de nieve**
star **la estrella**
storm **la tormenta**
stormy **tormentoso**

sultry **bochornoso**
sun / sunshine **hace sol**
sunny day **un día de sol**
(daily) temperature **la temperatura diurna**
thunder **el trueno**
it's thundering **hay truenos**
thunderbolt **el rayo**
thunderstorm **la tormenta eléctrica / de rayos**
torrent **el torrente**
torrential **torrencial**
tropical **tropical**
warm **cálido**
warm front **el frente cálido**
weather **el tiempo**
weather conditions **las condiciones climáticas**
weather forecast **el pronóstico del tiempo**
weather report **el informe del tiempo**
wet **mojado, húmedo**
What's the weather like? **¿Cómo es el tiempo?**
wind **el viento**
windy **ventoso**

The monsoon is now well established over southeast Asia.

El monzón ya está bien establecido en la zona sudeste de Asia.

The south of the country will be affected by tropical storms later tonight.

Durante la noche la zona sur del país se verá afectada por tormentas tropicales.

"Did you have a good vacation / holiday?"
"Yes, apart from the weather."
"I thought it was always hot and sunny on the Mediterranean."
"So did I. We must have chosen the one week when it was cold and rainy."

—¿ Lo pasaste bien en tus vacaciones?
—Sí, aparte del tiempo.
—Creía que siempre hacía sol y calor en el Mediterráneo.
—Yo también. Sin duda escogimos la única semana en que hizo frío y llovió.

THE ENVIRONMENT: THE NATURAL WORLD

24e Pollution

balance of nature **el equilibrio natural**
it becomes extinct **se agota, se extingue**
conservation **la conservación, la preservación**
conservationist **el conservacionista**
I conserve **conservo, preservo**
corrosion **la corrosión, la oxidación**
I consume **consumo**
consumption **el consumo**
I damage **daño, estropeo, perjudico**
damaging **perjudicial, dañoso**
danger (to) **peligro a**
I destroy **destruyo**
disaster **el desastre, el devastamiento**
disposal **el desecho**
I dispose of **desecho, [boto a la basura]**
I do without **no necesito, me arreglo sin**
ecology **la ecología**
ecosystem **el ecosistema**
emission **la emisión**
it emits **emite, desprende**

environment **el medio ambiente**
exhaust pipe **el tubo de escape**
garbage / rubbish **la basura**
harmful **perjudicial**
I improve **mejoro**
industrial waste **los residuos industriales**
I insulate **aíslo**
litter **la basura, los desperdicios**
I poison **enveneno**
poison **el veneno, el tóxico**
pollutant **el contaminante**
I pollute **contamino**
pollution **la contaminación**
I predict **pronostico**
I protect **protejo**
recyclable **reciclable**
I recycle **reciclo**
recycled paper **el papel reciclado**
reprocessing **el reprocesamiento**
residue **el residuo**
it runs out **se agota, se acaba**
I throw away **tiro**
waste *(domestic)* **la basura**
waste disposal unit **el triturador de basuras**
waste products **los productos de desecho, los productos desechables**

The city council / municipality provides facilities for recycling glass, cans, and newspapers.

El ayuntamiento [la alcadía] suministra facilidades para reciclar el vidrio, las latas y los periódicos.

Recent studies suggest the hole in the ozone layer will have serious consequences in the Northern Hemisphere.

Estudios recientes indican que el agujero en la capa de ozono tendrá consecuencias graves para el Hemisferio Norte.

On the earth

artificial fertilizer   **el fertilizante artificial**
biodegradable   **biodegradable**
deforestation   **la deforestación**
garbage / rubbish dump   **el vertedero de basura, [el relleno sanitario]**
nature reserve   **la reserva natural, el parque natural**
natural resources   **los recursos naturales**
nitrates   **los nitratos**
pesticide   **el pesticida**
radioactive   **radioactivo**
radioactive waste   **el residuo radioactivo**
rain forest   **la selva**
refuse   **el desperdicio, la basura, el desecho**
scrap metal   **la chatarra**
soil erosion   **la erosión del suelo**
weedkiller   **el herbicida**

In the atmosphere

acid rain   **la lluvia ácida**
aerosol *(system)*   **el aerosol**
aerosol can   **el tubo de aerosol, la botella de aerosol**
air pollution   **la contaminación del aire**

atmosphere   **la atmósfera**
catalytic convertor   **el catalizador**
CFCs   **los clorofluorocarbonos**
emission (of gas)   **la emisión (de gas)**
incinerator   **el incinerador**
skin cancer   **el cáncer de piel**
I spray   **pulverizo, atomizo, rocío, riego**
unleaded / lead-free gasoline   **la gasolina sin plomo**
waste gases   **los gases residuales**

In the rivers & seas

detergent   **el detergente**
drainage   **el drenaje, el desagüe**
drought   **la sequía**
flooding   **la inundación**
industrial wastes   **los residuos industriales**
oil slick   **la mancha de petróleo**
phosphates   **los fosfatos**
sea level   **el nivel del mar**
sewage   **la depuración de las aguas**
water level   **el nivel del agua**
water supply system   **el sistema de abastecimiento de agua**
water supply   **el suministro de agua**

"Do you think this awful weather is normal? Don't you think it's because of global warming?"

"Not really. It's just the normal cycle."
"Well, I think it's a combination of the greenhouse effect and nuclear testing in the last forty years."

— ¿ **Crees que este tiempo horroroso sea normal? ¿ No crees que sea resultado del recalentamiento mundial?**
— **No lo creo. Sólo se trata del ciclo normal.**
— **Bueno, yo creo que se trata de una combinación del efecto invernadero y de las pruebas nucleares que se hacen desde hace cuarenta años.**

Government & Politics

25a Political Life

I abolish **abolo, suprimo una ley**
act (of parliament) **la ley, la disposición parlamentaria**
administration **la administración**
I appoint **nombro, designo**
appointment **el nombramiento**
asylum seeker **el solicitante de asilo político**
it becomes law **cobra fuerza de ley, entra en vigor**
bill **la proposición / el proyecto de ley**
I bring down **derroco, derribo**
citizen **el ciudadano**
civil disobedience **la resistencia pasiva**
civil servant **el funcionario público**
civil war **la guerra civil**
coalition **la coalición**
it comes into effect **entra en vigor, rige**
common **civil**
constitution **la constitución**
cooperation **la cooperación**
corruption **la corrupción**
region **la región**
coup **el golpe de estado**

crisis **la crisis**
debate **el debate**
decree **el decreto**
delegate **el delegado, el diputado**
I demonstrate **participo en la manifestación**
demonstration **la manifestación**
I discuss **discuto**
discussion **la discusión**
I dismiss **destituyo**
I dissolve **disuelvo**
I draw up (a bill) **redacto**
duty **el deber**
equal opportunity **la igualdad de oportunidades**
executive **el ejecutivo**
executive (adj) **ejecutivo**
foreign policy **la política exterior**
I form a pact with **pacto con**
freedom **la libertad**
freedom of speech **la libertad de expresión**
I govern **gobierno**
government **el gobierno**
I introduce (a bill) **presento (un proyecto de ley)**
judiciary **la judicatura**
law **el derecho, la ley**

The Prime Minister summoned the Cabinet to an emergency meeting.

El Primer Ministro convocó una reunión extraordinaria del Consejo de Ministros.

The Minister of the Interior / Home Secretary said the Government was determined to halt the rise in juvenile crime.

El Ministro del Interior dijo que el Gobierno estaba resuelto a parar la subida en el nivel del crimen juvenil.

I lead   **encabezo**
legislation   **la legislación**
legislature   **la legislatura**
liberty   **la libertad**
local affairs   **los asuntos internos / locales**
local government   **el gobierno local**
long-term   **a largo plazo**
majority   **la mayoría**
meeting   **la reunión**
middle class   **la clase media**
ministry   **el ministerio**
minority   **la minoría**
nation   **la nación**
national   **nacional**
national flag   **la bandera nacional**
   Spanish national flag   **la bandera de España**
I nationalize   **nacionalizo**
I oppose   **me opongo**
opposition   **la oposición**
I organize   **organizo**
I overthrow   **derroco**
pact   **el pacto**
I pass *(a bill)*   **apruebo**
politics   **la política**
political   **político**
power   **el poder**
I privatize   **privatizo**
I protest   **protesto**
public   **el público**
   public *(adj)*   **público**
public opinion   **la opinión pública**
I ratify   **ratifico**

reactionary   **reaccionario**
I reform   **reformo, dimito**
reform   **la reforma**
I reject   **rechazo**
I repeal *(an act)*   **rechazo**
I represent   **represento**
I repress   **reprimo**
I resign   **dimito**
responsible   **responsable**
responsibility   **la responsabilidad**
reunification   **la reunificación**
revolt   **la revuelta, el levantamiento**
I rule   **rijo, dispongo**
sanction   **la sanción**
seat   **el escaño**
short-term   **a corto plazo**
solidarity   **la solidaridad**
speech   **el discurso**
state   **el estado**
statesman   **el hombre de estado**
I support   **apoyo**
I take power   **tomo el poder**
tax   **el impuesto**
taxation   **los impuestos**
term of office   **la duración del cargo**
I throw out (a bill)   **rechazo**
unconstitutional   **inconstitucional**
unilateral   **unilateral**
unity   **la unidad**
veto   **el veto**
I veto   **veto**
welfare   **el bienestar**
working class   **la clase obrera**

The Lower Chamber voted on the question of immigration controls.	**La Cámara Baja votó sobre la cuestión del control de inmigración.**
The Treasury promised to cut the proportion of national income taken in taxes to thirty per cent.	**El Ministerio de Hacienda prometió reducir a treinta por ciento la proporción de renta nacional recaudada en impuestos.**

GOVERNMENT & POLITICS

25b Elections & Ideology

Elections

ballot   **la votación**
ballot box   **la urna electoral / de votos**
ballot paper   **la papeleta de voto**
I hold an election   **celebro una elección**
campaign   **la campaña**
candidate   **el candidato**
constituency   **la circunscripción electoral**
count   **el recuento, la cuenta**
I elect   **elijo**
election   **la elección**
electorate   **el electorado**
I'm entitled to vote   **tengo derecho a votar**
floating vote   **el voto flotante**
four-year term of office   **el cargo de cuatro años**
general election   **la votación general**
I go to the polls   **voto**
I hold *(an election)*   **celebro**
local elections   **las elecciones regionales**
majority system   **el sistema mayoritario**
off-year elections / by-election   **la elección parcial**
opinion poll   **el sondeo de opinión**
party   **el partido**
poll   **el sondeo**
primary   **la primaria**

proportional system   **el sistema proporcional**
recount   **el recuento**
I recount   **vuelvo a contar**
referendum   **el referéndum**
right to vote   **el derecho de voto, el derecho a votar**
I stand for election   **me presento a la elección**
suffrage   **el sufragio**
swing   **el desplazamiento, el movimiento**
universal suffrage   **el sufragio universal**
vote   **el voto**
I vote (for)   **voto (por)**
voter   **el votante**

Political ideology

anarchist   **el anarquista**
anarchy   **la anarquía**
aristocracy   **la aristocracia**
aristocratic   **aristocrático**
capitalism   **el capitalismo**
capitalist   **capitalista**
center / centre ground   **los partidos de centro**
communism   **el comunismo**
communist   **comunista**
conservatism   **el conservadurismo, el conservatismo**
conservative   **conservador**
democracy   **la democracia**
democratic   **democrático**

Presidential elections in the United States occur every four years.

Las elecciones presidenciales en los Estados Unidos se celebran cada cuatro años.

The voters went to the polls today; it was a record turnout.

Los votantes acudieron a las urnas hoy; hubo un número récord de votantes.

dictator **el dictador**
dictatorship **la dictadura**
duke **el duque**
empire **el imperio**
emperor / empress **el emperador, la emperatriz**
extremist **extremista**
fascism **el fascismo**
fascist **fascista**
I gain independence **me independizo**
green party **el partido verde, el partido ecologista**
ideology **la ideología**
imperialism **el imperialismo**
imperialist **imperialista**
independence **la independencia**
independent **independiente**
king **el rey**
left **la izquierda**
left wing **el ala izquierda**
liberal **liberal**
liberalism **el liberalismo**
marxism **el marxismo**
marxist **marxista**
monarchy **la monarquía**
nationalism **el nacionalismo**
nationalist **nacionalista**
patriotic **patriótico**
patriotism **el patriotismo**
prince **el príncipe**
princess **la princesa**
queen **la reina**
racism **el racismo**
racist **racista**
radicalism **el radicalismo**

radical **radical**
republic **la república**
republicanism **el republicanismo**
revolutionary **el revolucionario**
right **la derecha**
right wing **el ala derecha**
royal **real**
royalist **monárquico**
socialism **el socialismo**
socialist **el socialista**

Representatives & politicians

chancellor **el canciller, el ministro**
congressman / woman **el diputado, la diputada, el / la congresista**
head of state **el jefe de estado**
leader **el líder**
mayor **el alcalde**
minister **el ministro**
minister of the interior / home secretary **el Ministro del interior**
party leader / leader of the party **el líder del partido político**
politician **el político**
prefect **el subsecretario**
president **el presidente**
prime minister **el primer ministro**
secretary of state / foreign minister **el ministro de asuntos exteriores**
senator **el senador**
speaker **el presidente de la cámara / del Parlamento**
spokesperson **el / la portavoz**

An opinion poll gave the Democrats a two point lead over the Republicans.

Un sondeo atribuyó a los Demócratas una ventaja de dos puntos sobre los Republicanos.

In the local elections, the Socialist party won a majority of seats on the town council.

En las elecciones locales, el Partido Socialista ganó una mayoría de escaños en el concejo municipal.

26 Crime & Justice

26a Crime

accomplice **el cómplice**
armed **armado**
assault **el asalto**
assault and battery **el maltrato y la agresión física**
battered baby **el bebé golpeado, el bebé maltratado**
burglar **el ladrón**
burglarize / burgle **robo en la casa**
burglary **el robo, el allanamiento de morada**
car theft **el robo de coche**
theft from car **el robo desde el coche**
child abuse **el abuso de menores**
I come to blows **me peleo a golpes**
I commit **cometo**
crime **el crimen, el delito**
crime rate **la tasa delictiva**
crime wave **la ola de crimen, la ola criminal**
criminal **el criminal, el delincuente**
criminal (adj) **criminal**
I deceive **defraudo, engaño**
delinquency **la delincuencia**

drug abuse **el abuso de drogas**
drug addict **el drogadicto**
drug barons **los capos de la droga**
drug dealer / pusher **el traficante de drogas, el camello**
drugs **las drogas**
drug trafficking **el tráfico de drogas, el narcotráfico**
I embezzle **desfalco, malverso**
embezzlement **el desfalco, la malversación**
extortion **la extorsión**
I fight **peleo, lucho, riño**
fight **la pelea, la lucha, la riña**
firearm **el arma de fuego**
I forge (banknote, signature) **falsifico**
forged **falsificado**
forgery **la falsificación**
fraud **el fraude**
gang **la banda**
gang warfare **la guerra de las pandillas**
grievous bodily harm **los daños corporales graves**
gun **la pistola**

Members of the public have begun to give information to the police about the rape of two teenage girls by a gang in west Buenos Aires last week.	**Miembros del público han empezado a dar información a la policía con respecto a la violación, la semana pasada, de dos chicas adolescentes por una pandilla en la zona del oeste de Buenos Aires.**

handbag snatching **el tirón del bolso**

handcuffs **las esposas**

Help! **¡Socorro!**

I hijack **secuestro (un avión)**

hijacker **el secuestrador aéreo**

holdup **el atraco, el asalto**

hooker **la prostituta, la fulana**

hostage **el rehén**

illegal **ilegal**

I importune **importuno, molesto**

I injure / wound **hiero, causo heridas**

I joy ride (stolen car) **conduzco un coche robado**

joy riding (stealing a car to go) **el robo de coches para la conducción temeraria**

I kidnap **rapto**

kidnapper **el raptor**

kidnapping **el rapto**

I kill **mato**

killer **el homicida**

knife **el cuchillo**

knifing **matar a cuchilladas**

legal **legal**

mafia **la mafia**

I mug **asalto**

mugger **el asaltador**

mugging **el asalto**

murder **el homicidio**

I murder **mato**

murderer **el asesino, el homicida**

I offend **cometo un delito**

pickpocket **el ratero, el carterista, el bolsista**

pickpocketing **el robo de cartera**

pimp **el proxeneta, el chulo, el alcahuete**

pimping **el proxenetismo, el chuleo**

poison **el veneno**

I poison **enveneno**

procuring **el proxenetismo, el chuleo**

prostitute **la prostituta, la fulana**

prostitution **la prostitución**

I rape **violo**

rape **la violación**

receiver **el receptador / receptor de bienes robados**

reprisals **la represalias**

shoplifting **el hurto en las tiendas**

I steal **robo**

stolen goods **los bienes robados, las cosas robadas**

terrorist **el terrorista**

torture **la tortura**

thief **el ladrón**

trafficking **el tráfico ilegal**

I traffic **trafico**

underworld **los fondos bajos, los bajos fondos**

victim **la víctima**

Pablo Escobar, the world's most infamous drug baron, was killed in a shoot-out with police and the army in Medellín.

Pablo Escobar, el magnate narcotraficante más infame del mundo, resultó muerto en un tiroteo con la policía y el ejército en Medellín.

He was stopped by the police for speeding in a residential area of Lugo.

Fue detenido por la policía por exceso de velocidad en una zona residencial de Lugo.

➤ TRIAL 26b; PUNISHMENT, CRIME PREVENTION 26c

26b Trial

accusation **la acusación**

I accuse **acuso**

accused person **el acusado**

I acquit **absuelvo**

I acquit for lack of evidence **absuelvo por falta de pruebas**

appeal **el recurso**

I appeal **recurro**

awaiting trial (in jail) **en prisión preventiva**

case for the defense **el discurso de la defensa**

compensation **la indemnización**

confession **la confesión**

I confess **confieso**

I convince **pruebo, convenzo**

costs **las costas**

counsel for the defense / defendant **el abogado defensor**

court **el juzgado, el tribunal, la corte**

court of appeal **el juzgado de apelación, la corte de apelación**

courtroom **la sala de juicios**

criminal court **el juzgado criminal, el juzgado (de lo) penal**

I cross-examine **interrogo**

I debate **debato, discuto**

defense / defence **la defensa**

I defend **defiendo**

I defend (myself) **me defiendo**

defendant **el demandado, el acusado**

diminished responsibility **la culpabilidad reducida**

I disagree **disiento**

I discuss **discuto**

district attorney **el fiscal de distrito**

dock **el banquillo de los acusados**

evidence **la prueba**

examining magistrate **el juez de instrucción**

extenuating circumstances **las circunstancias atenuantes**

eyewitness **el testigo ocular / presencial**

I find guilty **declaro culpable**

I give evidence **declaro**

for the defense **declaro en favor de la defensa**

for the prosecution **declaro en favor del cargo**

guilt **la culpa**

guilty **culpable**

high court of appeal **el tribunal supremo**

I impeach **acuso**

impeachment **la acusación**

indictment **el procesamiento**

indictment in court **el procesamiento ante el tribunal**

innocence **la inocencia**

The judge imposed a fine of two thousand pesos and ordered the accused to pay costs.

El juez le impuso al acusado una multa de dos mil pesos y le condenó con costas.

A man will appear in court today charged with the attempted murder of a fourteen-month-old baby boy.

Un hombre comparecerá hoy en el tribunal acusado de tentativa de asesinato de un nene de catorce meses.

innocent **inocente**
I inquire **pregunto**
judge **el juez**
juror **el miembro del jurado**
jury **el jurado**
jury box **el estrado del jurado**
justice **la justicia**
lawsuit **el proceso civil, el pleito, el litigio**
lawyer **el abogado, el letrado**
leniency **la clemencia**
life imprisonment **la condena a cadena/reclusión perpetua**
litigation **la litigación**
magistrate **el magistrado**
magistrate's court **el juzgado correccional/de paz**
mercy **la misericordia**
minor offense **la falta menor**
miscarriage of justice **el error de la justicia**
motive **el móvil, el motivo**
not guilty **inocente**
oath **el juramento**
offense **el delito**
order/writ **la orden, el decreto, el mandato**
I pass judgment **pronuncio sentencia**
perjury **el perjurio**
plea **el argumento de la defensa**
plea bargaining **las negociaciones para los cargos**
I plead not guilty **me declaro inocente**

premeditation **la premeditación**
I prosecute **acuso**
prosecution **la acusación**
public prosecutor **el fiscal**
public prosecutor's office **la fiscalía**
I put up/stand bail (for *someone*) **garantizo la fianza**
I question **pregunto**
retrial **la revisión del proceso**
I reward **recompenso, indemnizo**
speech for the defense/defence **el alegato de la defensa**
I stand accused **estoy acusado**
statement **la declaración**
I sue/I take to court **demando**
summons **la citación**
I suspect **sospecho**
suspicion **la sospecha**
Supreme Court **el tribunal supremo, la corte suprema**
sustained! **¡confirmado!**
I swear **juro**
I take legal action **empiezo un proceso**
trial **el juicio, el proceso**
unanimous **unánime**
verdict **el veredicto**
I witness **atestiguo**
witness **el testigo**
witness-box **el estrado de los testigos**

The case against the accused was dismissed on grounds of insufficient evidence.

El tribunal absolvió al acusado por falta de pruebas.

The accused had strong connections to the underworld.

El acusado tenía fuertes relaciones en el mundo del hampa.

CRIME & JUSTICE

26c Punishment

confinement **la reclusión**
  in solitary confinement **en régimen de aislamiento**
I convict **declaro culpable**
convict **el convicto, el reo**
death penalty **la pena de muerte**
I deport **deporto**
I escape **escapo**
fine **la multa**
I fine **multo**
I free **libero**
hard labor / labour **los trabajos forzados**
I imprison **hago prisionero, meto en prisión**
jailbird **el presidiario**
prison **la prisión, la cárcel**
prisoner **el prisionero**
I punish **castigo**
punishment **el castigo, la pena**
I am out on bail **salgo bajo fianza**
I reprieve a condemned prisoner **indulto**
I sentence to death **sentencio a muerte, condeno a muerte**
I serve a sentence **cumplo una condena**
sentence **la sentencia**

severity **la severidad, la dureza**
suspended sentence **la suspensión de sentencia**

The fight against crime

alarm **la alarma**
  burglar / car alarm **la alarma antirrobo**
autopsy **la autopsia**
arrest **el arresto**
I arrest **arresto**
baton / truncheon **la porra, el bastón**
chief of police **el comisario de policía, el jefe de policía**
civil law **el derecho civil**
clue **la pista**
come quickly! **¡venga rápido!**
crime prevention **la prevención del crimen**
criminal law **el derecho penal**
criminal record **los antecedentes penales**
customs **la aduana**
customs officer **el agente de aduana**
deportation **la deportación**
detective **el detective**
drug raid **la redada de drogas**

"What was the verdict in the trial?"

— **¿Cuál ha sido el veredicto en el proceso?**

"The defendant was sentenced to four years imprisonment."

— **El acusado fue condenado a cuatro años de cárcel.**

"Will he serve that long?"

— **¿Servirá tanto tiempo en la cárcel?**

"No, nothing like it. He'd already spent eight months awaiting trial."

— **No, nada de eso. Ya había pasado ocho meses en prisión preventiva.**

"Did he plead guilty?"

— **¿Se confesó culpable?**

"Yes, to manslaughter."

— **Sí. Se confesó culpable al homicidio sin premeditación.**

drug squad **la brigada antidrogas**
error **el error**
escape **la escapada, el escape**
I escape (to) **me escapo (a)**
examination **el examen, la prueba**
I examine **examino**
I extradite **extradito**
extradition **la extradición**
fingerprints **las huellas dactilares / digitales**
fugitive **el fugitivo**
guard dog **el perro guardián**
handcuff **la esposa**
identikit / photofit picture **el retrato robot**
informer **el informador, el confidente, el informante**
inquiry **el interrogatorio**
interview **el interrogatorio**
I interview **interrogo**
I investigate **investigo**
investigation **la investigación**
investigator **el investigador**
  private investigator **el investigador privado**
key **la clave**
law **el derecho, la ley**
lawbreaking **la contravención de la ley, el incumplimiento de la ley**

lock **la cerradura**
I lock **cierro con llave**
padlock **el candado**
plainclothes police **el policía vestido de paisano**
police officer **el policía**
police badge **la placa policial**
police record **el registro policial, los antecedentes penales**
  clean record **sin antecedentes penales**
police station **la comisaría [estación] de policía**
policeman **el policía**
policewoman **la mujer policía**
reward **la recompensa**
riot police **la policía antidisturbios [antimotines]**
security **la seguridad**
speed trap **el control de velocidad por radar**
traffic police **la policía de tráfico**
undercover **secreto, clandestino**
warrant **la orden**
  arrest warrant **la orden de prisión**
  search warrant **la orden de búsqueda**

He was convicted of breaking and entering and given a two-year sentence.

Fue declarado culpable de allanamiento de morada y condenado a dos años de prisión.

The government recommends more custodial sentences for serious offenders.

El gobierno recomienda que haya más condenas a la cárcel para los que son culpables de delitos graves.

Overcrowding is a serious problem in many prisons.

La masificación [superpoblación] es un problema grave en muchas cárceles.

▶ ADDICTION & VIOLENCE 12d

War & Peace

I abduct **rapto, secuestro, plagio**
aerial bombing **el bombardeo aéreo**
aggressor **el agresor**
air force **las fuerzas aéreas**
I airlift **me transporto por avión**
air raid **el ataque aéreo**
air raid shelter **el refugio antiaéreo**
air raid warning **la alarma antiaérea**
ambush **la emboscada**
antiaircraft **antiaviones**
army **el ejército**
I assassinate **asesino, mato**
assault **el asalto**
atomic **atómico**
I attack **ataco**
attack **el ataque**
barracks **las barracas, el cuartel**
battle **la batalla**
battlefield **el campo de batalla**
blast **la explosión**
I blockade **bloqueo**
blockade **el bloqueo**
I blow up **vuelo, hago explotar**
bomb alert **el aviso de bomba**
bombardment **el bombardeo**
brave **valiente**
I call up **llamo a filas**
camp **el campo**
campaign **la campaña**
I capture **capturo**
causes of war **las causas de la guerra**
I claim responsibility for **pido responsabilidad por**
I commit *(an act)* **cometo**
conflict **el conflicto**
confrontation **la confrontación**
I contaminate **contamino**

conventional *(weapon / warfare)* **convencional**
courtmartial **el consejo de guerra, el consejo militar**
cowardly **la cobardía**
the plane crashes **el avión se estrella**
I crush *(opposition)* **estrello**
I declare *(war)* **declaro**
defeat **la derrota**
I defeat **derroto**
I am defeated **estoy derrotado**
defense / defence **la defensa**
I defend **defiendo**
I destroy **destruyo**
I detain **detengo**
I detect **detecto**
devastating **devastador**
enemy **el enemigo**
espionage **el espionaje**
ethnic cleansing **la limpieza étnica**
I evacuate **evacúo**
evacuation **la evacuación**
I fight a battle **libro una batalla, lucho en una batalla**
I fight off **rechazo**
I flee **huyo, escapo**
front **el frente**
guerrilla warfare **la guerra de guerilleros**
harmful **dañino**
headquarters **los cuarteles generales**
hostilities **las hostilidades**
I interrogate **interrogo**
interrogation **el interrogatorio**
I intervene **intervengo**
intervention **la intervención**
intimidation **la intimidación**

I invade **invado**
invasion **la invasión**
I issue an ultimatum **doy un ultimátum**
I liquidate **liquido**
maneuvers/manoeuvres **las maniobras**
massacre **la masacre**
missing in action **desaparecido en acción**
military service **el servicio militar**
mobilization **la movilización**
I mobilize **movilizo**
morale **la moral**
multilateral **multilateral**
navy **la armada, la marina de guerra**
nuclear **nuclear**
occupation **la ocupación**
I occupy **ocupo**
offensive **la ofensiva**
  offensive *(adj)* **ofensivo**
I patrol **patrullo**
peace **la paz**
propaganda **la propaganda**
I provoke **provoco**
battle rage **el furor de la batalla**
raid **el ataque, la incursión**
rank **la fila**
reinforcements **los refuerzos**
reprisals **las represalias**
I resist **resisto**
resistance **la resistencia**
I review *(troops)* **paso revista a, revisto**

I revolt **me rebelo, me sublevo**
revolution **la revolución**
riot **el motín, la sublevación**
rubble **el escombro**
security check **la inspección de seguridad**
shell **el obús, el proyectil, la granada**
shelter **el refugio**
I sink the ship **hundo el barco**
the ship sinks **el barco se hunde**
skirmish **la escaramuza**
I spy **espío**
I start a war **comienzo una guerra**
strategy **la estrategia**
striking power **el poder ofensivo, el poder de ofensiva**
the vessel submerges **la nave se sumerge**
the vessel surfaces **la nave emerge**
survival **la supervivencia**
tactics **las tácticas**
terrorist attack **el ataque terrorista**
I threaten **amenazo**
trench **la trinchera**
underground **bajo tierra, subterráneo**
war **la guerra**
war breaks out **el estallido de guerra**
warmongering **el belicismo**
I win **gano**
wound **la herida**
I wound **hiero**

The Christmas truce was broken when hostilities resumed in Bosnia.

La tregua de Navidad fue infringida cuando se reanudaron las hostilidades en Bosnia.

Civil wars are the bloodiest of all.

Las guerras civiles son las más sangrientas de todas las guerras.

Total war is a concept of the twentieth century.

La guerra total es un concepto del siglo veinte.

WAR & PEACE

archer **el arquero**
assassin **el asesino**
casualty *(dead)* **la baja**
  casualty *(injured)* **el herido**
cavalry **la caballería**
civilian **el civil**
commandos **los comandos**
conscientious objector **el objetor de conciencia**
conscript **el conscripto**
convoy **el convoy**
deserter **el desertor**
division **la división**
foot soldier **el soldado de a pie**
general **el general**
guard **la guardia**
guerrilla **la guerrilla**
hostage **el rehén**
infantry **la infantería**
intelligence officer **el oficial de la inteligencia**
marines **la infantería de marina**
military personnel **el personal militar**
ministry of defense **el ministerio de defensa**
noncommissioned officer / NCO **el suboficial**
officer **el oficial**
orderly **el ordenanza, el asistente**
parachutist **el paracaidista**
prisoner of war **el prisionero de guerra**
rebel **el rebelde**

recruit **el reclutamiento**
regiment **el regimiento**
seaman / sailor **el marino, el marinero**
secret agent **el agente secreto**
sentry **el centinela, el guardia**
sniper **el francotirador**
soldier **el soldado**
spy **el espía**
squadron **el escuadrón**
staff **el personal**
terrorist **el terrorista**
traitor **el traidor**
troops **las tropas**
victor **el vencedor**

Weaponry & its effects

I aim (at) **apunto (a)**
aircraft carrier **el portaviones, el portaeronaves**
ammunition **la munición**
armaments **los armamentos**
armored car / armoured **el coche blindado / acorazado**
arms **las armas**
arms race **la carrera de armas**
artillery **la artillería**
bacteriological **bacteriológico**
barbed wire **el alambre de púas**
bayonet **la bayoneta**
I bomb(ard) **bombardeo**
bomb **la bomba**
bombardment **el bombardeo**
bomber *(aircraft)* **el bombardero aéreo**

In Sarajevo today, a man was shot dead by a sniper.

The explosion was several miles away, but it knocked everyone to the ground. Then the alert sounded for chemical weapons.

Hoy en Sarajevo, un hombre fue matado por un francotirador.

La explosión se produjo a varias millas de distancia, pero derribó a todo el mundo. Luego sonó la alarma de armas químicas.

bullet **la bala**
car bomb **el coche bomba**
crossbow **la ballesta**
chemical **química**
destroyer *(ship)* **el destructor**
I execute **ejecuto**
I explode a bomb **hago explotar una bomba**
explosive **el explosivo**
fighter plane **el caza**
I fire (at) **disparo a**
frigate **la fragata**
gas **el gas**
gas attack **el ataque de gas**
gun **la pistola**
hand grenade **la granada de mano**
H-bomb **la bomba H**
it hits **da contra, impacta, alcanza**
jet *(plane)* **el avión a reacción**
I kill **mato**
knife **el cuchillo, el puñal**
laser **el láser**
launcher **el lanzador**
letter bomb **la cartabomba**
machine gun **la ametralladora**
manufacturer **el fabricante**
minefield **el campo de minas**
minesweeper **el dragaminas**
missile **el misil**
mortar **el mortero**
neutron bomb **la bomba de neutrones**
nuclear test **la prueba nuclear**
nuclear warhead **la cabeza nuclear**

pistol **la pistola**
poison gas **el gas venenoso**
radar **el radar**
radar screen **la pantalla de radar**
radiation **la radiación**
radiation sickness **la enfermedad debida a la radiación**
radioactive **radioactivo**
radioactive fallout **el polvillo radioactivo**
revolver **el revólver**
rifle **el rifle**
rocket **el cohete**
rocket attack **el ataque con cohetes**
I sabotage **hago sabotaje, saboteo**
shell **el obús, el proyectil, la granada**
I shoot dead **mato de un tiro, mato a tiros**
shotgun **la escopeta**
shrapnel **la metralla**
siege **el sitio, el asedio**
I stockpile **formo una reserva**
submachine gun **la metralleta**
submarine **el submarino**
tank **el tanque**
target **el blanco, el objetivo**
torpedo **el torpedo**
torpedo attack **el ataque con torpedos**
I torpedo **torpedeo**
warship **el barco de guerra**
weapon **el arma**

The missile, which had been shot down, scattered debris over a wide area.

El misil que había sido derribado esparció escombros sobre un área extensa.

Six people were wounded when a shell landed in the old town.

Quedaron heridas seis personas al caer un proyectil sobre el barrio viejo del pueblo.

➤ CRIME 26

WAR & PEACE

27c Peace & International Relations

Peace

I ban *(the bomb)* **prohíbo**
cease-fire **el cese al fuego**
control **el control**
I declare peace **declaro la paz**
I demobilize **desmovilizo**
deterrent **la fuerza disuasiva**
I diminish tension **aminoro la tensión**
disarmament **el desarme**
exchanges of information **los intercambios de información**
free **libre**
I free **libero**
human rights **los derechos humanos**
I mediate **medio**
military service **el servicio militar**
negotiable **negociable**
negotiation **la negociación**
neutral **neutral**
neutrality **la neutralidad**
pacifism **el pacifismo**
pacifist **el pacifista**
peace **la paz**
peace plan **el plan de paz**
peace protester **el manifestante por la paz**

peace talks **las conferencias de paz**
peacekeeping force **las fuerzas para mantener la paz**
surrender **el rendimiento, la rendición**
I surrender **me rindo**
test ban **la suspensión de pruebas**
treaty **el tratado**
uncommitted **no comprometido**
victory **la victoria**

International relations

aid **la ayuda, la asistencia**
ambassador **el embajador**
arms reduction **la reducción de armamentos**
attaché **el agregado**
citizen **el ciudadano**
citizenship **la ciudadanía**
consul **el cónsul**
consulate **el consulado**
developing countries **los países en desarrollo**
diplomacy **la diplomacia**
diplomat **el diplomático**

The Spanish government was in danger of being embroiled in a diplomatic dispute.

El gobierno español corría el riesgo de enredarse en una disputa diplomática.

The Ministry of Defense announced cuts in the military budget today.

Hoy el Ministerio de Defensa anunció una reducción en el presupuesto militar.

Importers continue to take advantage of the low tariff rates.

Los importadores continúan apovechándose de las tarifas bajas.

---

206 ➤ COUNTRIES App. 20a; INTERNATIONAL ORGANIZATIONS App. 27c

diplomatic immunity **la inmunidad diplomática**
embassy **la embajada**
emergency aid **la asistencia de emergencia**
envoy **el enviado**
famine **el hambre**
foreign affairs **los asuntos exteriores**
foreign aid **la asistencia exterior**
foreigner **el extranjero**
I apply economic sanctions **empleo sanciones económicas**
I join *(organization)* **me afilio, me hago miembro de**
national security **la seguridad interior**
nonaligned **no alineado, neutral**
overseas **en ultramar, en el extranjero**
I ratify *(treaty)* **ratifico**
relief organization **la organización de beneficencia**
relief supplies **las provisiones de auxilio**
I represent **represento**
sanctions **las sanciones**
summit meeting **la cumbre**
Third World **el Tercer Mundo**
underdeveloped countries **los países subdesarrollados**

Trade

agricultural policy **la política agraria**
balance of payments **la balanza de pagos**
balance of trade **la balanza comercial**
common market **el mercado común**
currency **la moneda, la divisa**
customs **la aduana**
customs union **la unión aduanera**
European Union **la unión europea**
exchange rate **el tipo de cambio**
exports **las exportaciones**
floating currency **la divisa flotante**
it floats **flota**
foreign investment **la inversión extranjera**
free-trade zone **la zona franca**
gap between rich and poor **la diferencia entre ricos y pobres**
gross national product / GNP **el producto nacional bruto / PNB**
import controls **el control de importaciones**
imports **las importaciones**
tariff barriers **las tarifas aduaneras**
tariffs **las tarifas**
trade gap *(negative)* **el déficit exterior**

A spokesman for the Spanish Interior Ministry revealed the European Commission is investigating alleged unfair trading practices / practises.

It is hoped that the gap between rich and poor will decrease with the lifting of international trade barriers.

Un portavoz del Ministerio del Interior anunció que la Comisión Europea está investigando presuntas prácticas comerciales injustas.

Se espera que la diferencia entre ricos y pobres disminuya al suprimir las barreras al comercio internacional.

C

APPENDICES

Appendices

3b Clocks & Watches*

alarm clock   **el despertador**
clock   **el reloj**
cuckoo clock   **el reloj de cuco**
dial   **la esfera, la cara, el cuadrante**
digital watch   **el reloj digital**
egg timer   **el cronómetro para huevos**
grandfather clock   **el reloj de pie, el reloj de caja**
hand (of a clock)   **la aguja del reloj**
   minute hand   **el minutero**
   hour hand   **el horario**
   second hand   **el segundero**
hourglass   **el reloj de arena**
pendulum   **el péndulo**
stopwatch   **el cronógrafo**
sundial   **el reloj de sol**
timer   **el cronómetro de la cocina, el avisador**
watch   **el reloj de pulsera, el reloj de mano**
   watch strap   **la pulsera del reloj, la correa del reloj**
I wind up   **doy cuerda**

4d Mathematical & Geometrical Terms

acute   **agudo**
algebra   **el álgebra**
algebraic   **algebraico**
Arabic numerals   **los números arábicos**
arithmetic   **la aritmética**
arithmetical   **aritmético**
average   **el promedio**
axis   **el eje**
circumference   **la circunferencia**
complex   **complejo**

constant   **la constante**
cube   **el cubo**
cube root   **la raíz cúbica**
cubed   **al cubo**
decimal   **el decimal**
equality   **la igualdad**
factor   **el factor**
I factorize   **factorizo**
fraction   **la fracción, el quebrado**
function   **la función**
geometry   **la geometría**
geometrical   **geométrico**
imaginary   **imaginario**
integer   **el número entero**
irrational   **el número irracional**
logarithm   **el logaritmo**
mean   **la media**
median   **el medio, el número medio, el punto medio**
multiple   **el múltiplo**
nine is to three as . . .   **nueve es a tres como ...**
natural   **natural**
numerical   **numérico**
obtuse   **obtuso**
prime   **primo**
product   **el producto**
probability   **la probabilidad**
I raise to a power   **elevo a una potencia**
to the fifth power   **a la quinta potencia**
to the nth power   **a la enésima potencia**
radius   **el radio**
rational   **racional**
quotient   **el cociente**
real   **real**
reciprocal   **recíproco**
Roman   **romano**
set   **el conjunto**
square   **cuadrado**

* Appendices are numbered according to the most relevant Vocabulary.

square root **la raíz cuadrada**
symmetry **la simetría**
symmetrical **simétrico**
table(s) **las tablas**
tangent **la tangente**
trigonometry **la trigonometría**
variable **la variable**
vector **el vector**

5b Parts of the Body

ankle **el tobillo**
arm **el brazo**
back **la espalda**
backbone **la columna vertebral**
bladder **la vejiga**
blood **la sangre**
blood pressure **la presión arterial**
body **el cuerpo**
bone **el hueso**
bowel **los intestinos**
brain **el cerebro**
breast **el pecho, el busto, el seno**
buttock **las nalgas**
cheek **la mejilla**
chest **el pecho**
chin **el mentón, la quijada**
ear **la oreja**
elbow **el codo**
eye **el ojo**
eyebrow **la ceja**
eyelash **la pestaña**
face **la cara**
finger **el dedo**
fingernail **la uña**
foot **el pie**
forehead **la frente**
genitalia **los genitales**
gland **la glándula**
hair **el pelo, el cabello**
hand **la mano**
head **la cabeza**
heart **el corazón**
hip **la cadera**
hormone **la hormona**
index finger **el dedo índice**
jaw **la mandíbula**

kidney **el riñón**
knee **la rodilla**
knuckle **el nudillo**
leg **la pierna**
lid **el párpado**
lip **el labio**
liver **el hígado**
lung **el pulmón**
mouth **la boca**
muscle **el músculo**
nape of neck **la nuca**
neck **el cuello**
nose **la nariz**
nostril **la ventana de la nariz**
organ **el órgano**
part of body **la parte del cuerpo**
penis **el pene**
sex organs **los órganos sexuales**
shoulder **el hombro**
skin **la piel**
stomach **el estómago**
thigh **el muslo**
throat **la garganta**
thumb **el pulgar**
toe **el dedo del pie**
tongue **la lengua**
tooth **el diente**
vagina **la vagina**
waist **la cintura**
womb **la matriz**
wrist **la muñeca**

6a Human Characteristics

absentminded **despistado**
active **activo**
adaptable **adaptable, flexible**
affectionate **cariñoso**
aggression **la agresión**
aggressive **agresivo**
ambition **la ambición**
ambitious **ambicioso**
amusing **divertido**
anxious **ansioso, nervioso**
arrogant **arrogante**
artistic **artístico**
attractive **atractivo**

6a Human Characteristics (cont.)

bad-tempered **mal humorado**
bad / evil **malo, malvado**
boring **aburrido**
brave **valiente**
care **la atención, el cuidado**
careful **atento, cuidadoso**
careless **descuidado**
charm **encanto**
charming **encantador**
cheeky **caradura, fresco**
cheerful **alegre**
clever **listo, espabilado**
cold **frío**
comic **gracioso**
confidence **la seguridad en sí mismo**
confident **seguro de sí mismo**
conscientious **meticuloso**
courage **el valor**
courtesy **la educación, la cortesía**
cowardly **cobarde**
creative **creativo, imaginativo**
critical **crítico, exigente**
cruel **cruel**
cruelty **la crueldad**
cultured **cultivado, educado**
cunning **astuto**
curiosity **la curiosidad**
decisive (in-) **(in)decisivo, firme, tajante, (vacilante)**
demanding **exigente**
dependence (in-) **la (in)dependencia**
dependent (in-) **(in)dependiente**
distrustful **desconfiado**
eccentric **excéntrico**
energetic **enérgico, activo, vigoroso**
envious **envidioso**
envy **la envidia**
extroverted **extrovertido**
faithful (un-) **(in)fiel**
faithfulness **la fidelidad**
friendly (un-) **simpático (antipático)**

frivolous **frívolo**
generosity **la generosidad**
generous **generoso**
gentleness **la amabilidad, la ternura**
good-tempered **amable**
greed **la avaricia**
greedy **avaricioso, avaro**
hardworking **trabajador, laborioso**
helpful **servicial**
honest (dis-) **(des)honesto, (poco) honrado**
honesty (dis-) **la (des)honestidad**
honor / honour **el honor**
humane (in-) **(in)humano**
humble **humilde, modesto**
humorous **gracioso**
hypocritical **hipócrita**
idealistic **idealista**
imagination **la imaginación**
imaginative **imaginativo, creativo**
individualistic **individualista, independiente**
innocence **la inocencia**
innocent **inocente**
inquisitive **inquisitivo**
intelligence **la inteligencia**
intelligent **inteligente**
introverted **introvertido**
ironic **irónico**
kind **amable**
kindness **la amabilidad**
laziness **la pereza, la holgazanería**
lazy **perezoso, holgazán**
liberal **liberal**
likeable **simpático, fácil**
lively **animado**
lonely **solitario**
loveable **encantador**
mad **loco**
madness **la locura**
malicious **malvado**
mature (im-) **(in)maduro**

modest **modesto**
moody **voluble**
moral (im-) **(in)moral**
naive **ingenuo**
natural **natural**
nervous **nervioso**
nice **amable, simpático**
obedience (dis-) **la (des)obediencia**
obedient (dis-) **(des)obediente**
openness **la franqueza**
optimistic **optimista**
originality **la originalidad**
patience (im-) **la (im)paciencia**
patient (im-) **(im)paciente**
pessimistic **pesimista**
pleasant **agradable**
polite **educado, cortés**
politeness **la educación, la cortesía**
possessive **posesivo**
prejudiced **lleno de prejuicios**
pride **el orgullo**
proud **orgulloso**
reasonable (un-) **(poco) razonable**
rebellious **rebelde**
reserved **reservado**
respect **el respeto**
respectable **respetable**
respectful **respetuoso**
responsible (ir-) **(ir)responsable**
rude **maleducado, descortés, grosero**
rudeness **la mala educación, la descortesía, la grosería**
sad **triste**
sarcastic **sarcástico**
scornful **despreciable**
self-confident **seguro de sí mismo**
self-esteem **la autoestima**
selfish (un-) **(no) egoísta**
selfishness **el egoísmo**
self-sufficient **autosuficiente**
sensible **sensato**
sensitive (in-) **(in)sensible**

serious **serio, formal**
shy **tímido**
silent **silencioso**
silly **tonto, bobo**
sincerity **la sinceridad**
skillful **hábil**
sociable (un-) **(in)sociable**
stingy / mean **tacaño, agarrado**
strange **raro, especial**
strict **estricto**
stubborn **cabezota, tenaz, testarudo, terco**
stupidity **la estupidez**
suspicious **suspicaz**
sweet **dulce, cariñoso**
sympathetic (un-) **comprensivo, (in)compasivo**
sympathy **la compasión, la solidaridad**
tactful (-less) **(in)discreto**
talented **dotado**
talkative **hablador, charlatán**
temperamental **temperamental**
thoughtful **pensativo, considerado**
thoughtless **irreflexivo, desconsiderado**
tidy (un-) **(des)ordenado, limpio**
tolerance (in-) **la (in)tolerancia**
tolerant (in-) **(in)tolerante**
traditional **conservador, tradicional**
trust **la confianza**
trusting **confiado**
vain **vanidoso, engreído, vano**
vanity **la vanidad**
violent **violento, agresivo**
virtuous **virtuoso**
warm **cálido**
well-adjusted **equilibrado**
well-behaved **bueno, de buena conducta**
wisdom **la prudencia, la sabiduría**
wise **prudente**
wit **el ingenio**
witty **ingenioso, vivo, ocurrente**

8b Tools

ax / axe **el hacha**
bit **la barrena**
blade **el filo**
bolt **el tornillo**
bucket **el cubo**
chisel **el formón, el cincel**
crowbar **la palanca**
drill **el taladro**
file **la lima**
garden gloves **los guantes de jardinería**
garden shears **las tijeras de jardín**
hammer **el martillo**
hedge clippers **las tijeras podadoras**
hoe **la azada**
hose **la manguera**
ladder **la escalera, la escala**
lawnmower **el cortacésped, [la segadora]**
mallet **el mazo**
nail **el clavo**
nut **la tuerca**
paint **la pintura**
paintbrush **la brocha, el pincel**
pickax(e) **el pico, el zapapico**
plane **el cepillo de carpintería**
pliers **los alicates, las pinzas**
rake **el rastrillo**
sandpaper **el papel de lija**
saw **la sierra**
screw **el tornillo**
screwdriver **el destornillador**
shovel **la pala**
spade **la laya**
spirit level **el nivel de aire**
stepladder **la escalera doble / de tijera**
toolbox **la caja de herramientas**
trowel **el desplantador**
varnish **el barniz**
vise **el torno de banco**
weedkiller **el herbicida**

wrench / spanner (adjustable) **la llave (de tuercas)**

9a Shops, Stores & Services

antique store / shop **la tienda de antigüedades, el anticuario**
bakery / baker's **la panadería**
bank **el banco**
bookmaker's / betting shop **la agencia de apuestas**
bookstore / -shop **la librería**
boutique **la boutique**
butcher's **la carnicería**
candy store / sweetshop **la confitería, [la dulcería]**
car parts / spares store / shop **la tienda de repuestos / recambios**
charity shop / store **la tienda de sociedad benéfica / de caridad**
clothes store / shop **la tienda de modas / de ropa**
cosmetics store / shop **la tienda de estética, [el almacén de cosméticos]**
covered market **la plaza del mercado**
dairy **la lechería**
delicatessen **el delicatessen**
department stores **los (grandes) almacenes, [el centro comercial]**
dress store / shop **la casa de modas**
drugstore / chemist's **la farmacia, la droguería**
dry cleaners **la tintorería, [la lavandería]**
electrical store / shop **la tienda de material eléctrico / de electrodomésticos**
fast-food store / shop **la tienda de fast-food / [de comidas rápidas]**

fish store / fishmonger's **la pescadería**

fishstall **el puesto de pescado**

florist's **la floristería**

furniture store / shop **la tienda de muebles**

garden center / centre **el centro de jardinería**

greengrocer's **la verdulería, la verdurería, [la tienda de verduras]**

grocer **el tendero (de ultramarinos), el mantequero**

grocery / grocer's **la tienda de ultramarinos, la tienda de comestibles, [la tienda]**

hairdresser **el peluquero, la peluquera**

hairdresser's **la peluquería**

hardware store / shop **la ferretería**

healthfood store / shop **la tienda de alimentos naturales**

indoor market **la plaza del mercado cubierta**

insurance agent / broker **el agente de seguros**

jeweler's / jewelry store **la joyería**

kiosk **el quiosco, el kiosco**

laundromat / launderette **la lavandería automática**

market **el mercado**

men's shop / store **la tienda de ropa de caballero**

model shop / store **la tienda de juguetes / miniaturas**

music store / shop **la tienda de música**

newspaper kiosk **el quiosco de periódicos**

newsstand / newsagent's **el vendedor de periódicos**

optician's **la (tienda de) óptica**

outdoor / open-air market **el mercado**

pastry shop / cakeshop **la pastelería**

petshop / pet store **la pajarería**

pharmacy **la farmacia**

photographic shop / store **la tienda de fotografía**

post office **Correos, [la oficina de correos]**

pottery shop / store **la tienda de cerámica, [la alfarería]**

real estate / estate agent **el agente inmobiliario**

shoe repair shop / store **el zapatero remendón, [la remontadora de calzado]**

shoe store / shop **la zapatería, [el almacén de zapatos]**

shoemaker's / cobbler's **la tienda del zapatero remendón, [la remontadora de calzado]**

shop / store **la tienda**

shopping mall / shopping center **el centro comercial, la zona de tiendas**

souvenir shop / store **la tienda de recuerdos**

sports store / shop **la tienda de deportes**

stationer's / stationery store **la papelería**

store **la tienda, el almacén**

supermarket **el supermercado**

superstore / hypermarket **el hipermercado, [la supertienda]**

take-out / take-away food shop / store **tienda de comidas para llevar**

tobacconist's / tobacco store **el estanco, la tabaquería, [la cigarrería]**

toy store / toyshop **la juguetería**

travel agent **la agencia de viajes**

vendor **el vendedor, la vendedora**

vending machine **la vendedora automática**

video store / video-shop **la tienda de vídeo**

9a Currencies

dollar   el dólar
bolivar   el bolivar
peso   el peso
centavo   el centavo
euro   el euro
pound sterling   la libra esterlina
ruble   el rublo
yen   el yen

9c Jewelry / Jewellery

bangle   la esclava
chain bracelet   la pulsera
brooch   el broche
carat   el quilate
chain   la cadena
charm   el amuleto, [el dije]
cuff links   los gemelos, [las mancornas]
earrings   los pendientes
engagement ring   la sortija de pedida, [el anillo de compromiso]
jewel   la joya
jewelry / jewellery   la joyería
jewelry box   el joyero
medallion   el medallón
necklace   el collar
pendant   el medallón
precious stone / gem   la piedra preciosa
real   verdadero
ring   el anillo, la sortija
semiprecious stone   la piedra semipreciosa
tiara   la diadema
tie pin   el alfiler de corbata
wedding ring   el anillo de boda

9c Precious Stones & Metals

agate   el ágata
amber   el ámbar
amethyst   la amatista
chrome   el cromo
copper   el cobre
coral   el coral
crystal   el cristal
diamond   el diamante
emerald   la esmeralda
gold   el oro
gold plate   la lámina de oro
ivory   el marfil
mother-of-pearl   el nácar, la madreperla
onyx   el ónix
pearl   la perla
pewter   el peltre
platinum   el platino
quartz   el cuarzo
ruby   el rubí
sapphire   el zafiro
silver plate   la vajilla de plata
silver   la plata
topaz   el topacio
turquoise   la turquesa

10c Herbs & Spices

aniseed   el anís
basil   la albahaca
bay leaf   la hoja de laurel
caper   la alcaparra
caraway   la alcaravea
chives   el cebollino
cinnamon   la canela
clove   el clavo
cumin   el comino
dill   el eneldo
garlic   el ajo
ginger   el jengibre
marjoram   la mejorana
mint   la menta
mixed herbs   las hierbas finas
mustard   la mostaza
nutmeg   la nuez moscada

oregano el orégano
parsley el perejil
rosemary el romero
saffron el azafrán
sage la salvia
tarragon el estragón
thyme el tomillo

10d Cooking Utensils

alumin(i)um foil el papel
  aluminio / de estaño
baking tray la bandeja de horno
can / tin opener el abrelatas
carving knife el trinchante
colander el colador
food processor el robot de cocina
fork el tenedor
frying pan / fry-pan la sartén
grater el rallador
grill la parrilla
kettle el hervedor
knife el cuchillo
lid la cobertera, la tapa
pot la olla
rolling pin el rodillo
saucepan / casserole dish el cazo,
  la cacerola
scale la balanza
sieve la coladera
skewer la broqueta
spatula la espátula
spoon la cuchara
tablespoon la cuchara grande
tablespoonful la cucharada
teaspoon la cucharilla
teaspoonful la cucharadita
tenderizer el ablandador
wax paper / greaseproof el papel
  apergaminado

10d Smoking

ashtray el cenicero
box of matches la cajita de
  cerillas
cigar el puro

cigarette el cigarrillo
cigarette butt / stub la colilla
lighter el encendedor
matches las cerillas
pipe la pipa
smoke el humo
I smoke fumo
(no) smoking (no) fumadores
tobacco el tabaco
tobacconist's el estanco, la
  tabaquería, [la cigarrería]

11b Illness & Disability

AIDS el SIDA
angina la angina
appendicitis la apendicitis
arthritis la artritis
asthma el asma (f)
bacillus el bacilo
bacteria la bacteria
blister la ampolla
boil el divieso, el furúnculo
bronchitis la bronquitis
bruise la contusión, el cardenal,
  la magulladura, el magullón, el
  moretón
bubonic plague la peste bubónica
cancer el cáncer
catarrh el catarro
chicken pox la varicela
cholera el cólera
colic el cólico
cold el resfriado, el catarro
constipation el estreñimiento
corn el callo
cough la tos
deafness la sordera
death la muerte
depression la depresión
dermatitis la dermatitis
diabetes la diabetes
diarrhea la diarrea
diptheria la difteria
disease la enfermedad
dizziness el vértigo, el mareo
earache el dolor de oídos

217

eczema   **el eccema, el eczema**
epilepsy   **la epilepsia**
fever   **la fiebre**
fit   **el ataque**
fleas   **las pulgas**
flu   **la gripe**
food poisoning   **la intoxicación alimenticia, la toxinfección alimenticia**
gallstones   **el cálculo biliario**
German measles   **la rubéola**
gingivitis   **la gingivitis**
gonorrhea   **la gonorrea**
graze   **el roce, la abrasión, [la raspadura]**
hemorrhoids   **las hemorroides**
head louse   **el piojo**
headache   **el dolor de cabeza**
heart attack   **el ataque cardíaco**
hepatitis   **la hepatitis**
hernia   **la hernia**
high blood pressure   **la hipertensión**
HIV positive   **(el virus de la inmunodeficiencia humana) VIH positivo**
illness / sickness   **la enfermedad**
incontinence   **la incontinencia**
influenza   **la gripe**
infection   **la infección, el contagio**
jaundice   **la ictericia**
leukemia   **la leucemia**
louse   **el piojo**
malaria   **la malaria, el paludismo**
measles   **el sarampión**
meningitis   **la meningitis**
mental illness   **la enfermedad mental**
microbe   **el microbio**
migraine   **la jaqueca**
mumps   **las paperas, las parótidas**
nit   **la liendre**
overdose   **la sobredosis**
piles   **las almorranas, las hemorroides**
pneumonia   **la pulmonía**

polio   **el polio**
pregnancy   **el embarazo, la preñez**
rabies   **la rabia**
rheumatism   **el reumatismo**
salmonella   **la salmonelosis**
scabies   **la sarna**
seasickness   **el mareo**
sickness   **la enfermedad, el malestar**
smallpox   **la viruela**
stomachache   **el dolor de estómago**
stomach upset   **el trastorno estomacal**
stroke   **el ataque fulminante, la apoplejía**
stye   **el orzuelo**
syphilis   **la sífilis**
temperature   **la calentura, la fiebre**
tetanus   **el tétanos**
thrombosis   **la trombosis**
tonsillitis   **la amigdalitis**
toothache   **el dolor de muelas**
tuberculosis   **la tuberculosis**
ulcers   **las úlceras**
urinary infection   **la infección urinaria**
venereal disease   **la enfermedad venérea**
whooping cough   **la tos ferina**
yellow fever   **la fiebre amarilla**

11c Hospital Departments

admissions   **la secretaría, las admisiones**
blood bank   **el banco de sangre**
casualty   **(la sección de) accidentes**
consulting room   **el consultorio, la consulta**
coronary care unit   **la sección de asistencia cardíaca**
dialysis unit   **la sección de diálisis**

emergency **las urgencias**
geriatric **la geriatría**
gynecology **la ginecología**
infectious diseases **las enfermedades infectocontagiosas**
intensive care **la asistencia intensiva**
maternity **la maternidad**
medical ward **la sala médica**
mortuary **el mortuorio, el depósito de cadáveres, la funeraria, [el anfiteatro]**
oncology **la oncología**
operating room / theater **el quirófano, la sala de operaciones**
orthopedic **ortopédico**
outpatient department **el departamento de consulta externa**
pediatrics **la pediatría**
pathology **la patología**
pharmacy **la farmacia**
psychiatric **la psiquiatría**
reception **la recepción**
recovery room **la sala de posoperatorio / recuperación**
surgery **la cirugía**
treatment room **la sala de tratamiento / cura / medicación**
ward **la sala**
X rays **los rayos-X, la radiografía**

13b Holidays & Religious Festivals

All Saints (Nov 1) **el día de todos los santos**
All Souls (Nov 2) **el día de los difuntos**
Ascension Day **el día de la ascensión**
Ash Wednesday **el miércoles de ceniza**

Assumption Day (Aug 15) **el día de la asunción**
Candlemas **el día de la candelaria**
Christmas Day **el día de Navidad**
Christmas Eve **el día de Nochebuena**
Christmas **la Navidad**
at Christmas **en Navidad**
Corpus Christi **el Corpus Cristi**
Easter **la Semana Santa**
Easter Monday **el lunes de Pascua de Resurrección**
Easter Sunday **el domingo de Resurrección**
Eid **el Eid**
festival **el festival**
Good Friday **el Viernes Santo**
Hanukkah **el Hanukkah**
Labor / Labour Day **el día de los trabajadores, el día de San José obrero, el día del trabajo**
Lent **la cuaresma**
New Year's Day **el día de Año Nuevo**
New Year's Eve **el día de Nochevieja**
Palm Sunday **el domingo de Ramos**
Passover **la Pascua judía**
Pentecost / Whitsun **Pentecostés**
Ramadan **El Ramadán**
Sabbath **el sábado**
Shrove Tuesday / Carnival **el martes de carnaval**
Whitsuntide **la semana de Pentecostés**
Yom Kippur **el Yom Kippur**

14b Professions & Jobs

The arts

actor / actress **el actor, la actriz**
announcer **el presentador, el locutor, la presentadora, la locutora**
architect **el arquitecto, la arquitecta**
artist **el / la artista**
bookseller **el vendedor de libros, el librero**
cameraman **el cámara, el camarógrafo**
editor **el redactor**
journalist **el / la periodista**
movie / film director **el director de cine / la directora de cine**
movie / film star **la estrella de cine**
musician **el / la músico**
painter *(artist)* **el pintor, la pintora**
photographer **el fotógrafo / la fotógrafa**
poet **el poeta / la poetisa**
printer **el impresor**
producer (theater / theatre) **el productor / la productora de teatro**
publisher **el editor**
reporter **el reportero, la reportera**
sculptor **el escultor, la escultora**
singer **el cantante, la cantante**
television announcer **el presentador / la presentadora de televisión**
writer **el escritor, la escritora**

Education & research

headteacher / principal **el director, la directora, el rector, la rectora**
lecturer **el profesor universitario, la profesora universitaria**
physicist **el físico, la física**
primary school teacher **el profesor / la profesora de escuela primaria, el maestro, la maestra**
researcher **el investigador, la investigadora**
scientist **el científico, la científica**
secondary school teacher **el profesor / la profesora de escuela secundaria**
student **el / la estudiante**
technician **el técnico, la técnica**

Food & retail

baker **el panadero, la panadera**
brewer **el cervecero, la cervecera**
butcher **el carnicero, la carnicera**
buyer **el encargado / la encargada de compras**
caterer *(supplying meals)* **el abastecedor de comidas**
chemist **el químico, la química**
cook **el cocinero, la cocinera**
farmer **el granjero, la granjera**
fisherman **el pescador, la pescadora**
fishmonger **el pescadero, la pescadera**
florist **el / la florista**
greengrocer **el verdulero, la verdulera, [el vendedor / la vendedora de verduras]**
grocer **el tendero / la tendera (de comestibles)**
jeweler / jeweller **el joyero, la joyera**
pharmacist **el farmacéutico, la farmacéutica**
representative **el representante, el diputado, la diputada**
salesclerk / shop assistant **el dependiente / la dependienta de comercio**
storekeeper / shopkeeper **el tendero, la tendera**
tobacconist **el tabaquero, el estanquero**
waiter **el camarero, la camarera**
winegrower **el vinicultor, la vinicultora**

Government service

civil servant   **el funcionario, la funcionaria**
clerk   **el / la oficinista**
customs officer   **el / la agente de aduanas**
fireman   **el bombero, la mujer bombero**
judge   **el / la juez**
minister   **el ministro, la ministra**
officer   **el oficial, la oficial**
policeman   **el policía**
policewoman   **la mujer policía**
politician   **el político, la política**
sailor   **el marino, la marino, el marinero**
secret agent   **el agente secreto, la agente secreta**
senator / member of Parliament   **el senador, la senadora, el diputado, la diputada**
serviceman   **el / la militar**
soldier   **el / la soldado**

Health care

dentist   **el / la dentista**
doctor (Dr.)   **el médico, la médica, el doctor, la doctora**
midwife   **la comadrona**
nurse   **el enfermero, la enfermera**
optician   **el / la óptico, [el optómetra]**
physician   **el médico**
psychiatrist   **el / la psiquiatra**
psychologist   **el psicólogo / la psicóloga**
surgeon   **el cirujano, la cirujana**
veterinarian   **el veterinario, la veterinaria**

In manufacturing & construction

bricklayer   **el / la albañil**
builder   **el constructor**
carpenter   **el carpintero, la carpintera**
engineer   **el ingeniero, la ingeniera**

foreman   **el / la capataz**
industrialist   **el / la industrial**
laborer / labourer   **el trabajador, la trabajadora, el obrero, la obrera**
manufacturer   **el / la fabricante**
mechanic   **el mecánico, la mecánica**
metalworker   **el trabajador / la trabajadora del metal**
miner   **el minero, la minera**
plasterer   **el yesero, la yesera, el enlucidor, el albañil**
stonemason   **el cantero**

Services

accountant   **el / la contable, el contador, la contadora**
actuary   **el actuario / la actuaria de seguros**
agent   **el / la agente**
bank manager   **el director / la directora de banco**
businessman   **el hombre de negocios**
businesswoman   **la mujer de negocios**
caretaker   **el / la vigilante, el conserje**
cleaner   **el limpiador, la limpiadora**
computer programmer   **el programador / la programadora de ordenadores [de computadoras]**
counselor   **el asesor, la asesora, el consejero, la consejera**
draftsman   **el / la delineante**
electrician   **el / la electricista**
garbageman / dustman   **el basurero, la basurera**
gardener   **el jardinero, la jardinera**
gasman   **el trabajador / la trabajadora del gas**
guide   **el / la guía**

hairdresser **el peluquero, la peluquera**
insurance agent **el / la agente de seguros**
interpreter **el / la intérprete**
job counselor / careers adviser **el consejero / la consejera profesional**
labor / trade unionist **el / la sindicalista**
lawyer / solicitor **el abogado, la abogada, el letrado / la letrada**
librarian **el bibliotecario, la bibliotecaria**
mail carrier / postman **el cartero, la cartera**
mover / furniture remover **el empleado / la empleada de la mudanza**
office worker **el / la oficinista**
painter and decorator **el pintor, la pintora, el decorador, la decoradora**
plumber **el fontanero, la fontanera**
priest **el sacerdote**
receptionist **el / la recepcionista**
servant **el criado, la criada**
social worker **el / la asistente social**
stockbroker **el / la agente de bolsa**
surveyor **el topógrafo, la topógrafa**
tax inspector **el inspector / la inspectora de impuestos / hacienda**
translator **el traductor, la traductora**
travel agent **el agente de viajes**
typist **el mecanógrafo, la mecanógrafa**
undertaker **el director de pompas fúnebres**

Transportation

bus driver **el conductor / la conductora de autobuses**
driver **el conductor, la conductora**
driving instructor **el profesor / la profesora de autoescuela / conducción**

pilot **el / la piloto**
stewardess / air hostess **la azafata**
taxi driver **el / la taxista**
ticket inspector **el revisor, la revisora**
truck / lorry driver **el camionero, la camionera**

14b Places of Work

blast furnace **el alto horno**
branch office **la sucursal**
brewery **la cervecería**
business park **el centro de negocios**
construction site **la obra**
distillery **la destilería**
factory **la fábrica**
farm **la granja**
foundry **la fundición**
head office **la oficina principal**
hospital **el hospital**
mill **el molino**
  paper mill **la fábrica de papel**
  rolling mill **el taller de laminación**
  sawmill **el aserradero**
  spinning mill **la hilandería**
  steel mill **la fábrica de acero, la fábrica siderúrgica, la fundidura**
  weaving mill **la fábrica de tejidos**
mine **la mina**
office **la oficina**
plant **la planta**
public company **la empresa pública**
steel plant / steelworks **la fábrica de acero, la fábrica siderúrgica**
store / shop **la tienda, el almacén**
sweatshop **taller de trabajo afanoso y poco sueldo**
theme park **el parque temático**
vineyard / winery **la viña**
warehouse **el almacén, el depósito**
workshop **el taller**

14b Company Personnel & Structure

accounts department **el departamento de cuentas / contabilidad**
apprentice **el aprendiz, la aprendiza**
assistant **el ayudante, el asistente**
associate **el asociado, el socio**
board of directors **el consejo directivo, la junta de directores**
boss **el jefe**
colleague **el colega, el compañero de trabajo**
department **el departamento**
director **el director**
division **la división**
employee **el empleado**
employer **el empresario, el patrón / la patrona**
executive **el ejecutivo**
foreman **el capataz**
labor / labour **el trabajo**
line manager **el encargado de sección**
management **la dirección, la gestión, la administración, la gerencia**
manager **el director, el encargado, el gerente**
manager (f) **la directora, la encargada, la gerente**
managing director / CEO **el director / la directora general**
marketing department **el departamento de márketing / mercadeo**
personal assistant **el asistente personal**
president **el presidente**
production department **el departamento de producción**
sales department **el departamento de ventas**
secretary **el secretario, la secretaria**
specialist **el especialista**
staff / personnel **el personal**
team **el equipo**
trainee **el empleado en período de aprendizaje, el aprendiz**
vice president **el vicepresidente**

15c Letter-Writing Formulae

Dear . . . **Querido / a ...**
Dear Madam **Muy señora mía, Estimada**
Dear Mr. and Mrs. . . . **Estimados Señores ...**
Dear Peter **Querido Pedro, Mi querido amigo Pedro**
Dear Sir **Muy señor mío, Estimado señor**
greetings from **recuerdos de**
I am pleased that **Me alegro de**
I enclose **Remito adjunto / a**
All the best to **Recuerdos para**
Best wishes from **Saludos de**
Love from **Besos, Un abrazo de ..., Un cariñoso saludo de ...**
With best wishes from **Saludos de, Un cordial saludo de**
With kind regards **Con muchos recuerdos**
Yours faithfully **Lo / La saluda atentamente**
Yours sincerely **Lo / La saluda atentamente / cordialmente**

15d Computer Hardware

adaptor **el adaptador**
backlit screen **la pantalla a iluminación trasera**
battery **la pila, la batería**
brightness **el brillo**
brightness control **el botón de ajuste del brillo**
charger **el cargador**
central processing unit **la unidad procesadora central**

APPENDICES

chip   el chip, la micropastilla, el microplaquete, el circuito integrado
computer   el ordenador, la computadora
computer system   el sistema de ordenadores
delete key   la tecla de borrado
desktop   ... de escritorio
disk / disc drive   la unidad de disco, el disk drive
disk / disc   el disco
diskette   el disquete, el diskette, el disco flexible
display   la visualización, el despliegue
double density disk / disc   el disco de densidad doble
drive   la unidad de disco, el disk drive
escape key   la tecla de escape
exit key   la tecla de salida
flat screen monitor   la pantalla plana
floppy disk   el disco flexible, el floppy, el disquete, el diskette
floppy drive   la unidad de disco, el disk drive
function key   la tecla de función
hard disk   el disco duro
hard drive   la unidad del disco duro
hardware   el hardware, el material informático
high density disk   el disco de densidad alta
integrated circuit   el circuito integrado
interface   la interfaz, el interface
keyboard   el teclado
laptop   el ordenador portátil plegable
liquid crystal display   el visualizador de cristal líquido
local area network / LAN   la red de área local

Macintosh   Macintosh, una Mac
mainframe computer   la computadora central, el ordenador central
microprocessor   el microprocesador
minicomputer   el miniordenador, el minicomputador
modem   el módem
  dial-up   marcar
  DSL   DSL
  cable   cable
monitor   el monitor
mouse   el ratón
network   la red
personal computer / PC   el ordenador personal, el computador personal
plug-in drive   la unidad de disco enchufable
port   la puerta, el puerto, el port
portable   portátil
processor   el procesador
random access memory / RAM   el RAM / la memoria de acceso directo
resolution   la resolución, la definición
return key   la tecla de retorno
screen   la pantalla
scroll bar   la barra de desplazamiento
space bar   el espaciador, la espaciadora
terminal   la terminal
touch screen   la pantalla de toque
visual display unit / VDU   la unidad de presentación visual, la unidad de despliegue visual
viewdata system   el sistema de videodatos
wide area network / WAN   la red de área amplia

15d Computer Software

algebraic **algebraico**
algorithm **el algoritmo**
bug **el duende, el fallo, el error**
byte **el byte, el octeto**
coding **la codificación**
command **el comando**
compatible **compatible**
compatibility **la compatibilidad**
computer aided design / CAD **el diseño asistido por ordenador / DAO**
computer aided learning / CAL **la instrucción asistida por ordenador / IAO**
computer aided language learning / CALL **la enseñanza de lenguas asistida por ordenador**
computer animation **la animación por ordenador**
computer graphics **las gráficas por ordenador**
computer language **el lenguaje de ordenador**
computer literacy **la competencia en la informática**
computer literate **competente en la informática**
copy **la copia**
corrupted **degradado**
data **los datos**
data capture **la formulación de datos**
data entry **la entrada de datos**
data processing **el tratamiento de datos**
database **la base de datos**
default option **la opción por defectos**
double clicking **el doble pulsar, el doble clic (del ratón)**
drive **la unidad de disco**
escape **el escape**
exit **la salida del sistema**
file **el fichero**
flowchart **el diagrama de flujo, el**
organigrama, el ordinograma
format **el formato**
function **la función**
graphical **gráfico**
graphical application **la aplicación gráfica**
graphics **los gráficos**
graphics accelerator **el acelerador de gráficos**
help **ayuda, asistencia, auxilio**
help menu **el menú de asistencia**
incompatible **incompatible**
information technology / IT **la informática**
language **el lenguaje**
logic circuit **el circuito lógico**
low / high density **la densidad baja / alta**
macro **macro**
memory **la memoria**
menu **el menú**
operating system **el sistema de explotación, el sistema operativo**
on-line **on-line, en línea**
output **la salida, el output**
output unit **la unidad de salida, el dispositivo de salida**
password **la contraseña de acceso**
program(me) **el programa**
programmable **programable**
programmer **el programador**
programming **la programación**
pulldown menu **el menú desplegable**
reference archive **el archivo de referencias, el archivo de consulta**
return **el retorno**
software **el software, los elementos de programación**
software package **el paquete de programas**
sort **la ordenación**
space **el espacio**
spreadsheet **la hoja electrónica,**

la hoja de cálculo
statistics package el paquete estadístico
update la actualización
user friendly fácil de utilizar
virus el virus

15d Computer Printing

continuous paper el papel continuo
font la fuente, el tipo de letra
hard copy la copia impresa
ink cartridge el cartucho / el recambio de tinta
inkjet la impresora de chorro de tinta
laser printer la impresora (por) láser
paper feed el alimentador de papel
paper tray la reserva de papel
ribbon la cinta (de impresora)
roller el rodillo
sheetfeeder el alimentador de papel
style el estilo
toner el virador

16a Hobbies

angling la pesca con caña
archeology la arqueología
archery el tiro con arco
ballroom dancing el baile de salón
beekeeping la apicultura
birdwatching la ornitología, la observación de aves
carpentry la carpintería
collecting antiques la colección de antigüedades
collecting stamps la colección de sellos / [estampillas]
dancing bailar

fishing la pesca
gambling el juego
gardening la jardinería
going to the movies / cinema ir al cine
knitting el tejido de punto
listening to music escuchar música
photography la fotografía
playing chess jugar al ajedrez
reading la lectura
sewing la costura
spinning hilar
walking pasear
watching television mirar la televisión

17b Architectural Terms

alcove el hueco, el nicho
arch el arco
architrave el arquitrabe
atrium el atrio
bas relief el bajorrelieve
battlement la almena
buttress el contrafuerte
capital el capitel
caryatid la cariátide
colonnade la galería
column la columna
  doric dórica
  ionic jónica
  corinthian corintia
concave cóncavo
convex convexo
cornerstone la piedra angular
cupola la cúpula
diptych el díptico
drawbridge el puente levadizo
eaves el alero
facade la fachada
fanlight el montante de abánico
frieze / dado el zócalo, el friso
gable el frontón
gargoyle la gárgola
half-timbered con entramado de madera

haut relief **el altorrelieve**
headstone **la lápida**
herringbone *(adj)* **de espinapez**
molding / moulding **el zócalo**
nave **la nave**
ogive **la ojiva**
oval **ovalado**
overhanging **sobresaliente, voladizo**
pagoda **la pagoda**
pilaster **la pilastra**
pinnacle **el pináculo**
plinth **el plinto**
porch **el pórtico, la entrada**
portico **el pórtico, la arcada**
rear arch **el arco trasero**
roof **el tejado**
rosette **el rosetón**
rotunda **la rotonda**
sacristy **la sacristía**
spire / steeple **la aguja**
triumphal arch **el arco triunfal, de triunfo**
tryptych **el tríptico**
vault **la bóveda**
vaulted **abovedado**
volute **la voluta**
wainscot **el revestimiento**

17c Publishing

abridged version **la versión abreviada**
acknowledgment **el agradecimiento**
appendix **el apéndice**
artwork **la obra de arte**
author **el autor**
best-seller **el best-seller, el libro de más venta**
bibliography **la bibliografía**
book fair **la feria del libro**
catalogue **el catálogo**
chapter **el capítulo**
contents **el contenido**
contract **el contrato**
copy **la copia**

copyright **el derecho de autor**
cover *(of book)* **la cubierta, la tapa**
deadline **el plazo**
dedicated to **dedicado a**
edition **la edición**
    first edition **la primera edición**
    latest edition **la última edición**
editor **el redactor**
    literary editor **el redactor literario**
footnotes **las notas a pie de página**
illustrations **las ilustraciones**
manuscript **el manuscrito**
paperback **la cubierta rústica, el libro en rústica**
preface **el prefacio**
proofreading **la corrección de textos**
publication date **la fecha de publicación**
publisher **el editor**
publishing house **la casa editorial**
quote **la cita**
review **la revisión, la revista**
reviewer **el crítico, el reseñante**
subtitle **el subtítulo**
translation **la traducción**
version **la versión**
with a foreword by **con prólogo escrito por**

17d Musicians & Instruments

accordionist **el acordeonista**
alto *(singer)* **el contralto**
bagpipe **la gaita**
baritone **el barítono**
bass *(singer)* **el bajo**
bass clarinet **el clarinete bajo**
basset horn **el cuerno de bajo**
bassoon **el fagot**
bassoonist **el fagotista**
bells **las campanas tubulares**
bugle **la corneta, el clarín**
castanets **las castañuelas**

celeste **la celesta**
cellist **el violoncelista**
cello **el violoncelo**
cembalo **el cémbalo**
chorister **el corista**
clarinet **el clarinete**
clarinetist **el clarinetista**
clarion **la trompeta**
classical guitar **la guitarra clásica**
clavicord **el clavicordio**
conductor **el director de orquesta**
contralto **el contralto**
cornet **la corneta**
cymbal **el cimbal**
double bass **el contrabajo**
double bassoon **el contrafagot**
drum **el tambor**
drummer **el batería**
dulcimer **el salterio, el dulcémele**
flautist **el flautista**
flute **la flauta**
French horn **el cuerno francés**
grand piano **el piano de cola**
guitar **la guitarra**
guitarist **el guitarrista**
harmonica / mouth organ **la armónica**
harmonium **el armonio**
harp **el arpa** *(f)*
harpist **el arpista**
harpsichord **el clavicordio**
horn **el cuerno**
hurdy-gurdy **el organillo**
instrumentalist **el instrumentalista**
jews' harp **el birimbao**
librettist **el libretista**
lyre **la lira**
mandolin **la mandolina**
mezzo-soprano **la mezzosoprano**
oboe **el oboe**
oboe player **el oboe**
orchestra leader **el primer violín**
orchestra players **los músicos de la orquesta**
organ **el órgano**
organist **el organista**
percussion **los instrumentos de percusión**

percussionist **el percusionista**
pianist **el pianista**
piano **el piano**
pipe **la gaita, el tubo**
recorder **la flauta dulce, la flauta de pico**
saxophone **el saxofón**
saxophonist **el saxofonista**
soprano **el / la soprano**
spinet **la espineta**
accordion **la concertina**
string instruments **los instrumentos de cuerda**
strolling musician / busker **el músico ambulante**
synthesizer **el sintetizador**
tenor **el tenor**
tin whistle **la flauta metálica**
triangle **el triángulo**
trombone **el trombón**
trumpet **la trompeta**
tuba **la tuba**
tuning fork **el diapasón**
timpani **los tímpanos**
viol **la viola**
viola **la violeta, la viola**
viola player **el músico de viola**
violin **el violín**
violinist **el violinista**
violoncello **el violoncelo**
vocalist **el cantante**
Welsh harp **el arpa** *(f)* **galesa**
xylophone **el xilófono**

17d Musical Forms

aria **el aria** *(f)*
ballad **la balada**
cantata **la cantata**
canzonetta **la canzoneta**
chamber music **la música de cámara**
choral music **la música coral**
concerto **el concierto**
    piano concerto **el concierto para piano**
duet **el dúo**

fugue   **la fuga**
madrigal   **el madrigal**
march   **la marcha**
music drama   **el drama musical**
musical (comedy)   **la comedia musical**
nocturne   **el nocturno**
octet   **el octeto**
opera   **la ópera**
operetta   **la opereta**
oratorio   **el oratorio**
overture   **la obertura**
piano trio   **el trío de piano**
plainsong   **el canto llano**
prelude   **el preludio**
quartet   **el cuarteto**
quintet   **el quinteto**
recitative   **el recitativo, el recitado**
requiem Mass   **la misa de réquiem**
sacred music   **la música sagrada**
serenade   **la serenata**
sextet   **el sexteto**
septet   **el septeto**
sinfonietta   **la sinfonieta**
sonata   **la sonata**
song cycle   **el ciclo de canciones**
suite   **la suite**
symphony   **la sinfonía**
string quartet   **el cuarteto de cuerda**
trio   **el trío**

17d Musical Terms

accompaniment   **el acompañamiento**
accompanist   **el acompañante**
arpeggio   **el arpegio**
bar   **el compás**
beat   **el compás, el ritmo**
bow   **el arco**
bowing   **la técnica del arco**
cadence   **la cadencia**
chord   **el acorde**
clef   **la clave**
  bass   **de bajo**
  treble   **de soprano**
discord   **la disonancia**
improvisation   **la improvisación**

key   **la clave, la nota**
  major   **mayor**
  minor   **menor**
note   **la nota**
  breve   **la breve**
  half note / minim   **la blanca**
  quarter note / crotchet   **la negra**
  eighth note / quaver   **la corchea**
  sixteenth note / semiquaver   **la semicorchea**
mute   **sorda**
scale   **la escala**
score   **la partitura**
sharp   **sostenido**
sheet (of music)   **la partitura**

17e Movie / Film Genres

adventure movie / film   **la película de aventuras**
animation   **la animación**
black and white   **blanco y negro**
black comedy   **la comedia negra, el cine negro**
cartoons   **los dibujos animados**
comedy   **la comedia**
documentary   **el documental**
feature movie / film   **el largometraje**
horror movie / film   **la película de terror**
low-budget   **de bajo presupuesto**
sci-fi   **la ciencia ficción**
short film   **el corto de cine**
silent movies / cinema   **el cine mudo**
tearjerker / weepie   **la película lacrimosa**
thriller   **la película de intriga**
video clip   **el vídeo-clip**
war movie / film   **la película de guerra**
western   **la película del oeste**

19a Means of Transportation

by air   **por aire, por avión**
in an ambulance   **en una ambulancia**

229

by bicycle   **en bicicleta**
by bus   **en autobús**
by cable car   **en teleférico**
by car   **en coche**
by coach   **en autobús**
in a dinghy   **en barca**
by ferry   **en ferry**
by helicopter   **en helicóptero**
by hovercraft   **en hidrodeslizador /**
   aerodeslizador
by hydrofoil   **en hidroala**
by jumbo jet   **en jumbo**
by plane   **en avión**
by ship   **en barco, en buque**
by subway / underground   **por metro**
by taxi / cab   **en taxi**
by trolley / tram   **en tranvía**
by trolleybus   **en trolebús**
in a truck / lorry   **en camión**

19b Ships & Boats

aircraft carrier   **el porta(a)viones**
canoe   **la canoa**
cargo ship   **el barco de**
   mercancías, el buque mercante
dinghy   **el bote**
ferry   **el ferry**
hovercraft   **el hidrodeslizador**
hydrofoil   **el hidroala**
lifeboat   **el bote salvavidas**
merchant ship   **el barco mercante**
ocean liner   **el transatlántico**
oil tanker / petrol tank   **el tanque de**
   petróleo
rowing boat   **el bote de remo**
sailing boat   **el barco de vela**
ship   **el barco, el buque, la nave**
speedboat   **la lancha rápida**
submarine   **el submarino**
towboat   **el remolcador**
warship   **el buque de guerra**
yacht   **el yate**

19c Parts of the Car

air conditioning   **la**
   climatización
alternator   **el alternador de**
   corriente
automatic gear   **la marcha**
   automática, el cambio
   automático
back wheel   **la rueda de atrás, la**
   rueda trasera
battery   **la batería**
bodywork   **la carrocería**
brake   **el freno**
bumper / tender   **el parachoques**
carburetor   **el carburador**
catalytic converter   **el convertidor,**
   el catalizador
choke   **el obturador, el estárter**
clutch   **el embrague**
dashboard   **el cuadro de**
   mandos, el tablero (de
   instrumentos)
door   **la puerta**
   front   **delantera**
   passenger   **del pasajero**
engine   **el motor**
exhaust pipe   **el tubo de escape**
front seats   **los asientos**
   delanteros
front wheel   **la rueda delantera**
gearbox   **la caja de marchas / de**
   cambios
headlights   **los focos, los faros**
horn   **la bocina, el pito**
hood / bonnet   **la capota, el capó**
indicator   **el indicador de**
   dirección, el intermitente
license / number plate   **la matrícula**
lights   **las luces**
motor   **el motor**
passenger seat   **el asiento de**
   pasajero
pedal   **el pedal**
   accelerator   **el pedal de**
   aceleración, el acelerador

brake   **el pedal de freno, el freno**

clutch   **el pedal de embrague, el embrague**

rearview / rear mirror   **el espejo retrovisor**

registration number   **el número de matrícula, [las placas]**

roof   **el techo**

roof rack   **la baca, la canasta**

safety belt   **el cinturón de seguridad**

spares   **las piezas de repuesto**

　spare wheel   **la rueda de repuesto**

spark plug   **la bujía**

speedometer   **el velocímetro, el cuentakilómetros**

starter   **el arranque**

steering wheel   **el volante**

tank   **el depósito de gasolina**

throttle valve   **la válvula reguladora**

tire / tyre   **la cubierta, la llanta, la neumática**

　back tire / tyre   **la cubierta / llanta trasera**

　front tire / tyre   **la cubierta / llanta delantera**

　spare tire / tyre   **la cubierta / llanta de repuesto**

tire / tyre pressure   **la presión de las ruedas**

trunk / boot   **el maletero**

wheel   **la rueda**

windshield / windscreen   **el parabrisas**

windshield / windscreen wiper   **el limpiaparabrisas**

19c Road Signs

Cross now   **cruzar ahora**

Danger!   **¡peligro!**

Detour / Diversion   **la desviación**

End of detour / diversion   **fin de la desviación**

End of roadworks   **fin de las obras de la carretera**

End of speed zone   **fin de la regulación / señalización**

Free parking   **aparcamiento gratuito, parqueadero gratis**

Highway / Expressway entrance   **acceso a la autopista**

Junction   **cruce de autopistas**

Keep clear   **dejar libre el paso**

Loading bay   **la zona de carga y descarga**

Maximum speed   **la velocidad máxima**

No entry   **prohibida la entrada**

No parking   **no aparcar**

Pedestrians crossing   **el cruce de peatones**

Residents only   **sólo residentes**

Road closed   **carretera cerrada**

Roadworks   **carretera en obras**

Stop   **stop, parar**

Toll   **el peaje**

20a Tourist Sights

abbey   **la abadía**

playground   **el parque infantil**

amphitheater / amphitheatre   **el anfiteatro**

aquarium   **el acuario**

art gallery   **la galería de arte**

battlefield   **el campo de batalla**

battlements   **las almenas**

boulevard   **el bulevar**

castle   **el castillo, el alcázar**

catacombs   **las catacumbas**

cathedral   **la catedral**

cave   **la cueva**

cemetery   **el cementerio**

city   **la ciudad**

chapel   **la capilla**

church   **la iglesia**

concert hall   **la sala de conciertos**

convent   **el convento**

downtown / town centre   **el centro de la ciudad**
exhibition   **la exhibición**
fortress   **la fortaleza**
fountain   **la fuente**
gardens   **los jardines públicos**
harbor / harbour   **el puerto**
library   **la biblioteca**
mansion   **la mansión**
market   **el mercado**
monastery   **el monasterio**
monument   **el monumento**
museum   **el museo**
opera   **la ópera**
palace   **el palacio**
parliament building   **el edificio de las Cortes / [del Parlamento]**
pier   **el embarcadero**
planetarium   **el planetario**
ruins   **las ruinas**
shopping area   **la zona de tiendas**
square   **la plaza**
stadium   **el estadio**
statue   **la estatua**
temple   **el templo**
theater / theatre   **el teatro**
tomb   **la tumba**
tower   **la torre**
town hall   **el ayuntamiento, [la alcadía]**
university   **la universidad**
zoo   **el parque / jardín zoológico**

20a On the Beach

beach   **la playa**
beach ball   **la pelota de playa**
cabana / bathing hut   **la cabina, la cabaña, la caseta de playa**
deck chair   **la silla de lona**
I dive   **me tiro al agua**
diver   **el buceador**
pail and shovel / bucket and spade   **el cubo y pala**
sand   **la arena**
 grain of sand   **el grano de arena**

sandcastle   **el castillo de arena**
sandy *(beach)*   **arenoso**
scuba diving   **la natación submarina**
sea   **el mar**
seashore   **la costa**
snorkel   **el tubo snorkel, el esnórquel**
I snorkel   **nado respirando por un tubo**
suntan lotion   **la loción solar / bronceadora**
sunshade *(umbrella)*   **la sombrilla**
I surf   **hago surf**
surfboard   **la tabla deslizadora**
surfboarder   **el surfista**
surfing   **el surf, el acuaplano**
I swim   **nado**
waterskiing   **el esquí acuático**
windsurfing / sailboarding   **el windsurf, el surf a vela**
I go windsurfing   **practico el windsurf**

20a Continents & Regions

Africa   **Africa**
Antarctica   **Tierras Antárticas**
Arctic   **Ártico**
Asia   **Asia**
Australasia   **Australasia**
Balkans   **los Balcanes**
Baltic States   **los estados bálticos**
Central America   **América Central**
Eastern Europe   **Europa del este**
Europe   **Europa**
European Union   **la Unión Europea**
Far East   **el Extremo Oriente**
Middle East   **el Medio Oriente**
North America   **América del Norte**
Oceania   **Oceanía**
Scandinavia   **Escandinavia**
South America   **América del Sur**
former Soviet Union   **la ex-Unión Soviética**
West Indies   **las Antillas Occidentales**

former Yugoslavia **la ex-Yugoslavia**

20a Countries

Afghanistan **Afganistán**
Albania **Albania**
Algeria **Argelia**
Argentina **Argentina**
Austria **Austria**
Belgium **Bélgica**
Bolivia **Bolivia**
Bosnia **Bosnia**
Brazil **Brasil**
Bulgaria **Bulgaria**
Canada **el Canadá**
Chile **Chile**
China **China**
Colombia **Colombia**
Costa Rica **Costa Rica**
Croatia **Croacia**
Cuba **Cuba**
Cyprus **Chipre**
Czech Republic **la República Checa**
Denmark **Dinamarca**
Ecuador **Ecuador**
Egypt **Egipto**
England **Inglaterra**
Estonia **Estonia**
Finland **Finlandia**
France **Francia**
Germany **Alemania**
Great Britain **Gran Bretaña**
Greece **Grecia**
Guatemala **Guatemala**
Hungary **Hungría**
Iceland **Islandia**
India **India**
Indonesia **Indonesia**
Iran **Irán**
Iraq **Irak**
Ireland **Irlanda**
Israel **Israel**
Italy **Italia**
Japan **el Japón**
Jordan **Jordania**

Kampuchea **Kampuchea**
Kenya **Kenia**
Korea (North / South) **Corea (del Norte / del Sur)**
Kuwait **Kuwait**
Latvia **Letonia**
Lebanon **Líbano**
Libya **Libia**
Lithuania **Lituania**
Luxembourg **Luxemburgo**
Malaysia **Malasia**
Mexico **México**
Mongolia **Mongolia**
Morocco **Marruecos**
Netherlands **los Países Bajos**
New Zealand **Nueva Zelandia**
Nicaragua **Nicaragua**
Norway **Noruega**
Pakistan **Pakistán**
Palestine **Palestina**
Paraguay **Paraguay**
Peru **el Perú**
Philippines **las Filipinas**
Poland **Polonia**
Portugal **Portugal**
Romania **Rumania**
Russia **Rusia**
Saudi Arabia **Arabia Saudita**
Scotland **Escocia**
Serbia **Serbia**
Slovakia **Eslovaquia**
Slovenia **Eslovenia**
South Africa **Africa del Sur**
Spain **España**
Sri Lanka **Sri Lanka**
Sudan **Sudán**
Sweden **Suecia**
Switzerland **Suiza**
Syria **Siria**
Taiwan **Taiwán**
Tanzania **Tanzania**
Thailand **Tailandia**
Tibet **el Tibet**
Tunisia **Túnez**
Turkey **Turquía**
Uganda **Uganda**
Ukraine **Ucrania**

United States **los Estados Unidos**
Uruguay **Uruguay**
Venezuela **Venezuela**
Vietnam **Vietnam**
Wales **el País de Gales**
Zaire **Zaire**
Zimbabwe **Zimbabue**

20a Oceans & Seas

Adriatic Sea **el Mar Adriático**
Arctic Ocean **el Océano Glacial Ártico**
Atlantic Ocean **el Océano Atlántico**
Baltic Sea **el Mar Báltico**
Bay of Biscay **la Bahía de Vizcaya**
English Channel **el Canal de la Mancha**
Gulf of Mexico **el Golfo de México**
Indian Ocean **el Océano Indico**
Mediterranean Sea **el Mar Mediterráneo**
Pacific Ocean **el Océano Pácifico**

21a Main Language Families

Afro-Asiatic **afroasiático**
Altaic **altaico**
Austronesian **austronesiano**
Australian **australiano**
Caucasian **caucasiano, caucásico**
Central and South **central y del sur**
Eskimo **esquimal**
Indo-European **indoeuropeo**
 Baltic **báltico**
 Celtic **céltico**
 Germanic **germánico**
 Hellenic **helénico**
 Indo-Iranian **indoiraní**
 Italic **itálico**
 Romance **romance**
 Slavic **eslavo**
Independent **independiente**
North American Indian **indio norteamericano**

Paleo-Asiatic **paleoasiático**
Papuan **papúa**
Sino-Tibetan **sino tibetano**
Uralic **urálico**

21a Languages & Nationalities*

Afrikaans **el africano**
Albanian **el albanés**
Arabic **el árabe**
Armenian **el armenio**
Basque **el vasco**
Bengali **el bengalí**
Breton **el bretón**
Bulgarian **el búlgaro**
Burmese **el birmano**
Catalan **el catalán**
Chinese **el chino**
Coptic **el copto**
Czech **el checo**
Danish **el danés**
Dutch **el holandés**
English **el inglés**
Eskimo **el esquimal**
Estonian **el estonio**
Finnish **el finés, el finlandés**
Flemish **el flamenco**
French **el francés**
Gallegan **el gallego**
German **el alemán**
Greek **el griego**
Hebrew **el hebreo**
Hindi **el hindú**
Hungarian **el húngaro**
Icelandic **el islandés**
Indonesian **el indonesio**
Irish Gaelic **el gaélico irlandés**
Italian **el italiano**
Japanese **el japonés**
Korean **el coreano**
Kurdish **el kurdo**
Latin **el latín**
Majorcan **el mallorquín**
Mongolian **el mongol**
Norwegian **el noruego**
Persian **el persa**

➤ *Where applicable, the adjective of nationality (masculine form) is the same as the language.

Polish **el polaco**
Portuguese **el portugués**
Punjabi **el punjabí**
Rumanian **el rumano**
Russian **el ruso**
Scottish Gaelic **el gaélico escocés**
Slovak **el eslovaco**
Somali **el somalí**
Spanish **el español**
Swahili **el swahilí**
Swedish **el sueco**
Thai **el tailandés**
Tamil **el tamil**
Tibetan **el tibetano**
Turkish **el turco**
Urdu **el urdú**
Valencian **el valenciano**
Vietnamese **el vietnamita**
Welsh **el galés**

Latin American languages

Aztec **el azteca**
Guarani **el guaraní**
Inca **el inca**
Nahuatl **el nahuatl**
Pampa **el pampa**
Quechua **el quechua**

Other nationalities

Algerian **argelino**
American **americano**
American Indian **indio, indígena**
Argentinian **argentino**
Australian **australiano**
Austrian **austríaco**
Belgian **belga**
Bolivian **boliviano**
Brazilian **brasileño**
Canadian **canadiense**
Chilean **chileno**
Colombian **colombiano**
Costa Rican **costarricense**
Ecuadorean **ecuatoriano**
Egyptian **egipicio**
French Canadian
 francocanadiense

Guatemalan **guatemalteco**
Indian **indio**
Iraqi **iraquí**
Iranian **iraní**
Irish **irlandés**
Israeli **israelí**
Lebanese **libanés**
Mexican **mexicano, mejicano**
Moroccan **marroquí**
New Zealander **neozelandés**
Nicaraguan **nicaragüense**
Pakistani **pakistaní**
Palestinian **palestino**
Panamanian **panameño**
Paraguayan **paraguayo**
Peruvian **peruano**
Puerto Rican **puertorriqueño**
Saudi **saudí, saudita**
Scottish **escocés**
South African **sudafricano**
Swiss **suizo**
Syrian **sirio**
Uruguayan **uruguayo**

21b Grammar

accusative **el acusativo**
 accusative *(adj)* **acusativo**
adjective **el adjetivo**
adverb **el adverbio**
agreement **la concordancia**
it agrees with **concuerda con**
article **el artículo**
 definite article **el artículo definido**
 indefinite article **el artículo indefinido**
case **el caso**
case ending **la terminación del caso**
clause **la cláusula**
comparative **el comparativo**
conjunction **la conjunción**
dative **el dativo**
definite **el definido**
demonstrative **el demostrativo**
direct object **el objeto directo**

235

ending   la terminación
exception   la excepción
gender   el género
genitive   el genitivo
indefinite   el indefinido
indirect object   el objeto indirecto
interrogative   el interrogativo
negative   el negativo
nominative   el nominativo
noun   el nombre, el sustantivo
object   el objeto
phrase   la frase, la oración
plural   el plural
   plural *(adj)*   plural
possessive   el posesivo
prefix   el prefijo
preposition   la preposición
pronoun   el pronombre
   demonstrative   el pronombre demostrativo
   indefinite   el pronombre indefinido
   interrogative   el pronombre interrogativo
   personal   el pronombre personal
   relative   el pronombre relativo
   subject   el pronombre sujeto
reflexive   el reflexivo
   reflexive *(adj)*   reflexivo
rule   la regla
sequence   la concordancia, la sucesión
singular   el singular
suffix   el sufijo
superlative   el superlativo
   superlative *(adj)*   superlativo
word order   el orden de las palabras

Verbs

active voice   la voz activa
auxiliary   auxiliar
compound   compuesto
conditional   el condicional
defective   el defectivo

formation   la formación
future   el futuro
gerund   el gerundio
imperative   el imperativo
imperfect   el imperfecto
impersonal   el impersonal
infinitive   el infinitivo
intransitive   el intransitivo
irregular   irregular
passive voice   la voz pasiva
participle   el participio
past   el pasado
   past *(adj)*   pasado
perfect   el perfecto
present   el presente
reflexive   el reflexivo
   reflexive *(adj)*   reflexivo
regular   regular
sequence   la concordancia, la sucesión
simple   simple
strong   fuerte
subjunctive   el subjuntivo
system   el sistema
tense   el tiempo
transitive   el transitivo
use   el uso
verb   el verbo
weak   débil

21b Punctuation

apostrophe   el apóstrofe
asterisk   el asterisco
bracket   el corchete
colon   los dos puntos *(pl)*
comma   la coma
dash   el guión
exclamation mark   el signo de exclamación / admiración
quotation marks   las comillas
(in) parentheses   (entre) paréntesis
period / full stop   el punto final
question mark   el signo de interrogación
semicolon   punto y coma

22b Stationery

adhesive tape   la cinta adhesiva, el papel celo, [la cinta pegante]
blackboard eraser   el borrador de la pizarra
carbon paper   el papel carbón
card index   el fichero, el tarjetero
chalk   la tiza
clipboard   la tablilla con sujetapapeles
compasses   el compás
correction fluid   el líquido corrector
diary / datebook   la agenda
envelope   el sobre
eraser / rubber   la gomma de borra, la gomita
felt-tip pen   el rotulador
file   la carpeta archivadora
filing cabinet   el archivador
fountain pen   la pluma
glue   el pegamento, [el pegante]
highlighter   el rotulador fluorescente, el marcador
hole punch   la taladradora, el taladro, [la perforadora]
ink   la tinta
ink refill   la mina de bolígrafo
in tray / out tray   la bandeja de entradas / de salidas
label   la etiqueta
letter opener / scalpel   el escalpelo
marker   el rotulador
note book   el cuaderno, el block
overhead projector / OHP   el proyector de transparencias
paper   el papel
paper clip   el clip, el sujetapapeles
paper cutter / guillotine   la guillotina
pen   el bolígrafo
pencil   el lápiz
photocopier   la fotocopiadora
pocket calculator   la calculadora de bolsillo
protractor   el transportador de ángulos

ring binder   la carpeta de anillos
rubber band / elastic band   la gomilla, la gomita
ruler   la regla
scissors   las tijeras
screen   la pantalla
T- / set square   el juego de escuadra y cartabón, el cartabón, la escuadra
sheet of paper   la hoja de papel
shredder   la trituradora de papel, el desfibrador
stamp   el sello, el tampón, la estampilla
stapler   la grapadora, la cosedora
staple remover   el quitagrapas
textbook   el libro de texto
thumbtack / drawing pin   la chincheta, el chinche
typewriter   la máquina de escribir
typewriter ribbon   la cinta de la máquina de escribir
transparency   la transparencia
wastepaper basket   la papelera
whiteboard   la pizarra blanca
workbook / exercise book   el cuaderno de ejercicios

23a Scientific Disciplines

applied sciences   las ciencias aplicadas
anthropology   la antropología
astronomy   la astronomía
astrophysics   la astrofísica
biochemistry   la bioquímica
biology   la biología
botany   la botánica
chemistry   la química
geology   la geología
medicine   la medicina
microbiology   la microbiología
physics   la física
physiology   la fisiología
psychology   la psicología
social sciences   las ciencias sociales

APPENDICES

technology   la tecnología
zoology   la zoología

23b Chemical Elements

aluminum / aluminium   el aluminio
arsenic   el arsénico
calcium   el calcio
carbon   el carbono
chlorine   el cloro
copper   el cobre
gold   el oro
hydrogen   el hidrógeno
iodine   el yodo
iron   el hierro
lead   el plomo
magnesium   el magnesio
mercury   el mercurio
nitrogen   el nitrógeno
oxygen   el oxígeno
phosphorus   el fósforo
platinum   el platino
plutonium   el plutonio
potassium   el potasio
silver   la plata
sodium   el sodio
sulfur   el sulfuro
uranium   el uranio
zinc   el zinc, el cinc

23b Compounds & Alloys

acetic acid   al ácido acético
alloy   la aleación
ammonia   el amoniaco
asbestos   el amianto, el asbesto
brass   el latón
carbon dioxide   el dióxido de carbono
carbon monoxide   el monóxido de carbono
copper oxide   el óxido de cobre
hydrochloric acid   el ácido clorhídrico
iron oxide   el óxido de hierro
lead oxide   el óxido de plomo

---

nickel   el níquel
nitric acid   el ácido nítrico
it oxidizes   oxida, se oxida
ozone   el ozono
propane   el propano
silver nitrate   el nitrato de plata
sodium bicarbonate   el bicarbonato de sodio
sodium carbonate   el carbonato de sodio
sodium chloride   el cloruro de sodio
sulfuric acid   el ácido sulfúrico
tin   el estaño

23c The Zodiac

Aries   Aries
Taurus   Tauro
Gemini   Géminis
Cancer   Cáncer
Leo   Leo
Virgo   Virgo
Libra   Libra
Scorpio   Escorpión
Sagittarius   Sagitario
Capricorn   Capricornio
Aquarius   Acuario
Pisces   Piscis

23c Planets & Stars

Earth   Tierra
Venus   Venus
Mercury   Mercurio
Pluto   Plutón
Mars   Marte
Jupiter   Júpiter
Saturn   Saturno
Uranus   Urano
Neptune   Neptuno
North star   la Estrella Polar
Big Dipper / Great Bear   la Osa Mayor
Halley's comet   el Cometa Halley
Southern Cross   la Cruz del Sur

24b Wild Animals

baboon   **el mandril**
badger   **el tejón**
bear   **el oso**
beaver   **el castor**
bison / buffalo   **el búfalo**
camel   **el camello**
cheetah   **el leopardo cazador**
chimpanzee   **el chimpancé**
cougar   **el puma**
coyote   **el coyote**
deer   **el ciervo, el venado**
elephant   **el elefante**
elk   **el alce, el anta**
fox   **el zorro**
frog   **la rana**
giraffe   **la jirafa**
gorilla   **el gorila**
grizzly bear   **el oso pardo**
hare   **la liebre**
hedgehog   **el erizo**
hippopotamus   **el hipopótamo**
hyena   **la hiena**
jaguar   **el jaguar**
leopard   **el leopardo**
lion   **el león**
lizard   **el lagarto**
lynx   **el lince**
mink   **el visón**
mole   **el topo**
monkey   **el mono**
moose   **el alce de América**
mouse   **el ratón**
otter   **la nutria**
panther   **la pantera**
polar bear   **el oso polar**
puma   **el puma**
rat   **la rata**
reindeer   **el reno**
rhinoceros   **el rinoceronte**
snake   **la serpiente, la culebra**
squirrel   **la ardilla**
tiger   **el tigre**
toad   **el sapo**
whale   **la ballena**
wildcat   **el gato montés**

wolf   **el lobo**
zebra   **la cebra**

24b Birds

albatross   **el albatros**
blackbird   **el cuervo**
bluetit   **el herrerillo**
chaffinch   **el pinzón**
crow   **el grajo, la corneja**
dove   **la paloma**
eagle   **el águila** *(f)*
    golden eagle   **el águila real**
emu   **el emú, el dromeo**
hawk / falcon   **el halcón**
heron   **la garza**
hummingbird   **el colibrí, el picaflor**
kingfisher   **el martín pescador**
magpie   **la urraca**
osprey   **el águila** *(f)* **pescadora**
ostrich   **el avestruz**
owl   **el búho, la lechuza, el mochuelo**
parrot   **el loro**
peacock   **el pavo real, el pavón**
pelican   **el pelícano**
penguin   **el pingüino**
pigeon   **la paloma**
robin   **el petirrojo**
seagull   **la gaviota**
sparrow   **el gorrión**
starling   **el estornino**
swallow   **la golondrina**
swan   **el cisne**
swift   **el vencejo**
thrush   **el tordo**
woodpecker   **el pájaro carpintero**
wren   **el troglodito**

24b Parts of the Animal Body

beak   **el pico**
claw   **la garra, la zarpa**
comb   **la cresta**
feather   **la pluma**
fin   **la aleta**
fleece   **la lana, el vellón**

fur   el pelo
gills   la branquia, la agalla
hide   el pellejo, la piel
hoof   la pezuña
mane   la melena, la crin
paw   la pata, la garra
pelt   el pelo, el pelaje
scale   la escama
shell *(oyster, snail)*   la concha
  shell *(tortoise, crab)*   el caparazón
tail   el rabo, la cola
trunk   la trompa
tusk   el colmillo
udder   la ubre
wing   el ala

24c Trees

apple tree   el manzano
ash   el fresno
beech   la haya
cherry tree   el cerezo
chestnut   el castaño
cypress   el ciprés
eucalyptus   el eucalipto
fig tree   la higuera
fir tree   el abeto
fruit tree   el árbol frutal
holly   el acebo
maple   el arce, el maple
oak   el roble
olive tree   el olivo
palm   la palmera
peach tree   el melocotonero
pear tree   el peral
pine   el pino
plum tree   el ciruelo
poplar   el chopo, el álamo
redwood   la secoya
rhododendron   el rododendro
walnut tree   el nogal
willow   el sauce
yew   el tejo

24c Flowers & Weeds

azalea   la azalea
cactus   el cactus, el cacto
carnation   el clavel
chrysanthemum   el crisantemo
clover   el trébol
crocus   la flor del azafrán
daffodil   el narciso
dahlia   la dalia
daisy   la margarita
dandelion   el diente de león
fern   el helecho
flax   el lino
foxglove   la dedalera
geranium   el geranio
hydrangea   la hortensia
lily   la azucena
nettle (stinging)   la ortiga
orchid   la orquídea
poppy   la amapola
rose   la rosa
snowdrop   la campanilla de invierno, la flor de nieve
sunflower   el girasol
thistle   el cardo
tulip   el tulipán
violet   la violeta

25b Political Institutions

assembly   la asamblea
association   la asociación
cabinet   el gabinete
  shadow cabinet *(UK)*   el gobierno en la sombra
confederation   la confederación
congress   el congreso
council   el consejo, la junta
federation   la federación
House of Representatives   la cámara de los representantes
local authority   la autoridad local
Lower House / Lower Chamber   la cámara baja
parliament   el parlamento
party   el partido político

Senate   **el senado**
town council   **la junta local, el consejo de gobierno local**
town hall   **el ayuntamiento, [la alcadía]**
Upper House   **la cámara alta**

27b Military Ranks

admiral   **el almirante**
air marshal   **el mariscal de aire**
brigadier   **el brigadier, el general de brigada**
captain   **el capitán**
captain *(Naval)*   **el capitán de navío**
commander   **el capitán general del ejército**
commander *(Naval)*   **el capitán de fragata**
commanding officer   **el comandante**
corporal   **el cabo**
field marshal   **el mariscal de campo**
general   **el general**
lieutenant   **el teniente**
lieutenant commander   **el capitán de corbeta**
major   **el comandante**
private   **el soldado raso**
rear admiral   **el contraalmirante**
sergeant   **el sargento**
sergeant major   **el sargento mayor, el brigada**
sergeant major *(US)*   **el primer sargento**

27c International Organizations

ASEAN / Association of South-East Asian Nations   **ANSA / Asociación de Naciones del Sudeste Asiático**
Council of Europe   **el Consejo de Europa**

EC / European Community   **CE / la Comunidad Europea**
EU / European Union   **UE / la Unión Europea**
IMF / International Monetary Fund   **FMI / el Fondo Monetario Internacional**
NATO / North Atlantic Treaty Organization   **OTAN / la Organización del Tratado del Atlántico Norte**
OECD / Organization for Economic Cooperation and Development   **OCDE / la Organización de Cooperación y Desarrollo Económico**
OPEC / Organization of Petroleum Exporting Countries   **OPEP / la Organización de Países Exportadores de Petróleo**
Security Council   **el Consejo de Seguridad**
UNO / United Nations Organization   **ONU / la Organización de las Naciones Unidas**
WHO / World Health Organization   **OMS / la Organización Mundial de la Salud**
World Bank   **el Banco Mundial**

D

SUBJECT INDEX

Subject Index

Numbers refer to Vocabularies

A

abroad, going   19b
accidents   11a
accommodation(s)   8a, 12c; on
   vacation / holiday   20b
addiction   12d
advertising   18d
age   5a, 7c
agreeing   15b
agriculture   24c
airplane / aeroplane   19d
animals   24b; wild animals App. 24b;
   farm animals 24c
animal body, parts of   App. 24b
appearance, physical   5a
appreciation, artistic   17a
approval   15b
architecture   17b; features App. 17b
arguing   6d
army   27a, 27b
art, fine   17b
artistic criticism   17a
artistic styles   17a
arts   17; jobs App. 14b
asking directions   2b
automobiles   19c; parts App. 19c

B

banking   14e
bathroom   8c
beach   App. 20a
beauty   11d
beliefs, political   25b; religious 13a
birds   24b, App. 24b
birth   7b
boats   19b; travel by 19b
bodily functions   11d
body, parts of   5b, App. 5b
booking, vacation / holidays   20b
books   17c
buildings   17b; features 17b; sights
   App. 20a
business   14

C

calculations   4d
calendar   3b
camping   20c
car   19c; parts App. 19c
cause & effect   6d
character, human   6a, App. 6a
chemical elements   App. 23b
chemistry   23b
children   7b
chores, household   8d
church   13b
cinema   17e; film genres App.17e
civil service, jobs   App. 14b
clarifying meaning   15b
classroom   22b
climate   24d
clothing   9c; for sports & leisure 16c;
   fabrics 5f
college   22d
colors / colours   5b
commerce   27c
communicating   15
company personnel &
   structure   14b
comparing   5e, 6d
compass, points of   2b
compounds, chemical   App. 23b
computers   15d; hardware App. 15d;
   software App.15d
conditions of work   14c
congratulating   15a
conjunctions   1a
construction   14b; jobs App.14b
continents   App. 20a
cooking   10d
cosmetics   9b
countries   App. 20a; nationalities
   App. 21a
countryside   24a
crime   12d, 26; crime fighting 26c
criticism, artistic   17a
crockery   8c
cuisine, traditional   10b, 10c
currencies   App. 9a
cutlery   8c

D

daily life   8
dance   17d
date   3b
days of week   3b
death   7c
decline, economic   14e
dentist   11c
descriptions   5; people 5a; things 5c
dessert   10c
dining out   10a
dining room   8c
direction(s)   2
disability   11b, 12b
discrimination   12e
discussing   6d
diseases   App. 11c
doctors   11c
doctrines, religious   13a
do-it-yourself / DIY   8d; tools App. 8c
domestic animals   24b
domestic goods   9b
drama   17e
drinks   10a
drug abuse   12d

E

earth   23c, 24a, 24e
eating   10d
eating out   10a
economics   14a, 14d, 14e
economy   14d
education   22; jobs App.14b
elections   25b
electrical goods   8c
electricity   23b
elements, chemical   App. 23b
emergencies   11a
emotions   6b
emphasizing   6d
energy sources   23c, 23b
environment   24, 23c
equipment, sports & leisure   16c
etiquette   15a; letter writing App.15c
evaluating   5d
examinations   22c
examples, giving   6d
exclamations   15b
existence   2b
expressing views   6d

F

fabrics   5f
factory   14b
faculties, human   5b; educational 22d
family   7
farewells   15a
farming   24c; farm animals 24c
feelings   6b
festivals, religious   App. 13b
films   17e; genres App. 17e
finance   14d; personal 14e
fine arts   17b
first aid   11a, 11b
fish   10b
fitness   11d
fittings & fixtures   8b, 8c
flowers   App. 24c
food   10, 9b; preparation 10d; jobs
    App.14b
foodstuffs, basic   9b
fractions   4c
friends   7a
fruit   10c
fuel sources   23c
functional words   1a
funerals   7c
furnishings   8b, 8c
furniture   8b, 8c
further education   22d

G

games   16b, 16c
gardening   24c; tools App. 8c
gems   App. 9c
geography   24a
geology   23c
geometrical terms   App. 4d
good-byes   15a
government   25; jobs App. 14b
grammar   App. 21b, 1a
growth, economic   14e; human 7c

H

hair care   11d
handicapped   11b, 12b
hardware, computer   App. 15d
health   11d
health care, jobs   App. 14b
herbs   10c

hesitating   15b
higher education   22d
hobbies   16a, App. 16a, 20a
holiday   20; beach App. 20a
holidays   App.13b
home   8
homelessness   12c
horticulture   24c
hospital   11c; jobs App. 14b;
   departments App. 11c
hotel   20b
house   8
household   8b, 8c
household goods   9b
housework   8d
housing   8a, 12c
how much?   4
human body   App. 5b
human character   6, App. 6a
human life cycle   7c
human relationships   7
hygiene   11d

I

ideology, political   25b; religious 13a
illness   11b
illnesses   App. 11b
industrial relations   14a
industry   14d, 14b; jobs App. 14b
insects   24b
institutions, political   App. 25a
international organizations   27c
international relations   27c
interview for job   14c
introductions   15a

J

jewelry / jewellery   App. 9c
job application & interview   14c
jobs   App. 14b
journalism   18
justice   26b, 26c

K

kitchen   8c
knowing   6c

L

labor / labour relations   14a
language   21

language families   App. 21a
languages   App. 21a
leisure time   16; hobbies App. 16a
length   4a
letter writing   15c, App. 15c
life cycle, human   7c
life sciences   23a
listening   21b
literature   17c
location   2b
lounge   8c
love   7b

M

mail   15c
man-made features   24a
manufacturing   14b; jobs App. 14b
marriage   7b
materials   5f
mathematics   4d, App. 4d
meals   10a
meaning, clarifying   15b
means of transportation   App. 19a
measuring   4b
meat   10b; meat dishes 10b
mechanics   23b
media   18
medical science   23a
medical treatment   11c
meetings   15a
mental activity   6c
metals   App. 23b, App. 9c
military personnel   27b
military ranks   App. 27b
minerals   23c
money   14e, App. 9a; spending 9a
months   3b
movement   2
movies   17e; genres App. 17e
music   17d
musical forms & terms   App. 17d
musicians & instruments   App. 17d

N

nationalities   App. 20a
natural features   24a
newspapers   18b
nuclear physics   23b
numbers   4c

APPENDIX H-S

O

obligation   15b
oceans   App. 20a
office   14b; departments App. 14b;
    personnel App. 14b
optician   11c
old age   7c

P

packaging   4b
parliament   25, App. 25a
parties, political   25b
parts of the body   5b, App. 5b;
    animal   App. 24b
past, present & future   3a
pastimes   16a, App. 16a
patterns (clothing)   9c
pay (work)   14c
paying, for vacation / holiday   20b
peace   27c
permission   15b
peoples   App. 20a
periods, artistic   17a
personnel   App. 14b
pets   24b
physical relief   24a
physical sciences   23b
physics   23b; nuclear 23b
place   2
places of work   App. 14b
planets   App. 23c
plant life   24c, App. 24c
pleasantries   15a
police   26c
political institutions   App. 25b
politicians   25a
politics   25
position   2
possessive adjectives & pronouns
    1a
post   15c
poultry   10b
poverty   12b
precious stones   App. 9c
prejudice   12e
prepositions   1a; of place 2a, of time
    3a
press   18b
prison   26c

professions   App. 14b
progam(me)s, TV & radio   18c
pronouns   1a
publishing   17c, 18b
puddings   10c
punctuation   21c
punishment   26c

Q

quantity   4, 9b
question words   1a

R

radio   18c
rail(road)   19e
ranks, military   App. 27b
reading   21b
recipes   10d
regions, geographical   App. 20a
relationships   7
relatives   7a
religion   13
religious beliefs   13a
religious festivals   App. 13b
religious practice   13b
representatives, political   25a
research, scientific   23a; space 23c;
    jobs App. 14b
reservations, expressing   6d
restaurants   10a
retail, jobs   App. 14b
road signs   App. 19c
road travel   19c
rooms   8b, 8c
routine   8b, 8d

S

school   22a, 22b, 22c
school subjects   22c
science   23
scientific disciplines   App. 23a
scientific research   23a
sea   24b; seas App. 20a; pollution
    24e
sea travel   19b
seafood   10b
sealife   24b
seasons   3b
self-catering holiday   20c

SUBJECT INDEX

self-catering holiday   20c
self-service vacation   20c
senses   5b
services   App. 9a; jobs App. 14b
sexuality   12e, 7b
shape   4a
ships   19b
shoes   9c
shopping   9; food 9b; clothes 9c
shops   App. 9a
sickness   11b
sights, tourist   App. 20a
singers   App. 17d
size   4a
smoking   App. 10d
social discourse   15a, 15b
social issues   12
social services   12b
society   12
software, computer   App. 15d
space   23c
speech   21b
sport   16b, 16c
sporting equipment   16c
stars   App. 23c
stationery   App. 22b
stores   App. 9a
strikes   14a
subjects, academic   22c, 22d
substances   5f
superlatives   5e
surprise   15b
sweet *(dessert)*   10c

T

telecommunications   15c
telephone   15c
television   18c
temperature   4b
thanking   15c
theater / theatre   17e
thought processes   6c
time   3
time of day   3b
timepieces   App. 3b
toiletries   9b

tools   App. 8c
tourist sights   App. 20a
trade   27c
trains   19e
transportation   19; means App. 19a;
    jobs App. 14b
travel   19, 2c; by air 19d; by rail 19e;
    by road 19c; by sea 19b
treatment, medical   11c
trees   App. 24c
trial   26b

U

unemployment   12b, 14c
universe   23c, App. 23c
university   22d

V

vacation   20; on the beach 20a
vegetables   10c
verbs   App. 21b
views, expressing   6d
violence   12d, 26a, 27a, 27b
vocabulary   21a
volume   4b

W

war   27a, 27b
watches & clocks   App. 3b
wealth   12b
weapons   27b
weather   24d
weeds   App. 24c
weight   4b
what sort of?   5
when?   3
where?   2
wildlife / animals   24b, App. 24b
word processing   15d
words   21a
working conditions   14c
workplaces   App. 14b
writing   21b, 17c; letters App. 15c

X, Y, Z

zodiac   App. 23c